THE 5 DISCIPLINES OF INCLUSIVE LEADERS

UNLEASHING THE POWER OF ALL OF US

ANDRÉS T. TAPIA & ALINA POLONSKAIA

Foreword by KEVIN CASHMAN, Global Leader of CEO and Executive Development, Korn Ferry

Berrett–Koehler Publishers, Inc.

Berrett-Koehler Publishers, Inc.
1333 Broadway, Suite 1000
Oakland, CA 94612-1921
Tel: (510) 817-2277
Fax: (510) 817-2278
www.bkconnection.com

ORDERING INFORMATION
Quantity sales. Special discounts are available on quantity purchases by corporations,
associations, and others. For details, contact the "Special Sales Department" at the Berrett-
Koehler address above.
Individual sales. Berrett-Koehler publications are available through most bookstores. They
can also be ordered directly from Berrett-Koehler: Tel: (800) 929-2929; Fax: (802) 864-7626;
www.bkconnection.com.
Orders for college textbook / course adoption use. Please contact Berrett-Koehler:
Tel: (800) 929-2929; Fax: (802) 864-7626.

Distributed to the U.S. trade and internationally by Penguin Random House Publisher
Services.

Berrett-Koehler and the BK logo are registered trademarks of Berrett-Koehler Publishers, Inc.

Printed in Canada

Berrett-Koehler books are printed on long-lasting acid-free paper. When it is available, we
choose paper that has been manufactured by environmentally responsible processes. These
may include using trees grown in sustainable forests, incorporating recycled paper, minimizing chlorine in bleaching, or recycling the energy produced at the paper mill.

Library of Congress Cataloging-in-Publication Data

Names: Tapia, Andrés, 1960- author. | Polonskaia, Alina, author.
Title: The 5 disciplines of inclusive leaders : unleashing the power of all
    of us / by Andrés T. Tapia and Alina Polonskaia.
Other titles: The five disciplines of inclusive leaders
Description: 1st Edition. | Oakland : Berrett-Koehler Publishers, 2020. |
    Includes bibliographical references and index.
Identifiers: LCCN 2020023162 | ISBN 9781523088201 (hardcover) | ISBN
    9781523088218 (adobe pdf) | ISBN 9781523088225 (epub)
Subjects: LCSH: Leadership. | Diversity in the workplace. | Employee
    motivation. | Organizational change. | Korn/Ferry International (Firm)
Classification: LCC HD57.7 .T377 2020 | DDC 658.3008--dc23
LC record available at https://lccn.loc.gov/2020023162

First Edition
25 24 23 22 21   10 9 8 7 6 5 4 3 2

Book production and design: Seventeenth Street Studios
Cover design: Daniel Tesser, Studio Carnelian
Copyeditor: Todd Manza
Author photos by: John Reilly Photography (page 267) and Inna Testolini (page 268)

CONTENTS

Contents

FOREWORD

I N A TIME WHEN WALLS AND EXCLUSION too often define and divide us, it is critical to rise above our limiting mindsets, and even more importantly, to transcend constricted heart-sets. The human spirit, our deepest, most authentic humanity, cannot be denied or minimized by judgments that tend to restrict our collective worth. In the end, synergy supersedes separateness and eventually prevails. Inclusion is the soul of synergy.

Diversity and inclusion are foundational to both creativity and innovation. Our research, and the research of others, has demonstrated that the essence of innovation is grand collaboration. The broader and more diverse the dots included and connected, the more profound the innovative breakthrough. Diversity and inclusion fosters this by hearing, appreciating, and including new, unique voices to create new, unique possibilities. However, our technological innovations have too often outpaced our human innovations. As Mastercard's Chief Executive Officer, Ajaypal Banga, reflected, "We have the Internet of Everything but not the inclusion of everyone."[1]

Great leaders transform by reconciling polarities and paradoxes into new, more unified possibilities. Inclusive leaders bridge the seeming polarities while honoring the spectrums and breadth of diversity and uniqueness. The Reverend Jesse Jackson captured this beautifully: "Our premise is that inclusion leads to growth. So for those who are locked out, they lose development, and those who are in power lose market and growth."[2] Whether we are running a global organization or dealing with our families, being inclusive, appreciating both unity and diversity, is a constant human challenge.

A while ago, a very seasoned global CEO reflected on his career with me:

> I always thought of our company as truly global, truly inclusive of the world. The truth is, we were not. We were a US-centric, internationally located firm. Unintentionally, we divided more than we included. Why? Because I had not made my own inside-out leadership shift to be more open, more inclusive, within myself. Until I examined my own boundaries, my own biases, my own lack of openness in my life story, I could not even see it, much less appreciate and value it, in others.
>
> As I opened, the world opened. As I included more of myself, I became more inclusive of others.

We all have boundaries, we all have our walls, built brick by brick through our life experience. Break down the walls from the inside and the world enters. CNN news anchor Anderson Cooper put it well: "While as a society we are moving toward greater inclusion and equality for all people, the tide of history only advances when people make themselves fully visible."[3] The goal of diversity and inclusion is to unleash potential by making ourselves, and all those around us, more visible and more authentic contributors.

The 5 Disciplines of Inclusive Leaders is a profound leadership experience. It inspired me to deeply reflect on my own leadership and on some of the original research I presented in *Leadership from the Inside Out* more than twenty-five years ago. While inclusion and diversity were just taking hold in the corporate world back then, the principles of authenticity, courage, agility, purpose, interpersonal trust, resilience, and value creation were present. While reading Andrés and Alina's great work, I was struck that the core principles for both world-class leadership and inclusive leadership are so foundationally connected.

Each of our stories, to various degrees, is full of diverse people, influences, experiences, cultural impacts, biases, traumas, and triumphs. Knowing our deeper, unique stories helps us to be more open, more empathetic, and more curiously connected to the diverse stories of others. Once we know our own story and deeply appreciate the stories of others, separateness recedes. Like reading a great novel and empathizing with all the characters, once we understand someone's story, our heart opens and our harsh judgment disappears.

Inclusive leadership is no longer just a desirable thing to have or to add to our leadership. It is crucial to be it, to embody it, to achieve greater purpose-driven performance through it. As a result, I would encourage you to pause deeply with this great book. If you do so, it will be much more than an interesting and engaging intellectual exercise; it will be a rich, transformative leadership experience. Go slowly and go deeply on this journey with Andrés and Alina. They are true masters in this field. Andrés and Alina, along with their world-class colleagues in Korn Ferry's diversity and inclusion practice, have distilled many decades of research and insights from countless clients to deepen and accelerate your journey to inclusive leadership.

Leadership changes everything; it is a causal force, intolerant of the status quo, compelled to transform everything it touches. But while leadership changes everything, it can accelerate change in one of two ways: change for the better or change for the worse. *The 5 Disciplines of Inclusive Leaders* will ensure that you are a force for changing our world to a much more sustainable, innovative, purposeful, and peaceful place!

Kevin Cashman

Global Leader of CEO and Executive Development, Korn Ferry

Bestselling author, *Leadership from the Inside Out* and *The Pause Principle*

PREFACE

THESE SHOULD BE BREAKTHROUGH TIMES FOR THE work of diversity and inclusion. Companies are spending more than $8 billion a year on diversity programs.[1] Sixty-three percent of today's diversity professionals were appointed or promoted to their roles between 2016 and 2019. CEOs have signed multiple pledges and sought various diversity and inclusion certifications.[2] Efforts to create more inclusive organizations are clearly not suffering from a lack of attention.

But those efforts are suffering from a lack of results.

Despite the massive investments and statements full of bravado, female and non-White talent is still woefully underrepresented in many sectors. Boards of Fortune 500 companies are made up of only 8.6% Blacks, 3.8% Latinos, and 3.7% Asians, while women represent 22.5% in these same companies and 15% in the top global companies.[3] Of the senior leadership roles at Fortune 500 companies, Blacks occupy only 3.2%, Asians 2%, Latinos 4%, and women 10%.[4] Meanwhile, those from indigenous groups across all of the Americas, and in places like Australia, for example, are nearly invisible. They don't even show up in most of the reporting. And those who are LGBTQ+ or differently abled continue to wrestle with the not unrealistic fear that disclosing their true selves could hurt their career advancement and even job retention chances.

Furthermore, in what is assumed to be the relatively progressive nonprofit arena, the percentage of non-Whites in executive director roles were either only marginally better or even worse than in the corporate world. One US study had the collective representation of African Americans, Asians, and Hispanics at 13%, while another put the number at 8%. (On the brighter side, while the percentage is not yet at parity, the story on women in nonprofits is significantly better than in the for-profits, with 42% representation.)

Something is not working.

In more than twenty years of work in internal diversity and inclusion (D&I) roles, as well as in global management consultancies, we (Andrés and Alina) have been both witnesses to and participants in this exploding attention to addressing the lack of representation and the inequities that different talent groups experience in our organizations. Our work in the trenches has led us to discover the fundamental missing ingredient that is needed to go from effort and attention to results.

To be clear, we are both deeply mission- and values-driven leaders. So, yes, we believe greater diversity and inclusion is the right thing to do from a fairness, equality, democracy, and human dignity perspective. These things bring inherent purpose and humanity in themselves.

But our strategic starting point is always discerning what organizations want to achieve and what enablers and barriers will help or hinder progress toward those goals. From an outcomes perspective, there is a *So what?* that must be explored. So what if an organization is more diverse and inclusive? Specifically, how will this help it achieve its vision, mission, and concrete objectives of better service, better products, better quality of life, better financials? In other words, how do organizations use D&I to unleash the power of all of us?

When it comes to diversity and inclusion, the answers are compelling, as we explain in this opening section.

The *So what?* then invites the *Now what?* What does an organization need to do to become more diverse and inclusive? There are various key elements, but here we make the case that they all revolve around an organization having skilled, inclusive leaders.

We are believers in adult-based-learning training that is experiential, relevant, and actionable. We have seen the powerful results this can have on participants' beliefs, mindsets, and skills around the topic and realities of diversity and inclusion. We are believers in programs such as mentoring (both the traditional kind and the reciprocal mentoring between two parties), and we wholeheartedly embrace the findings that sponsorship is an even more effective way to accelerate the advancement of traditionally underrepresented talent.

We also believe in the effectiveness of differentiated development that is designed to address head-on the particular challenges and headwinds that talent from traditionally underrepresented groups often face, such as how to overcome systemic and legacy exclusions to access, opportunities, development, and rewards. This means that while organizations must do the heavy lifting of addressing the reduction of structural barriers, we believe there is a "power of choice" within each individual to also enhance the opportunities that they can open up for themselves.

To determine the optimal interventions for these best practices, we also firmly believe they must be discerned through proof points emerging from deep, root cause diagnostics that employ quantitative and qualitative research methods to surface the reasons for exclusionary dynamics in an organization.

However, even after listing best practices that have been researched, documented, and proven to work, our work in the trenches has led us to discover one fundamental missing ingredient: the role of leaders of the organization.

The missing ingredient was not leader buy-in. The best practice of CEOs and other leaders as champions of diversity is clearly understood, not only by the grassroots but also by the leaders themselves. It is common knowledge that without CEO and top leadership involvement, nothing much happens. That's why so many have signed that CEO pledge, and why they have been so public in their declarations of support.

The missing ingredient we found is in what is being asked of the leader.

Top and aspiring leaders can't just be vocal supporters of diversity. They can't just be sponsors of D&I programs. They can't just be the ones who provide the budget. They can't just delegate it to their chief diversity officer, or just show up at the designated heritage month event, or just attend the banquet where they receive the latest award.

They need to actually *lead* the effort.

This is why we set out to discern what it takes to be an inclusive leader and how we can help leaders at all levels become effective at it. The work entailed both quantitative and qualitative research. We collaborated with psychometric assessment scientists and with deeply grounded and experienced diversity and inclusion experts. Together, we mined the data, tested the assumptions, and validated the findings.

We then assessed our own clients, debriefed them, heard their first-hand stories, and coached them. We joined them on individual and organizational transformation journeys.

We learned that inclusive leadership is not just about an attitude of openness. It is about a set of skills and ways of being that can be assessed, coached, and put into action to bring about the equitable, inclusive, and diverse organizations to which so many aspire.

This book is about what we discovered that works. And we are eager to share it with you.

■   ■   ■

INTRODUCTION
Defining the Inclusive Leader

WHAT DOES AN INCLUSIVE LEADER LOOK LIKE? There's plenty of opinion in the public square about this, as well as many inspiring stories. But we wanted to start with the science. What do the 3 million leadership assessments in our Korn Ferry database tell us about the unique elements of inclusive leaders? Here, we lay out the scientific approach that led to our traits- and competencies-based Inclusive Leader model. We also touch on the role of life experiences in the inclusive leader's formation and development.

Let's look at the compelling ways that organizations use D&I to unleash the power of all of us.

CONTEXTUALIZING INCLUSIVE LEADERSHIP

First things first. Let's explain what we mean by *diversity, inclusion,* and *equity*. Diversity is about getting a mix of different people in the door, inclusion is about ensuring that mix is working well, and equity is fulfilling the promise that they all have equal access, opportunity, support, and rewards.

While headlines deluge us with the disturbing news that our societies are increasingly polarizing, a massive diversity, inclusion, and equity movement is afoot within corporations and nonprofit organizations. This countertrend to polarization is fueled by both altruism and self-interest.

On the altruistic side, many employers in all sectors—including industrials, the consumer sector, financial services, technology, health care, pharmaceuticals, the legal professions, government, nonprofits, and the military—have a genuine concern for ensuring that their talent feels valued, respected, and safe in the midst of divisions. They seek to have equitable organizations where disparities at any level, including access, opportunity, support, and reward, don't exist. They want to deliver on their promise of equality, that no one will be favored or disfavored on the basis of who they are.

On the self-interest side, a tsunami of demographic changes has presented organizations with unprecedented challenges and opportunities. Organizations are desperately trying to figure out the answers to these vexing questions:

- How do we attract the best talent from talent pools that have never before been tapped?
- How do we ensure that all talent, including women; people of different races, ethnicities, and socioeconomic status; and those with different physical and cognitive abilities, sexual orientations, or personalities, can rise to the fullness of their potential and into the highest levels of leadership?
- How do we ensure that the increased complexity of more diverse workforces does not lead to destructive conflict?
- How do we tap into our organization's diversity to reach previously unreached consumers and markets?
- How do we optimize diversity for greater innovation and organizational growth?

This long and comprehensive list of challenges underscores the notion that organizational competitiveness now and long into the future requires us to leverage diversity and inclusion.

Hard financial metrics back this up. In a study of one thousand companies across twelve countries, McKinsey & Company found strong associations between diversity and financial performance. Companies in the top quartile for racial and ethnic diversity were 36% more likely to have financial returns above their respective national industry medians, while those in the top quartile for gender diversity were 25% more likely to have financial returns above their medians. Furthermore, inclusive organizations were found to be 70% more likely to capture new markets, 75% more likely to see ideas become productized, and 87% more likely to make better decisions, while enjoying 19% higher innovation revenue (figure 1).[1]

The case is clear: whether for altruistic or self-interested reasons, leaders need to design organizations that equitably meet the needs of all their talent. And this exciting movement toward building tomorrow's equitable organizations is dependent on a new type of leader: the inclusive leader.

The inclusive leader is collaborative and facilitative rather than command and control. They are transparent rather than operating

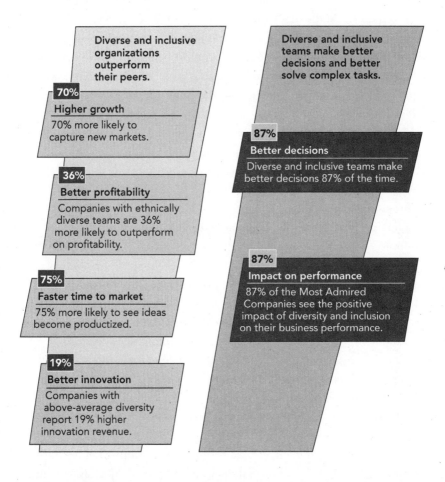

Figure 1. Done well, diversity and inclusion maximizes performance of individuals, teams, and organizations. *Sources:* McKinsey; Boston Consulting Group; Center for Talent Innovation; Erik Larson; Korn Ferry. For exact sourcing see endnote 1 for this chapter.

within the shadows of closed doors. They are culturally agile rather than anchored in their own worldview. They are able to fully embrace and leverage the vast diversity of today's workforces. They can create a safe space, regardless of what is happening externally, where people feel accepted and empowered to give the best of their talents. They unleash the power of all of us.

INCLUSIVE LEADERSHIP IS NOT JUST ABOUT DIVERSITY AND INCLUSION

Let's set diversity and inclusion aside for a moment and look at the research on the skills that future leaders need. A Korn Ferry study of perceptions of investors on whether leaders in organizations are rising to the challenge of massive disruption ("self-disruptive leaders") confirmed for us that inclusive leadership is not only the key to more equitable organizations; it is the foundation of broader leadership effectiveness.

Not only were investors in companies dissatisfied with what they saw (70% argued that short-term pressures stripped leaders of the ability to push through innovation, digitization, and transformative change), but they also considered current leadership styles to be in urgent need of change. As Dennis Baltzley, Korn Ferry's Global Leadership Practice leader, summarized the implications of the findings: "If you love consistency, the future will be hard for you." Those surveyed indicated that this includes the majority of leaders, as two-thirds (67%) of them identified current leadership norms as "not fit for the future."

Our self-disruptive leader research also found that if companies are to avoid being swept away by today's massive changes, leaders must "disrupt" themselves—their thoughts, their values, their actions. The disruption of markets can only be met with a disruption of the current leadership approach.

The study identified self-disruptive leaders as exceptionally good at partnering with diverse people across their organization's internal and external ecosystems and effective at creating the trust that helps establish inclusive environments and unlocks the full power of all the talent.

Sound familiar?

These inclusive leadership behaviors naturally tumbled out of research that was *not* about diversity and inclusion but rather was about how to be a successful leader in these tumultuous times. There is a 40% overlap in the traits and competencies required of self-disruptive leaders and of inclusive leaders.

What the study shows is that an inclusive leadership mindset and skills are necessary for effective leadership today and for the future. For the twenty-first-century leader of the future, inclusiveness is the new currency of power, influence, and effectiveness. It is the catalyst for unleashing talent to the fullness of its potential—the power of us all—which in turn provides the jet fuel that companies require to seize unprecedented opportunities and maneuver through daunting challenges. Figure 2 shows the clear logical connections between business performance and inclusive leadership.

Figure 2. The business case for inclusive leadership. *Source:* Andrés T. Tapia and Alina Polonskaia, *The Inclusive Leader White Paper* (Korn Ferry, 2020).

INCLUSIVE LEADERS AS CHANGE AGENTS

Inclusive leadership allows for more effective leadership across the board while still being change agents in addressing specific diversity and inclusion challenges.

Inclusive leaders can be effective advocates for diversity, fully embracing the business case as it is laid out in figure 2. They can champion initiatives that make inclusion an organizational priority by ensuring they are addressing both behavioral and structural inclusion, a distinction to which we devote a full chapter in part 3. They can help to identify the root causes of the barriers to retaining and promoting underrepresented employees. They can demand diverse slates of candidates, hold leaders accountable for increasing the pipeline of underrepresented talent, elevate the visibility of affinity groups, and act as role models and advocates for the programmatic and structural changes needed to create an equitable organization.

In our survey of talent management, human resources (HR), and diversity and inclusion experts, there was near consensus on the positive impact inclusive leaders have on their talent, including enabling them to feel free to bring their authentic selves to work, providing them with a sense of empowerment, and reassuring them that there is fairness and that they will be challenged with stretch opportunities (see appendix B, table B-1). Respondents also were in agreement about the impact of inclusive leaders on their organizations, such as fostering greater innovation, marketplace growth, and inclusive management practices plus encouraging the organization's embrace of diversity as a vital part of an economic business case (see appendix B, table B-2).

For all the upside, however, there still is a large gap between the embracing of diversity and inclusion, and its promise of better business performance, and the actual ability to lead inclusively toward these organizational outcomes.

Organizations do not become more diverse and inclusive automatically. An intent to be more diverse doesn't necessarily lead to increased diversity. Furthermore, greater diversity in and of itself doesn't necessarily lead to better business results. Inclusive leadership is the necessary bridge to both greater diversity and the enhanced business performance that greater diversity promises. And being an effective inclusive leader requires specific skills, mindsets, experiences, and self-knowledge. Fortunately, these attributes can be defined, measured, assessed, coached, and developed—which takes us to what we have learned, through science and fieldwork, about what is required to be an inclusive leader.

WHY GREATER DIVERSITY DOES NOT AUTOMATICALLY LEAD TO BETTER RESULTS

Leaders in general have not yet been able to fully achieve the promise that greater diversity is good for the organization. A study by Nancy J. Adler demonstrated that while diverse teams do indeed outperform and out-innovate homogeneous teams, they also can be significantly less effective (see figure 3).[2] Why? Because diversity by itself is not enough. Rather, it must be skillfully managed in an inclusive way. Without inclusion and equity, diversity has a high chance of becoming chaotic, leading to lower productivity and engagement, higher turnover, and even litigation.

It is no wonder, then, that homogeneity is so attractive. It is relatively easy to manage a group of people with similar backgrounds and experiences. It is significantly more difficult to convince teams made up of individuals of varying differences to understand each other's thought patterns and behaviors, and to value them at a deep and

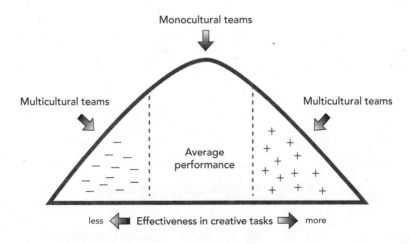

Figure 3. Impact of diversity on team performance. *Source*: Joseph DiStefano and Martha Maznevski, "Creating Value with DiverseTeams in Global Management,"*Organizational Dynamics* 29, no. 1 (2000): 45–63.

personal level. But inclusive leaders who are skilled at navigating these differences, and whose organizational values back them up, are able to optimize their performance to the point that those differences become leveraged assets that lead to better performance.

Interestingly, even when diverse teams are managed well, homogeneous teams still outperform diverse ones in the early stages because of the disruption and conflict that can result when different perspectives, experiences, backgrounds, thinking, and communication styles are merged. But over time, diverse teams managed well by inclusive leaders significantly outperform well-managed homogeneous ones (see figure 4).

WHAT DOES AN INCLUSIVE LEADER LOOK LIKE?

First, let us share how we determined what an inclusive leader looks like, thanks to the deep expertise and scientific knowledge of our PhD statisticians and industrial and organizational psychologists at the Korn Ferry Institute.

Since 2015, we have assessed more than three thousand leaders on inclusive leadership. We began with working assumptions grounded in Korn Ferry's vast knowledge and research on leadership, diversity, and inclusion. We tested our assumptions through fieldwork and

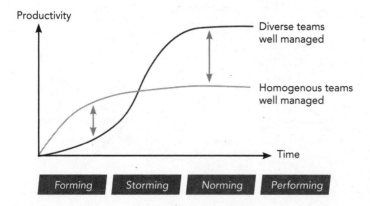

Figure 4. Impact of diversity on team performance. *Source*: Joseph DiStefano and Martha Maznevski, "Creating Value with Diverse Teams in Global Management,"*Organizational Dynamics* 29, no. 1 (2000): 45–63. Graph is adapted from three different sources: DiStefano and Maznevski, Katherine Phillips, and Bruce Tuckman.

then through the rigorous analysis of data collected from thousands of leaders. Over time, our knowledge deepened and evolved into our Inclusive Leader model.

With this experiential and quantitative grounding we mapped out a clear, inclusive leader profile of competencies and traits, this time based on a thorough analysis of Korn Ferry's database of more than 3 million leadership assessments. We then used a variety of additional qualitative testing strategies, which included an Inclusive Leader survey of talent professionals, in-depth interviews with inclusive leaders, focus groups in Argentina, Colombia, Germany, India, and the United States, and one virtual focus group with five participants from different African countries. This rich and diverse data provided us with profound insight into what it takes to be an inclusive leader. (See appendix B for details on each of the research methodologies.)

We determined that inclusive leadership can be defined empirically and experientially by looking at specific inclusive leader competencies—what leaders do to be inclusive—and traits—who they are that leads to their being inclusive. Therefore, inclusive leadership can be assessed, coached, and developed.

We define inclusive leaders as leaders who interact with the diversity around them, who build interpersonal trust, who take the views of others into account, and who are adaptive. These abilities increase their effectiveness and the impact they have on individuals, teams, clients, customers, and communities—and therefore on the organization as a whole.

TRAITS—INNER ENABLERS OF INCLUSIVE LEADERSHIP

Traits are how we are wired. They indicate our personality characteristics, which heavily influence how we think, feel, and act. In the Inclusive Leader model, traits are the enablers that support the inclusive leader competencies. Taken as a whole, these traits help answer the following question: What is a leader's natural disposition toward differences?

We found five trait clusters (authenticity, emotional resilience, self-assurance, inquisitiveness, and flexibility) that enable inclusive leadership, and each contains several subtraits:

- **Authenticity** requires humility, setting aside ego, and establishing trust in the face of opposing beliefs, values, or perspectives.
- **Emotional resilience** requires the ability to remain composed in the face of adversity and difficulty, including when one is around others with differences. It also requires situational awareness, to be able to pivot and change behaviors to effectively manage diversity.
- **Self-assurance** requires a stance of confidence and optimism.
- **Inquisitiveness** requires openness to differences, curiosity, and empathy.
- **Flexibility** requires the ability to tolerate ambiguity and to be adaptable to diverse needs.

Later, we will explore these enabling traits in more detail and look at why all of the listed traits are essential to leading inclusively, with skill and impact.

COMPETENCIES—THE FIVE DISCIPLINES OF INCLUSIVE LEADERS

Traits such as an openness toward differences are must-haves, but they are not enough to make an inclusive leader. An inclusive leader must also possess the skills to lead inclusively.

Korn Ferry found and used empirical analysis to organize these competencies into the clusters that we call the five disciplines. The inclusive leader builds interpersonal trust, integrates diverse perspectives, optimizes talent, applies an adaptive mindset, and achieves transformation.

- **Builds interpersonal trust.** The inclusive leader embraces perspectives that differ from their own; they are honest and authentic.
- **Integrates diverse perspectives.** The inclusive leader considers all points of view and the needs of others and skillfully navigates conflict situations
- **Optimizes talent.** The inclusive leader motivates others, supports their growth, and joins forces for collective success.

- **Applies an adaptive mindset**. The inclusive leader takes a broad worldview, adapts behavior to suit the situation, and creates new approaches.
- **Achieves transformation**. The inclusive leader confronts difficult topics and brings people along to achieve results.

The five disciplines, based on competencies, are enabled by the five trait clusters. Figure 5 shows how these are related. Leaders can have expanding spheres of impact that flow from self, team, and organization. If we follow the Inclusive Leader model in figure 5 clockwise,

Figure 5. The Inclusive Leader model. *Source*: Korn Ferry Institute, 2020.

the spheres of influence widen as one moves along the model. *Builds interpersonal trust* primarily involves the spheres of self and team, while *integrates diverse perspectives* moves more fully into the realm of impact on the team. *Optimizes talent* has a major impact on both the team and the organization, but both still primarily relate to the direct impact on talent. It's in the last two disciplines, *applies an adaptive mindset* and *achieves transformation*, where the impact lies heavily on the organization—not only on people strategies and experiences but also on other business imperatives, such as innovation, globalization, brand and reputation, and growing market share.

In part 1, we will devote full chapters to each of the five disciplines, complete with stories of how they were put into action and the results they yielded.

BIOGRAPHY MATTERS

There is a vital wrapper around our Five Disciplines model: biography. A leader's formative and lived experiences create a unique, irreplicable story that in essence makes them "diverse"—though the term *diverse* is commonly misused. People often will refer to "diverse candidates" or "diverse talent" when they really are referring to talent that has been traditionally underrepresented. But these people are no more or less diverse than those from the majority culture. Diversity is about the full range of differences. Instead of talking about diverse employees, then, it is much better to talk about diverse workforces and teams. Every person is diverse in their own way, and it is useful to embrace this notion because it can be potently effective in helping those in the majority culture—in many cases the White male—to begin to feel included in the inclusion journey.

In any event, because biography matters, it is important to recognize that each person's "diversity" confers on them advantages or disadvantages that create inequity in society and the workplace. Addressing this disparity is what leads us to the work of inclusion and equity.

We have found that knowing clients' biographies as well as their experience with diversity can help in how we coach them on the five disciplines. Experiences that expose one to a variety of geographies, to people with all kinds of differences and a range of contexts, can have a profound impact in challenging leaders' assumptions and ways of doing things. It also helps them realize the power of approaching problems by unconventional paths and to recognize that customer and employee needs cannot be effectively addressed the same way across the board. Instead, solutions may be varied and sometimes counterintuitive.

Formatively, a leader may have grown up in a different country or region from the one in which they live and work today. They may have experienced being in the minority, in the majority, or in a fully racially or ethnically mixed environment. Their parents may have done an overseas stint in business, nonprofit, government, military, or missionary organizations. While in school, leaders may have studied abroad or participated in a service program. They may have undertaken an extended stay in a different culture, whether within or outside of their native country. Their professional development might have included expatriate assignments. Work assignments across varied (cross-functional, cross-divisional, or cross-market) contexts also may have forced leaders to operate outside their comfort zones and to challenge their own assumptions.

In our Inclusive Leader survey of talent professionals, there was unanimous consensus that inclusive leaders must seek to gain new and diverse experiences in the present and the future. It also was seen as valuable if leaders had been actively involved in "giving back," such as by sponsoring or mentoring people from different backgrounds (68%), or if they had worked in an organization with a meaningful amount of diversity (48%).

Biography matters because exposure to different experiences, coupled with deliberate development and discussion about what they mean, can be transformative. This can help leaders get comfortable seeing the world from other points of view. Inclusive leaders learn to more profoundly leverage their biographies, with savvy, to lead others inclusively. And for those who did not have early life exposures to diverse experiences, it's not too late for short- or long-term immersion experiences, or even lifestyle changes. Throughout this book you will come across leaders who have done both.

HOW THIS BOOK IS ORGANIZED

In the next section, "The Core of Inclusive Leadership," we will explore the traits that enable leaders to develop and practice each of the five disciplines. These traits, which are made of strands of personal beliefs, values, and personality, are leaders' source of energy for building the full range of skills that the five disciplines require.

Following that summary, part 1 focuses on each of the five disciplines of inclusive leaders, one chapter at a time, using quantitative and qualitative research to unpack each of the competencies that compose the disciplines.

Part 2 focuses on the exemplars, the individuals and organizations that are standouts in living inclusive leadership. We tell these stories from the point of view of impact—how inclusive leadership led to business outcomes, how their actions and behavior with their diverse workforces helped them to optimize results.

Part 3 lays out some of the most intractable diversity and inclusion challenges that inclusive leaders must confront to design the equitable organizations of the future.

And finally, in the conclusion, we zero in on the key takeaways from our journey together, and then leave the last word to the next generation of leaders among Millennials (born roughly between 1980 and 1994) and Generation Z (born between 1995 and 2015), in terms of what they understand inclusive leadership means for them and how that understanding will shape the further evolution of inclusive leadership.

There is one other essential element to how we put this book together. We invited more than a dozen current or recent Korn Ferry consultants to write sidebars that illustrate various aspects of how the five disciplines and their enabling traits play out in reality. These contributors reflect diversity across geographies, abilities, religion, gender, race and ethnicity, generation, and areas of experience. We did this in the spirit of inclusive leadership, because of our deep-seated belief that the collective intelligence of a diverse team would yield greater value to the work and to your reading experience. The individuals they choose to focus on—organizational executives, historical figures, artists, athletes, or public servants—as well as their interpretation of how these individuals lead inclusively, is unique to them. We could not have come up with these sidebars on our own. Not only did each contributor add richness at face value with their bylined sidebar, but also their contributions further the synthesis of our thinking about what it takes to be an inclusive leader.

So here we are, with the case for inclusive leadership laid out and an introduction to a verified model for what this kind of leadership looks like. Ready to dive in?

It takes a comprehensive plan to foster inclusive leadership that achieves the promises of a more diverse workforce. We invite you to dig deeper into what it means to be an inclusive leader and to learn from those who have started to crack the code.

■   ■   ■

THE CORE OF INCLUSIVE LEADERSHIP: THE ENABLING TRAITS

OUR RESEARCH ON INCLUSIVE LEADER TRAITS HAS taken us to the land of *Of course*. Of course inclusive leaders need to be authentic, self-assured, and inquisitive. Of course they are emotionally resilient and flexible. Our research uncovered these traits, and our colleagues, as well as those we asked in surveys and focus groups, confirmed that they make sense (see appendix B, table B-1).

But leaders who exhibit these vital personality characteristics without the actionable behaviors and competencies embodied in the five disciplines will remain as feel-good leaders who failed to lead transformation through diversity (getting the mix in the door), inclusion (ensuring the mix is working well), and equity (ensuring that all have equal access, opportunity, support, and reward). Conversely, leaders who focus only on "Tell me what to do and I'll do it," without cultivating the enabling traits of inclusive leadership through deeper personal work, will be lacking the energy and credibility sources that enable all of the five disciplines.

We have identified eleven enabling traits that reside within the five enabling trait clusters mentioned. As part of the validation process we surveyed talent and diversity and inclusion professionals (see table 1, next page). Next, we explore each cluster, calling out some of their less obvious implications for inclusive leadership.

ENABLING TRAIT CLUSTER	DEFINITION	ENABLING TRAITS	RESPONDENTS WHO RATE TRAIT CLUSTER *EXTREMELY IMPORTANT*	RESPONDENTS WHO RATE TRAIT CLUSTER *VERY IMPORTANT*	TOTAL
Authenticity	Expectations of forthrightness in relationships; humility; freedom from arrogance	Trust Humility	63%	29%	92%
Emotional resilience	Calm and composed under stress; aware of self in the moment	Composure Situational self-awareness	63%	21%	84%
Self-assurance	Believes in own capabilities; has positive expectations for the future	Confidence Optimism	25%	42%	67%
Inquisitiveness	Inquisitive; seeks understanding and sense-making; wants to know how others think and feel	Openness to differences Curiosity Empathy	58%	38%	96%
Flexibility	Comfortable when the path forward is not clear	Tolerance for ambiguity Adaptability	38%	42%	80%

Table 1. Korn Ferry Validated Traits Associated with Inclusive Leadership

AUTHENTICITY

EXPECTATIONS OF FORTHRIGHTNESS IN RELATIONSHIPS; HUMILITY; FREEDOM FROM ARROGANCE

- Trust
- Humility

The literature on contemporary leadership is replete with research that indicates that **authenticity** is one of the most valued traits in leaders. Generation X, Millennials, and Gen Z, having grown up in a time without an expectation of personal privacy, are cynical about leaders and institutions because of all that has been exposed about what happens behind closed doors. They expect that the truth about ethical lapses, corporate greed, or government corruption will come out sooner or later.

To create *trust*, leaders must be transparent about who they are, how they make decisions, and how their thinking may be evolving as it is challenged. This is why we begin inclusive leader work with individuals sharing their personal biographies and cultural identities.

We start out with the (true) assumption that everyone is diverse. Everyone has a unique, irreplicable story, including those in the majority. Of course, each person also needs to have a grasp on what advantages and disadvantages their diversity has provided them with—this is the work of inclusion and equity.

To share and disclose requires *humility*. While there are indeed leaders who grew up privileged, many have stories of growing up poor or in abusive homes. Some of the executives we have coached in the United States were members of White minorities in Black or Latino communities. Others were Black, Latino, or Asian minorities in White communities. Even those who grew up privileged often have mixed feelings about whether their lack of exposure to diversity has stunted their ability to be inclusive. There are myriad permutations. When leaders begin to be open about their stories and their implications, first to themselves and then by sharing them with others, it begins a process of establishing and deepening trust with those within a team or an organization.

But this kind of openness does not come easily at all, and this is not true just for leaders. Much of the failure to leverage diversity comes from the fact that those in the minority often feel the need to downplay or cover who they are because of a lack of trust in the majority culture. *Covering* is a term that was first used by sociologist Erving Goffman to describe how people with "known stigmatized identities" consciously choose to "mute" those identities.[1]

Sixty-one percent of leaders queried in a Deloitte University survey said they cover at work. This includes people of different races, ethnicities, personalities, physical and cognitive abilities, and sexual orientations. Even 45% of straight White males—a group that historically hasn't been the subject of diversity and inclusion studies—reported covering.[2]

This generates a Catch-22: I won't show who I am because it's not safe, but I won't trust you if you don't show me who you are. Inclusive leaders break this cycle by uncovering their identities and being authentic. When they do, this act of humility and of trusting those around them, is an enabler to the heavy lifting of each of the five disciplines.

EMOTIONAL RESILIENCE

CALM AND COMPOSED UNDER STRESS; AWARE OF SELF IN THE MOMENT

- Composure
- Situational self-awareness

Diversity and inclusion can elicit a significant amount of hidden panic among leaders. After all, they often are the cited evidence that an organization is not diverse or inclusive.

In addition, the topics to address are fraught in the social and political discourses of our day, as captured in hashtags such as #BlackLivesMatter, #TimesUp, #NoBanNoWall, #MarchForOurLives, #TakeAKnee, #Dreamers, #LoveIsLove, or #ÉCoisaDePreto (#It'sABlackThing, which was to laud the achievements of Afro-Brazilians). Each of these draws not only fervent supporters who retweet but also fierce opponents who troll. With the power of social media to make any misstatement or action go viral, many leaders are reluctant to go near these trending diversity topics within their organizations.

For this reason, the trait of **emotional resilience** is a must-have for leaders who seek to be inclusive. But this work is not for the faint of heart. Across countries, industries, and functions, leaders scored low on this enabling trait cluster in our global inclusive leadership analysis. That is because one of the hardest things about diversity is adapting to unfamiliar people and situations and keeping it together in the midst of the complexities of differences.

As inclusive leaders make declarations of the vitalness of diversity and inclusion to the organization, hopes will be raised, but backlash also will ensue. Voices that have long been covered and repressed will begin to be heard; they will begin to challenge and question more openly (as they should). The organization and its leaders will need to listen and be ready to respond.

In this environment, *composure*—the ability to remain calm and in control in the midst of stress and challenge—is vital. Employees understand that the issues are fraught. All sides, for the most part, seek out and value the leaders who can keep it together as the tugs and pulls take place.

Inclusive leaders also require *situational self-awareness* to tune in to the context in which they are about to speak or make a decision. But the contexts they need to be aware of are not just the ones within organizational boundaries; they also need to be tuned in to what is going on in the world at large and how it is affecting their employees. (See chapter 12 for more on managing when the outside comes inside.)

SELF-ASSURANCE

BELIEVES IN OWN CAPABILITIES; HAS POSITIVE EXPECTATIONS FOR THE FUTURE

- Confidence
- Optimism

We all know it's difficult for people to change in their personal lives, and this is no less true of people within organizations. When favored or legacy behaviors have been institutionalized through processes, structure, policies, and requirements, it becomes clear how audacious a declaration to become more diverse and inclusive really is.

Consider the *confidence* and *optimism* all pioneers exhibit in the face of uncertainty and long odds. Examples include NASA, in its quest to get a man on the moon; the Polynesians who embarked on rafts to see where the massive Pacific Ocean currents took them, and landed in South America; Polish-French physicist and chemist Marie Curie, who remains the only person to win the Nobel Prize in two different scientific fields; or gymnast Simone Biles, who performed the first-ever triple double tumbling pass. None of these achievements would have been possible without the people involved possessing the **self-assurance** that they could be done.

Inclusive leaders also require this trait for the very hard, perilous, and long-haul work of diversity and inclusion. Employees may be cynical about the prospect of change, but they also are receptive to those who charge forward with the confidence and optimism to make it happen anyway.

INQUISITIVENESS

SEEKS UNDERSTANDING AND SENSE-MAKING; WANTS TO KNOW HOW OTHERS THINK AND FEEL

- Openness to differences
- Curiosity
- Empathy

Inquisitiveness is the heart and soul of the enabling trait composites. It's this inquisitive demeanor that pries things wide open when it comes to unleashing the power of diversity in an inclusive way. For all the talk about how organizations need differences for all sorts of compelling reasons, the propulsion inherent in this diversity often remains bottled up—like the fuel in a rocket that sits ready to be ignited and to cause liftoff but never does.

The only way to ignite diversity and all the power it brings is to tap into it, explore it, and understand it through inquisitiveness.

Paradoxically, one of the greatest inhibitors to diversity and inclusion is an early concept of D&I that required the opposite of inquisitiveness: blindness to differences. Among its most hallowed manifestations is Dr. Martin Luther King Jr.'s wish that his children "will not be judged by the color of their skin but by the content of their character." There is no denying the healing power this approach has had in breaking down the judgments against differences, which often are even codified into law and training solutions. But this uplifting message of unity could potentially make us noninclusive, because this assumption of similarity can mask ways in which we are different and thus can cause us to ignore each individual's diverse life experiences.

Lack of *curiosity* and *openness to differences* can lead to a form of bias, an assumption that everyone is the same. The result can be the dismissal or minimization of other people's feelings, ways of thinking, and experiences.[3]

Furthermore, when openness is limited to just an embrace of those who are different, without an accompanying *empathy* for their different experiences, people may be reticent to bring their whole selves to work, as they have been invited to do. It negates the very benefits we seek out in attracting greater diversity.

This is the moment where many start to bump into cognitive dissonance. If we call out differences this way—even in the constructive spirit in which it's meant—what about unity? Does this not create a separation, the very antithesis of what we are after in inclusion? Therein lies the inclusion paradox: in order to achieve inclusion, rather than just focusing on what we have in common, we need to proactively surface our differences as well.[4]

The only way to navigate this paradox and be truly inclusive is to be inquisitive through an openness to the implications of people's differences, curiosity about who they are and the choices they have made about individual and group identity, and empathy that not only seeks to understand but honors and respects the choices people have made about who they say they are.

A study of inclusive leadership by Catalyst shows that people want both unity with others *and* to have their differences recognized. As the research authors, Jeanine Prime and Elizabeth R. Salib, explain, perceiving similarities with coworkers engendered a feeling of belongingness, while perceiving differences led to feelings of uniqueness. Across the six different countries studied (Australia, China, Germany, India, Mexico, and the United States), these perceptions were strong predictors of inclusion. Employee feelings of uniqueness and belonging contributed, on average, more than 20% to employees' perceptions of inclusion. Meanwhile, uniqueness accounted for 18% to 24% of an employee's perception of inclusion, and belonging accounted for 27% to 35%.[5]

FLEXIBILITY

COMFORTABLE WHEN THE PATH FORWARD IS NOT CLEAR

- Tolerance of ambiguity
- Adaptability

Certainty can be comforting. But when it comes to organizations made up of a diversity of humans, there are way too many situational variables, way too much mystery about human emotions and motivations, and way too many unknowns about what has shaped people's worldviews to be certain about the best way to achieve greater D&I.

Inclusive leaders understand that there is no one answer or set of practices that will achieve their goal of diversity and inclusion and unleash the power of all of us. That is because D&I is always about testing and questioning the status quo. (If the status quo were already equitable, there would not be any need for diversity and inclusion

THE CHALLENGE WITH TRAITS: CAN PEOPLE REALLY CHANGE WHO THEY ARE?

Sarah Hezlett, Minneapolis

The very definition of a trait, as a personal, distinguishing characteristic or quality, makes it seem immutable and enduring. But can people change and develop their traits? A growing body of research says yes. While your traits may be relatively stable, they are not fixed in stone.

Through adulthood, our personalities continue to change. On average, people tend to become warmer. They grow more responsible. Calmer. More confident. And these trends suggest that personality change is not always short-term or temporary. Personality changes can stick.[6] Evidence suggests that these changes are not just a function of maturing or aging but of life events. Individuals' traits shift, both in anticipation of and as a consequence of life experiences.[7]

This is good news for those seeking to be more inclusive leaders. Not only is it possible to develop the disciplines of inclusive leadership but also people can shift their traits to be more enabling and supportive of inclusive behaviors.

Melinda Gates, Cochair of the Bill & Melinda Gates Foundation, is an example of someone who has changed something fundamental about who she is. In her book *The Moment of Lift*, she writes, "I am a private person—in certain ways, a bit shy. I was the girl in school who raised her hand to speak while other kids bellowed their answers from the back row. I like to work offstage."[8]

interventions.) This means that inclusive leaders must be adept at moving from a place of organizational and individual certainty to one of exceptional **flexibility**. They must have a *tolerance for ambiguity*, because the contexts in which they find themselves are not always clear and we really don't know what the future holds. They must demonstrate *adaptability* to situations in which the information is always incomplete and vital voices often are missing from the room.

In martial arts, a stiff stance sets one up for an easy takedown. So, too, with leading inclusively. Instead, assume a flexible crouch and you will have the greatest set of options to counter the next strike of injustice, inequity, and exclusion.

But personal and public experiences led her to change. She wrestled with the unresolved impact of a previous abusive relationship in her life and went through an identity crisis as she transitioned from being a corporate leader to a stay-at-home mom. Then, as the leader of a high-profile organization, she came face to face with realities that called for her to be more outspoken. She opted to transform herself into a highly visible public advocate for empowering women—a huge shift for her.

Despite her fears about being the focus of public controversy, particularly as a Catholic, Gates considered the importance of serving as a role model for her children, the previous experiences she valued and wanted to honor, the beliefs she learned from her mother, and the morality of failing to act. As a profile of her in the *Christian Science Monitor* described it, "The more she learned about the struggles of poor women in Africa and Asia—including the discrimination and abuse they faced from husbands who, for example, beat their wives for using birth control—the stronger her voice became."[9]

Developing new traits involves disruption. We need to step out of established routines and get uncomfortable. We need to critically reflect on what habits and beliefs serve us, and what gets in our way—often with guidance from others. And we need to embrace new experiences.

Yes, it is possible for people's traits to change. And as Melinda Gates's story demonstrates, growing one's enabling traits builds the capacity for inclusive leadership.

TRAITS AND DISCIPLINES GO HAND IN HAND

Leaders who exhibit the vital personality traits of authenticity, emotional resilience, self-assurance, inquisitiveness, and flexibility are critical to D&I efforts. But without the actionable behaviors embodied in the five disciplines, these leaders will fall short in achieving D&I transformation. In part 1, we will explore the five disciplines that operationalize inclusive leadership and unleash the power of us all.

If traits are the soul of inclusive leaders, the five disciplines—those key competency composites—are the inclusive leaders in action. The five disciplines are what inclusive leaders achieve through skill, persistence, and practice. As the leaders master the inclusion competencies, they go through the same process as when they learn any other set of skills. There are things to learn and apply. There is trial and error. There is feedback and coaching. There is role modeling. There is learning from others. There are risk assessment, trade-off decisions, and bold actions. And these efforts are mobilized at the interpersonal, team, and organizational levels.

The great news is that leaders seeking to be inclusive come to this work already possessing many strengths. They are accomplished in their fields, they are already leading others, and they have been recognized, promoted, and rewarded according to their leadership abilities. But as with mastering any other discipline, whether it be archery, cooking, playing the clarinet, gardening, home building, or you name it, there is always more to learn; there is more knowledge, more insights, and more experiences to be acquired on the road to a deep and nuanced understanding of what inclusive leadership entails and the ability to evaluate the capabilities of inclusive leaders.

In part 1, we plumb the meaning of each of the five disciplines and unpack each of the competencies within them. We bring the science behind the disciplines to life with the perspectives of inclusive leaders and informative sidebars highlighting others who exemplify the competencies.

PART 1

THE FIVE DISCIPLINES

DISCIPLINE 1

Builds
Interpersonal Trust

INSTILLS TRUST
VALUES DIFFERENCES

A T TWENTY-EIGHT YEARS OLD, JUAN GALARRAGA WAS asked to take a high-risk assignment. He was charged with turning around a high-volume, high-visibility, and severely underperforming Target store in South Florida. An ambitious Venezuelan immigrant, he accepted the turnaround assignment and within a week had moved to Naples, three hours away.

The situation was even worse than he had thought. He had seen the poor financials before arriving, but not the depth of low morale and hostile finger pointing. Recognizing the skepticism aimed at him due to his relative youth and his being an unknown, and given that he had precious little time to show he could turn things around, Galarraga's top priority was to quickly build interpersonal trust—not just between him and his new associates but also among the team members themselves.

During his first week, Galarraga called a mandatory all-team meeting behind the store, before the doors opened to customers. When people arrived, they saw a big bonfire. Galarraga instructed them to sit in a circle around it. He asked everyone to write down a story about a disappointment or frustration with something that was going on at the store.

> **BUILDS INTERPERSONAL TRUST:**
>
> *is honest and follows through; establishes rapport by finding common ground while simultaneously able to value perspectives that differ from own.*

One after the other, each read what they had written. When they were done, Galarraga had them throw their pieces of paper into the bonfire and watch them go up in smoke.

"No more," he said. "It's a new day, a new life. Let's have each other's back. Today, we start anew!"

That Target store became one of the most successful in the region.

Builds interpersonal trust is a foundational discipline of inclusive leaders. In fact, 100% of the talent professionals who responded to our Inclusive Leader survey said building interpersonal trust is either extremely or very important to being an effective inclusive leader.

Trust leads to credibility and an increased willingness to listen and adhere to directions. It creates a reciprocity between leaders and team members in which both feel comfortable sharing themselves and their perspectives.

Two competencies make up this first discipline: the ability to *instill trust* and the ability to *value differences*. Interestingly, each initially leans in the opposite direction of the other, but then they come full circle to reinforce each other, for optimal inclusive impact.

Instilling trust requires finding common ground across differences, while valuing differences requires surfacing the implications of differences to better understand others. As we saw in the previous chapter, this is the paradox of inclusion: inclusive leaders must focus on what we have in common and also proactively unearth our differences.

Finding common ground comes first, before the harder work of surfacing differences constructively. To do so, leaders often highlight the organizational mission and values employees are meant to live, and they communicate the shared short- and long-term goals they are working toward together. As in Juan Galarraga's story, the messages tend to emphasize that "We are all in the same boat," "We are family," and "There is no *I* in *team*."

But focusing on commonalities as a way of establishing trust has its clear limits. There is a point of diminishing returns, where the drive to find commonality as an act of solidarity devalues differences. When this happens, the trust born out of the discovery of similarities begins to erode.

When differences are brought out into the open, inclusive leaders can shape more inclusive practices and procedures to achieve that often touted but often elusive goal of greater diversity leading to greater creativity and innovation.

This is how *instills trust* and *values differences* end up reinforcing one another. Finding commonalities instills the initial trust that allows for the higher-risk exploration of differences. Then, as leaders surface and embrace differences, they build further trust with all their team members.

INSTILLS TRUST

He who does not trust enough, will not be trusted.

Lao Tzu

There are plenty of strong leaders who are very good at instilling trust in people like themselves. Inclusive leaders, however, are distinguished by their ability to *instill trust* in the face of all forms of difference. This is particularly difficult because, biologically and neuroscientifically, we are programmed to be less trusting and more critical of those who are not like us.[1]

The following leaders, in very different organizations and from very different cultures, instilled trust in similar ways: by focusing on what their very different team members had in common.

Hengliang Pan, General Manager of the Global After-market Business at LiuGong Machinery, headquartered in China, said:

> I was leading a project on global cost pricing and
> one of the VPs [vice presidents], also from China, was
> much older than me and had significantly more global
> experience. We were so different from each other
> that there was a lot of conflict; it affected the other
> team members, who were from other countries and

functions as well. We had a meeting where we got to
air our different points of view, but the turning point
was when we talked about how we all were working
for the same business and we all wanted to grow it. It
is important to find a common goal, because everything we do, we do not do for ourselves but for the
business to grow.

Gabor Gonda, Managing Director–Central Europe at Hewlett
Packard Enterprise (HPE), related, "I have had to restructure various
projects or start them from scratch. Every time I grant 100% trust
from day one, with the assumption that people are good. I assume that
everyone will respect if others take the risk of sharing something vulnerable about themselves. It makes you look human. If you are willing
to do this, the others become more comfortable in doing the same."

Freada Kapor Klein, founder of SMASH and co-founder of Kapor
Capital with her husband, said:

I am completely underwhelmed by people who lead
with where they work and where their degrees are
from. I'm much more interested in their stories and the
emotional, social, and geographic distances they have
traveled. We look for people whose lived experience
actually leads them to identify problems and solutions
that those in the majority don't see. We ask them not
what they believe but what have they done to work on
diversity and inclusion. If they can't tell us specifically
what they did yesterday or last week toward greater
equity, I don't believe them. We found that in the entrepreneurs we fund, if they have been confronted by the
injustices of the criminal justice system, the education
system, the credit system, this is what has driven them
to create a business to solve those very problems.

Of course, the universal experience of eating is a surefire way to
break down walls and build inclusion. Mervi Lampinen, a Director
of Information Technology (IT) at MSD Sharp & Dohme in Germany,
shares her inclusive approach, which is in some ways countercultural
to her German context: "I cook! Any time we have people coming
to Germany I always invite them to my home, where I cook. The

food and home environment is very informal and inclusive. It brings people together by bringing down barriers. This is especially helpful in German culture, which has a very strong hierarchy. Food helps dismantle the hierarchy and brings everyone to the same level."

Frode Berg, Managing Director of Nordics at Experian, zeroes in on people's common desire for those around them to be reliable:

> It's important to really do what you say you are going to do and be fanatical about it. Do not change your story line; if you have promised something, then you better deliver it. That is the way you build a bridge of trust with someone, who may have every reason to be a bit biased against you if there are cultural or language differences. And if for some reason you cannot do what you said you were going to do, be quick with acknowledging it, and share how you will fix and address the situation—and abide by the new time frame.

Anil Sachdev, CEO of the School of Inspired Leadership (SOIL), in Gurgaon, India, told us how common it is for people to long for transparency and reliability; even when the truth is painful, it instills trust. He shares his story of heading operations when the market was in very bad shape and cash for salaries and other spending was very tight: "We were transparent about the current state and made a commitment that we would not lay off the workers as long as there is cash. Further, once cash shortages began to cut into payroll, we started reducing compensation at the top with layoffs as the last resort."

Missteps in building trust may arise when people build on shaky or irrelevant ground. Lou Nieto, former president of Consumer Foods at ConAgra, shares how people often build trust by building teams around them with people similar to them: "I was a director-level person reporting to a VP who was not a very strong performer. He tried to build trust with me on the basis that we went to the same fraternity, though in different schools. But this wasn't a social setting, it was a business setting, and at the end of the day my loyalty was to the business. The commonality that needed to matter to build trust was high performance, not both of us knowing the same secret handshake."

Instilling trust also requires learning to be discerning when, even when valuing differences, it would be best not to highlight differences. Sachdev from SOIL tells this story:

> I was in Japan with people from twelve different countries in a fellowship program to learn about the Japanese culture of productivity. In the evening, after the fellowship program was done for the day, my Mitsubishi colleagues would entertain me. On the bus the next morning with the fellowship participants, I would be asked what I did in the evenings.
>
> Then one day a Japanese woman brought this up to me in that most gentle of Japanese ways: "Anil, do you know that when you share those stories, it makes the other

STORYTELLING GOES TO THE HEART OF TRUST

INSTILLS TRUST ▪ *Kevin Cashman, Minneapolis*

Two enterprise CEOs from the same company I was coaching came onstage, one after the other, to unveil their new agendas tied to the organization's already-declared transformational change.

The first CEO bombed in front of that audience of three thousand. The second one soared. Both were highly skilled and experienced. Both had attractive and well-put-together presentation slides. Both spoke to organizational values as the keys to the desired transformation. But one left the audience cold and cynical, the other engaged and inspired.

What was the difference?

The first CEO, who had a reputation of being a fact-finding leader, assumed his job was to inform. He listed the five values he felt were critical to the organization: value 1 . . . value 2 . . . value 3 . . . value 4 . . . value 5. . . . The group, which had been poised to hear fresh, different, and engaging ideas, was stunned. A resistant quiet blanketed the room. People moved back from the edges of their seats and leaned into their seatbacks with a disappointed, distrustful thud.

people feel sad?" She explained that because most of them came from poor countries, "when you share about your lavish experiences, you are reminding them that they are poor." I had no idea! This really helped me to be sensitive to intercultural sensitivities and what other people might feel and what you should and should not share in groups.

For Deena Al-Faris, founder of fashion brand Qamrah and cofounder of Caviar Court sturgeon fish farm and caviar factory in Saudi Arabia, instilling trust begins with trusting yourself first: "When you know what you want, you will know better what you should ask and what you shouldn't ask."

Is this all you have? Do you really care about these so-called values, or are you just mouthing the words from HR? Do I really want to entrust my career and creative energies to this leader . . . to this organization?

Sensing the flat response, the CEO tried to rally. "Okay. Let me list these values again." So he went through them a second time, in exactly the same dry way. Not a glimmer of engagement remained. Instead, there was disconnection and disillusionment. Likely, many LinkedIn profiles were updated that evening.

The second CEO, who had a reputation of being an inspiring and authentic leader, took a much different approach. He, too, had five core values; however, instead of reading them off as a list, he told an authentic, real-life story related to each one. The PowerPoint melted into the background as each of the core values came to life. The audience was perched on the edge of their chairs, absorbed in the authenticity and relevance of the CEO's inspired messages. He had tapped into the collective heart of the organization, and trust was pumping through the entire group!

The difference between the two CEOs is that the second understood how authentic, relevant stories move us from intellectually transmitting information to emotionally inspiring transcendent trust. Powerful stories inspire us to connect, to contribute, and to include. Storytelling goes to the heart of trust.

VALUES DIFFERENCES

Strength lies in differences, not in similarities.

> Stephen R. Covey, American
> educator

Getting out of the "find commonality" and into the *"value differences"* mode can be difficult, as it is so much easier to trust the familiar than the unfamiliar. The best antidote inclusive leaders use to overcome this barrier is to fully go against this primal current of distrust of the different. Instead, they lean into their differences, leveraging the enabling traits of curiosity, empathy, and humility.

 ### FROM STAR TO DIRECTOR: HOW INCLUSIVE LEADERS LEVERAGE DIFFERENCES

VALUES DIFFERENCES ▪ *Wayland Lum, Austin*

I was coaching a VP at a well-known global publishing company who had an impressive track record of managing team sales performance. It was easy to see why Scott had been so successful: he was a bright, big-picture thinker with healthy doses of charisma and drive. He knew how to win, but his victories usually involved him imposing his own will on the people he was leading. It was always the *Scott Show*, and he was the star.

Once he stepped into the VP role, Scott's team grew frustrated with how he led team discussions. Without realizing it, Scott had put himself in the position of spokesperson for all issues, challenges, and concerns that he thought required attention. It made his team feel like supporting players to the lead actor.

Korn Ferry research shows that valuing differences starts with the leader. When a leader recognizes the uniqueness of team members and creates a sense of shared purpose and belonging, a climate of inclusion is fostered and sustained. And that's when you get the best out of your people.

To truly value the different talents, perspectives, values, and aspirations in his people, Scott had to first *see* them. Through our coaching work, he gained insights and increased self-awareness of how he was coming across to others, especially his direct reports. Now it was

Hengliang Pan of LiuGong Machinery, a Chinese multinational that makes construction equipment, shares this story of valuing personality differences:

> I tend to be very calm and not have a passionate demeanor; therefore, I have ended up being more distant from the people who work with me. But then I started working with Mr. Wang, who was very energetic, highly encouraging of the people around him, and much older than me. He was also a very good critical thinker who approached problems systemically, first diagnosing their root causes and then developing ways with others on how to solve those problems.

time to become a student of his people; he needed to gain a deeper understanding of who they were, what motivated them, what they valued, and how they wanted to make their best contribution at work.

Scott channeled the same commitment and energy that made him a winning sales manager into becoming an effective talent developer. He began documenting the personal development of each of his people and discussing their progress with them. It sent a strong message that he was committed to their growth.

In team meetings, Scott stopped leading with his thoughts on the business and what needed to be done. Instead, he led with examples of performance-related successes, followed up with public and private recognition of each person's work.

In one of our coaching sessions, I asked Scott how this had made a difference in his team's performance.

"My team is better at taking charge and moving forward with confidence," he answered. His efforts to value differences helped each team member elevate their performance and contributions.

Valuing differences was a mindset shift for Scott. He no longer waited for managers to share their needs with him. He actively asked how he could support them in the unique ways that they needed his support. Talent management went from being a twice-yearly discussion to an ongoing conversation about their challenges, obstacles, and wins.

Scott was now the director of the show, and his people were the stars.

———————— ■ ————————

While I valued his technical and problem-solving know-how, I especially noticed how he engaged others both emotionally and intellectually. I learned from him how to be more energetic with my team and show them that I was passionate about the business plan.

Gabor Gonda at HPE told us about how he learned to value nationality diversity, while acknowledging the extra work this difference requires to build trust:

When I was appointed as the managing director of this Central Europe region, I had talent from three different countries. They were not getting along with each other and it was hindering the work. I encouraged them to be explicit yet sympathetic about the obstacles caused by their differences. It turns out that some did not feel comfortable talking and problem-solving in English, our corporate global language, in front of customers. Our solution was to create a guide that documents our processes and selling points that everyone could use instead of having to explain things on the fly in an unfamiliar tongue.

For Jenny Ni, Human Resources Director of Dow China, her lesson came from valuing generational diversity:

My team is over 90% Millennials. One example of their different way of thinking was when we launched the annual campus recruitment campaign. We had always gone on campuses for campus recruiting, so I was surprised when they suggested we don't. Instead, they wanted to stage a big pop music concert to bring the students to one venue in the city. They also created a social media campaign to invite students to come to our corporate campus or join via live webcast to discuss "life experience with students." A lot of our more senior leaders did not really understand any of this, and I was a bridge between our younger talent and older leaders. Ironically, though, sometimes with the Millennials I had to just use my seniority to keep the ideas manageable!

Tram Trinh, CEO of VITANLINK, in Paris, describes herself as patient and as having an indirect style of communication. She learned to value a board member who had an opposite temperament: impatient and direct.

"I learned that a lot of time can be wasted trying to be polite when it is clear it's time to walk away."

Frode Berg from Experian calls himself the archetypically brooding Norwegian. His client was the archetypal optimistic American from Florida. Their phone and video call negotiations were not going well, and just when it felt like things could not get any worse, the American announced, "I am going to jump on a plane and fly to London so we can get this deal across the line."

"I didn't see where that would help, as we were so far from each other's positions," Berg shares. But the sixty-year-old American would not take no for an answer from the thirty-year-old Scandinavian. He came to London and they overcame their differences. "His optimism and can-do attitude rolled away the fog of my own pessimism and overcautiousness."

Inclusive leaders confront their own conscious and unconscious biases, open themselves up to approaches that they are uncomfortable with, and lean into their differences with others. And when they do—despite the discomfort, the friction, and the conflict—good things happen.

Building interpersonal trust requires learning how to instill trust and to value differences on a one-to-one and a one-to-group basis.

Next, we will discuss the discipline of *integrates diverse perspectives*. It requires the leveraging of differences in a manner that expands the spheres of impact beyond self and team to the wider organization.

■   ■   ■

Integrates Diverse Perspectives

MANAGES CONFLICT
BALANCES STAKEHOLDERS

W HEN TRAM TRINH, NOW CEO OF VITANLINK, was reporting to the chief operating officer at Johnson & Johnson, she was responsible for leading the rollout of a new software program. But this was more than just an IT project. It required working with many people, from all different types of backgrounds and at all levels, from executive to operational, in seven different European countries. Both the functional roles and cultural dispositions of the stakeholders led them toward very different priorities, styles of communication, and views on how to address nearly every aspect of the rollout. To further complicate the dynamics, they had only four months to do what usually would take seven.

Not everyone was in agreement with the aggressive timeline. It had been a corporate decision, but the finance and logistics directors in another location resisted it. People were being pulled by a hard, full-speed-ahead push, on the one hand, and tugged by a fierce push-back to slow down or even stop, on the other. The Reply All email threads captured the flow of passive-aggressive stances on all sides all too well.

> INTEGRATES DIVERSE PERSPECTIVES:
>
> *considers all points of view and needs of others; skillfully navigates conflict situations.*

Trinh needed to be in tune with the various stakeholders—their aspirations, needs, and worries—and to find a way to resolve the inherent conflicts that arose from their differences. Through various conversations in which she listened openly, she found the fulcrum of the resistance was one leader. Since this person was senior to her—and more than twice her age—Trinh first sought him out via email in to arrange a meeting, but he ignored her.

"I tried to see who around him could influence him. No one wanted to dare do that. It all became very toxic," Trinh recalls.

Trinh wanted to avoid escalating to the resister's boss. Since formality was not achieving the desired results, she decided to use a more direct approach. This executive was a morning person who got to the office long before anyone else did.

"So I started showing up when he did, with two cups of coffee," Trinh shares. "During this time, I brought up some of the key issues we were facing and I asked for his experienced help about what we should do."

The executive settled into the coach role as Trinh involved him in every one of the steps of the rollout. When she sent team emails, she made it clear they were the result of these joint conversations. This helped him feel valued, and it also helped the team; the emails, with their united stand, had eliminated the passive-aggressive tone of earlier exchanges, which previously had made the team ill at ease and unclear on how to move forward.

"He was not an easy person to work with," Trinh says of this resistant stakeholder, "but we found a way."

And in the end, the software was released on time.

In our Inclusive Leader survey of talent professionals, 100% of respondents said that **integrating diverse perspectives** was either extremely or very important. At the same time, we have found that this inclusive leadership discipline is one of the most difficult to master.

It requires patience and humility to *balance stakeholders* and effectively *manage conflict*. But most executives and their teams have a bias for action and are driven by near-term results. Explains Peggy Hazard, Korn Ferry senior client partner, who has worked extensively with executive teams to help them be more inclusive leaders:

> When asked about the value of leveraging diversity, they say, "But we have targets to meet; we don't have the luxury." Inclusive leaders, on the other hand, invest time and encourage voicing differences as an invaluable source of fresh solutions. They understand that the extra time they spend working through conflict on the front end not only saves time in the long run; it also leads to better results. They know groupthink can lead to poor and sometimes costly decisions. They listen more than they talk. They are patient and calm, to work through the surfaced or underground conflict caused by divergent opinions and then skillfully guide the team to converge to a better decision.

The findings of Dr. Katherine Phillips, from the Columbia University School of Business, support this view. "The mere presence of people on the team who we know are different in a significant way makes the team more creative, diligent, and successful," Phillips writes in *Scientific American*. "Simply interacting with individuals who are different forces group members to prepare better, to anticipate alternative viewpoints, and to expect that reaching consensus will take effort."[1]

BALANCES STAKEHOLDERS

> *In my experience, the most effective professionals in business and government have the ability to get things done. They're trained to work with multiple stakeholders, to understand how to identify a problem, devise solutions, to compromise and work well with others.*
>
> Henry Paulson, former US
> Secretary of the Treasury

In every organization, within each project or endeavor, there are multiple stakeholders who are active players in the initiative and/or will be affected by it. They have ideas, opinions, perspectives, hopes, and fears. While they are not all equally helpful or well-founded, they are real to the holders of those thoughts and feelings in ways that will affect their behaviors in either helpful or unhelpful ways.

Inclusive leaders *balance stakeholders* very well. They recognize that inclusion is about listening to all voices—after all, what is the point of diversity and inclusion if voices are ignored, marginalized, or shut down? Yet balancing stakeholders does not mean abdicating leading the way forward by falling prey to the paralysis of trying to satisfy all. This is not possible. Hence, the qualifier *balances*.

How can leaders ensure that their teams are producing what their customers need, efficiently and on time? That their employees are trained, enabled, appreciated, and rewarded well? That everyone is in the safest environment possible? That the company is in compliance throughout? That innovation keeps happening? That financial expectations are achieved? . . .

Balancing the needs of various stakeholders requires masterful leadership, and it is not about trying to satisfy everyone. Some needs will gain primacy over others, but over time the input of all leads to a better overall output and work environment.

Here's how one leader balances the various stakeholders *within* a group.

Johannes Koch, Managing Director Germany, SVP Global Sales DACH-region at Hewlett Packard Enterprise, has a team with twenty-three different nationalities and a good mix of men and women. Some of this diversity he inherited, due to the nature of his geographic responsibility, but he also has been deliberate in ensuring a strong gender and nationality mix so that no one group dominates.

In listening to how he balances this complex group of stakeholders, we discerned some principles that have served him well: *everyone participates* and there are *no stupid jokes*. To ensure everyone participates, Koch purposefully does not use PowerPoint slides in his staff calls. This puts the focus on the exchange of everyone's thoughts and ideas. Stakeholders of certain cultural backgrounds found this difficult at first. The Germans, Central Europeans, and Russians expect the boss to be the one giving direction, Koch explained.

Clearly, the prohibition of stupid jokes blunts exclusionary comments made in the guise of "just kidding." For women, who historically and still today have been objectified, this approach closes off negative comments and behaviors directed toward them and ensures a more level playing field for both women and men.

Jenny Ni, from Dow Chemical, discusses the additional need to balance stakeholders across various groups.

"As a human resources leader, I try to understand the different functions' perspectives before offering them solutions. There are two key things I seek to understand: One, where are they coming from in what they believe and want? And two, how to add value to what is going on."

With this approach, Ni ends up hearing things that she had not thought about, despite all her expertise. It also unearths stakeholder incompatibilities that will need to be resolved so she can address them proactively.

For those like Jenny Ni who are in a minority group, it can be very difficult to be responsive to various constituents while remaining true to themselves. She shares how she had to adapt to lead an all-male team in India:

> My initial style was to be quiet and humble around all my male colleagues. They were straightforward in their communications, and initially, to me, it seemed quite aggressive and I felt I could not talk. But it was not fair to say that they were aggressive and that I couldn't talk. In reality, they were just very passionate about their ideas and expressive in how they communicated. Since I was working in an all-male, all-Indian team, I started to adapt to the team more. I told them directly that I wanted to express my ideas—and they welcomed that! We developed a great relationship through our differences, and I was recognized as a good leader who represented their views well to the other parts of Dow.

Deena Al-Faris, cofounder of two very different companies in Saudi Arabia, shares how she uses her relationship-building skills to balance stakeholders as a minority.

"Throughout most of my career, I was the youngest leader and the only woman in the room, so I needed to invest time early with each of

ROHINI ANAND AT SODEXO: BALANCING STAKEHOLDERS TO DRIVE SOCIAL JUSTICE INITIATIVES

BALANCES STAKEHOLDERS ▪ *Ömer Ongun, Ottawa*

Who doesn't love a feel-good story? Like the one where Sodexo chefs regularly volunteer their time to provide healthy cooking workshops for Latino immigrants in central Florida's Hillsborough County.

For this workshop series, Sodexo, the food services and facilities management company, partners with the Mexican American Legal Defense and Educational Fund to present essential health and nutrition information aimed at helping Latino families lead a healthy lifestyle. And you can thank Rohini Anand, Sodexo's former chief diversity officer, who balanced the needs of multiple internal and external stakeholders—immigrant families, the fund, Sodexo's chefs, operational leaders, and employees—to create and sustain this inclusive social justice initiative.

"The key was creating a clear connection between the social service impact and the company's vision," says Anand. "You also have to be practical in implementation, do it in a way that builds a practical bridge between vision and aspiration."

For these health and wellness workshops, Anand's team had to do the heavy lifting as well as the funding, the first time around. She knew she could count on key stakeholders having a genuine interest in participating at least once, especially since it did not require funding or an ongoing commitment from them.

the stakeholders. I wanted to establish relationships and share what is on each other's minds, rather than allowing things to roll like a snowball based on assumptions. Before trying to influence them and reassure them that their various needs and expectations are being taken into account, I learned it was so important to first see and hear how people talk and think."

A key element of how Al-Faris and Ni addressed the challenge of being in the minority was by demonstrating cross-cultural agility in balancing stakeholders. This is something that Frode Berg from Experian also zeroed in on. He balances stakeholders by adapting to their various cultural and communications preferences.

"And once they see and experience it," Anand says, with the assurance of someone who has pulled this off time and time again, "they will do more." The firsthand experience of the impact they can have on their communities inspires commitment in stakeholders.

The cheering students and happy parents, now better equipped to live healthy lives, tug at the heartstrings and strengthen the key stakeholders' sense of mission. The ability to serve also elevates employee engagement. In addition, Anand directly links the program to the businesses' economics.

"Our clients then see the mutual benefits and they want to partner with us on several impact programs we have," says Anand. "This approach is embedded into a business development strategy."

Once stakeholders buy in and take ownership of these programs, sponsorship begins to stick. To ensure accountability and to keep these programs going, Anand and her team prepare diversity and inclusion scorecards with qualitative metrics that give managers credit for whatever steps they have taken, such as demonstrating inclusive behaviors with tangible actions.

This successful approach has now been replicated many times throughout Sodexo worldwide, serving refugees, empowering women, and contributing to economic development. And that's how Anand, an inclusive leader, balanced stakeholders to establish Sodexo's enduring contribution to social justice.

———————————▪———————————

"When we deal with Germans, we need to be more loud, show we can take direction, and show that we are in control in a variety of ways, including by never being late to a meeting. But in other parts of Europe we can be more relaxed in a meeting, to the point of not being involved much. It's a humbler stance."

In balancing stakeholders, it's not about the right way or wrong way to do things but about engaging players with different priorities in ways that keep the project moving forward.

For Rita Estevez Luaña of Experian, balancing stakeholders is simple: "No politics, no flashy talks, no hidden agendas! It's a waste of time." Her strategy is to listen carefully to each stakeholder's point of view and to clearly convey it to the others, so all carry the burden of resolving the dilemmas in ways that benefit the collective.

Balancing stakeholders is, in effect, well, a balancing act. No set of stakeholders is the same, but all of the inclusive leaders interviewed were clear about the same keys to success:

- Have a common goal.
- Listen to what people see and want.
- Be open with all about the various stakeholders you are needing to balance.
- Make them part of the solution.
- Be decisive once the input has been heard and considered.

MANAGES CONFLICT

In the middle of difficulty lies opportunity.

Albert Einstein, German-born
Nobel Prize–winning physicist

Most of us would rather avoid conflict than confront it. Conflict is tense, messy, and scary, and in fact can lead to very bad things. No wonder we wish it would just disappear.

But in organizational life, conflict is unavoidable.

"If it's important to someone, it has the potential to cause conflict," writes Heather Barnfield, Director, Intellectual Property Development at the Korn Ferry Institute, in its competency development guide, *FYI for Your Improvement*. "Handled badly, conflict can entrench, disrupt productivity, and damage relationships."

Inclusive leaders not only *manage conflict* but also take into account the inherent diversity of what is fueling the conflict. They go further by seeing it as a catalyst for even better solutions.

"Conflict doesn't have to be a bad thing. It surfaces previous undiscussables, highlights not just the disconnects but also the intersection of ideas. Managed well, conflict provides a forum for finding better alternatives, even breakthroughs in building relationships and solving problems," Barnfield explains.

CONFLICT BASED ON NATIONAL CULTURE DIFFERENCES

The Hewlett Packard Enterprise Europe, Middle East, Africa team struggled with Germans who thought the Saudis were too rude, with Saudis who thought the Dutch were too direct, with Dutch who thought. . . . And so it went.

HPE's Koch managed this conflict by helping all sides understand the different ways that different cultures express disagreement. For example, the Dutch value clear and direct peer-to-peer feedback, while for the Saudis that is considered a "deadly sin."

"I found myself coaching my team members to be more sensitive and to stop making it about being right. We all needed to stitch Russian to Arabic to Western European to US styles. I told them that if you don't have that ability, I am not convinced you would be good for the job. It will exhaust you and the team." In effect, Koch made this inclusive behavior a requirement on his team.

CONFLICT BASED ON CULTURE DIFFERENCES WITHIN A COUNTRY

So much of managing national cultural differences, as described in the previous section, deals with understanding different styles and learning how to accommodate them. When it comes to racial and ethnic differences within a country, there is much to be said about applying those same principles.

But within a country, cultural differences can be sharper and more heated. Think of the long histories of racial strife in places like the United States, where Native Americans were subject to ethnic cleansing, Blacks to slavery and Jim Crow laws, the Japanese Americans to internment, and Latinos to discriminatory immigration policies. This historical canvas is always in the background when conflict arises across racial and ethnic lines—and it can be destructive.

At least there are ways to prevent conflict when the polarizations are well known, as Deena Al-Faris shares. Her father successfully recruited to his nascent company Sunni and Shia Muslims, whose people have been feuding for centuries—a company that eventually she ended up running.

"Since Shia are in the minority in Saudi, many won't say they are Shia, for fear they may be treated differently. But then, when it's time to pray, they don't say where they are going. My father recruited a lot from the Shia. He gained their trust by going to where they lived and speaking about their reputation of dedication to work. Then, at work, we made sure they had their own prayer rooms and could go whenever they needed to, without bringing it up."

Besides race and ethnicity, social class and generational divisions within cultures often arise. Anil Sachdev, founder and Chairman of the School of Inspired Leadership, explains how he managed the conflict that arose from accusations of class discrimination:

THE COUNTERINTUITIVE POWER OF SLOWING DOWN

MANAGES CONFLICT ▪ *Peggy Hazard, New York City*

Everyone expected the meeting to unfold as most did at this company: introductory comments by the CEO, issue for discussion put on the table, and a few aggressive and dominant people monopolizing the conversation.

This dynamic had created a culture that stifled many points of view. It created both overt and covert conflict, which left most leaders with the pervasive feeling that disagreement with the few dominant leaders was too risky.

But this time the script played out differently. I had been working as executive coach to this organization's CEO. Given specific developmental conversations we had had, he chose this moment to break the status quo norm.

Rather than passively allowing the alpha leaders to dictate the course and outcome of the discussion, the CEO paused the person driving toward a conclusion and respectfully said, "Our success and transformation depends on thinking differently and creatively. I'd like us to slow down a bit and widen our lens. I want to be sure each of you is giving your best thinking before we make any final decisions. I know it will take more time, but I want to hear all perspectives."

He then solicited input from everyone at the table, deftly drawing out those who were quiet, and firmly, but politely, keeping the dominant team members in check. Despite that, at one point, as others kept interrupting one of them, the CEO helped stay the course of the new dynamic he was seeking to instill: "Please let him finish his point." He

An employee was accused of stealing, which, according to company policy, would mean disciplinary action that included firing. People in the union thought the person was being victimized due to their social class, and management did not. There was so much conflict in how people interpreted the situation that we decided to form a five-person team consisting of reps from union and management to talk to various parties in this dispute.

demonstrated skill, sensitivity, and determination in ushering each person into the dialogue and making everyone feel heard.

What emerged was extraordinary. The discussion pivoted away from the initial topic to addressing the culture of exclusion and how many didn't feel safe to speak up. Rather than shut it down because of the agenda, the CEO encouraged people to share their experiences. One person mentioned that, in his culture, interrupting or grandstanding in meetings was taboo; another said that, as an introvert, it was too difficult to compete with the extroverts; a third said if they had listened to more people who understood a target customer, they wouldn't have failed with a recent product launch.

Then another member spoke up, his voice tight. "I am ashamed to admit this, but I knew [a major strategic play] was stupid and would be an expensive mistake. But because I did not want to be ridiculed, I did not speak up." He paused, and then added, "I deeply regret it to this day."

You could hear a pin drop. But rather than run from the conflict, the CEO leaned in. He said, "This is so valuable to hear. I didn't realize. So what more do we need to do? How should we change our meetings?" And then he devoted the rest of the meeting to defining new, more inclusive team norms.

At the close of the meeting, the CEO stated that they would invest time in all meetings to hear everyone's perspectives; that inclusive team behavior would become a central part of the culture, moving forward.

The positive impact on the team's engagement and on the quality of the dialogue and the decisions that came of it was so strong that each member conducted similar sessions, using this same principle of integrating diverse perspectives with their teams.

They found this person not guilty, which made some in management unhappy. But the long-term outcome was good. Rather than adopting a straightforward action and taking legal action, we involved the community in the resolution, which was respected.

At a young age, Martin Moser, HPE's Senior Director of Hybrid IT Hardware, Central Europe, Russia, Turkey, and Africa, had to grapple with age-related conflict:

"When I was twenty-three, I got my first job to manage a group of people who were fifty to fifty-five years old, and experienced. I was leading them because I had knowledge about computers and they didn't. But at the beginning everything I said created conflict, because I wasn't accepted. I realized I could not just come in and tell them what to do. I slowed down and focused on being consistent, showing up week after week. I learned to play captain, and they slowly learned to accept me."

These examples make it clear that managing conflict means engaging the very diversity at the center of it, where it can take shape in a variety of ways, from passive to assertive, from urgent to patient, from gentle to firm. Deena Al-Faris zeroes in on the essence of how best to develop strategies for managing conflict. Whenever there are differences of opinion, she gets her team to set aside the solutions they are arguing about, and they go back to the vision and purpose of the organization and what they are about.

"Once we are reset on common purpose, all ideas, no matter how different, I would give it a chance," she says. "This is where the team feels they are valued and they can start to pull and rethink things and feel a responsibility, and sometimes they revise or bring more innovative answers."

Diverse perspectives welcome.

Integrating diverse perspectives equips leaders to better manage their diverse teams as well as the various other diverse parts of the organization they interact with. It means tending to what others need to feel seen and heard, not only in their ideas but also in their pain. This sets the stage to get the most of the team's contributions, which we'll discuss in the next chapter.

■ ■ ■

DISCIPLINE 3

Optimizes Talent

DRIVES ENGAGMENT
DEVÉLOPS TALENT
COLLABORATES

ARLIER IN HER CAREER AS A GLOBAL Vice President of Human Resources, Sue Sun-LaSovage had noticed that "Nancy," a director of engineering, was consistently excluded from vital informal conversations that took place during meetings among the other members of her engineering leadership team. In addition, Nancy was being passed up for promotions and denied the pay increases for which she was qualified. Nancy had immigrated from Asia to the United States and was the only woman on an otherwise all-White, male team. For Sun-LaSovage, a female immigrant from Asia herself, the interactions between Nancy and the others leaders were littered with telltale signs of conscious and unconscious biases that led the men to misjudge and underestimate her.

Sun-LaSovage realized that being an inclusive leader required taking risks and stepping in as an assertive advocate and sponsor of talent that was being treated unfairly and suboptimized. Advocating for change would benefit both the organization and Nancy, so Sun-LaSovage pushed the leader of the group to take a closer look at Nancy.

> OPTIMIZES TALENT:
>
> *motivates others and supports their growth; joins forces for collective success across differences.*

"We can't just select overconfident men who talk assertively," Sun-LaSovage told the leader. "Instead of looking for the same kind of articulate people who can't deliver, we have to notice the people who deliver, even if they are quiet."

The leader listened respectfully but still he kept comparing Nancy to the type of outspoken leaders he had historically promoted—and finding Nancy lacking. Sun-LaSovage explained to the leader that different cultural backgrounds lead to different communication styles and that these differences can lead to misjudgments. For instance, Nancy's high-context, indirect, and nuanced communication style was being misperceived as imprecise and inarticulate by her colleagues because they valued a low-context communication style.[1]

The leader tilted his head, trying to grasp what Sun-LaSovage was trying to explain to him. Rather than take her at her word, he got curious and spent more time with Nancy and really listened to her. Once he did, he found Nancy quite impressive. Not only was she just as capable a leader as the others, but also she was able to see beyond the surface of most issues because of her multicultural life and work experiences.

Nancy was promoted soon thereafter.

Much of the promise of diversity as a catalyst for organizational value stalls at the stage of unrealized potential. This is because most leaders and managers find themselves trapped by their own unresolved biases and lack of inclusive skills.

To **optimize talent**, inclusive leaders need to *drive engagement*, *develop talent*, and generate *collaboration* with *all* talent, but with particular attention to underrepresented and overlooked groups and individuals. In our Inclusive Leader survey, 96% of survey respondents said that this was either extremely or very important for inclusive leaders.

Environments that generate high engagement are by definition addressing the aspirations of employees. When people feel seen and valued, they have a sense of belonging. For talent that is often over-looked, this can have a particularly potent positive effect. Their resulting commitment to the organization fuels a virtuous cycle of reciprocity.

With this deepening of mutual commitment and trust, leaders and managers are in a good position to establish relational and goal-oriented connections. The pieces click into place, where they can do the more difficult but vital work of developing talent.

Inclusive leaders who drive engagement and develop talent also set their teams up to collaborate in a way that leverages the diversity of all members. Collaboration is when a team's collective intelligence kicks in and the promise of diversity and inclusion is really fulfilled. In this third discipline, leaders are still operating in the influence realm of leading self and team.

DRIVES ENGAGEMENT

> *People will forget what you said, they will forget what you did,*
> *but they will never forget how you made them feel.*
>
> Maya Angelou, American writer

The link between high employee engagement and organizational performance is clear. Our research also establishes the connections between diversity and high engagement and a concept, completing the chain reaction of how diversity drives organizational results:

As organizations attract more diversity,

inclusive leaders seek and value the diversity around them.

As a result, employee engagement increases,

and higher engagement leads to better organizational results.

This is a good moment to explain both *engagement* and *enable-ment*, which we group into the concept of employee "effectiveness." Think of engagement as an employee's degree of commitment to the organization they work for and their willingness to expend their discretionary effort beyond the minimum amount required by the job. And think of enablement as how well equipped employees are with the tools and processes that can, on the one hand, actively address their frustrations, and on the other, enhance their ability to give that extra effort if they feel highly engaged.

In our 2020 study on workforce diversity and engagement, Korn Ferry found the following:

- Companies with better gender balance (30% to 70% of the workforce is women) have, on average, 8.4% more effective employees than those companies that are less gender diverse (where more than 70% of the total workforce is either women or men).

INSPIRING MODELS OF LEADERSHIP IN OVERLOOKED PLACES

DRIVES ENGAGEMENT ▪ *Cecilia Pinzón, Bogotá*

One way leaders engage is by modeling. Strong, successful leaders inspire others. When we think about leadership, we usually imagine top executives in multinational companies or those who are at the top of their game in entertainment, sports, and politics. But inspiring leaders also show up outside these obvious corridors of power.

Growing up in Bogotá, Colombia, I was deeply inspired by three influential women in my life: my two grandmothers and my mother. Despite all of them having been raised in a *machista* society where women faced all kinds of discrimination, they challenged gendered notions of what women can and cannot do. It was their inclusive leadership that inspired me to engage my own talents and become a successful professional.

My paternal grandma, Mama Illa, was born in Kutná Hora, Czech Republic, in the middle of World War I. She had to flee her country during World War II because her parents were discovered helping Jews hide from Hitler's troops. With no clear destination, she landed in Colombia, met my grandfather, and decided to stay. She had to learn a whole new language and way of living, and she faced those challenges with a great deal of optimism.

- Employees of color, both male and female, when compared with Whites, are 6.5% more likely to be effective.
- Leaders that are seen as fair and respectful, encourage collaboration, and value different ideas and opinions are 2.5 times more likely to have effective employees on their teams.[2]

The leaders we interviewed bring these statistics to life. This diverse cross section of inclusive leaders had one thing in common: a passionate drive for highly motivated teams. They pursued with equal intensity the means and the ends of strong engagement. The means: ensuring that people on their teams felt truly valued for their unique abilities. The ends: using those unique abilities to contribute to the group and its purpose. They know that by valuing diversity they will

My maternal grandma, whom I call Agüe or Bita, worked side by side with my *abuelo* (grandfather), who had his own architectural firm. He was the architect, but she was the one who made sure the office worked smoothly, that the finances were in order, and that all the challenges an entrepreneurial company faces in a developing economy were addressed.

And then, my *mamá*. When she graduated with her degree in economics, she walked onstage to receive her diploma with me and my sister; I was four and my sister was one year old. She was equally proud of being an economist and a mother. Her career included many high-prestige jobs typically reserved for men, like the general manager of a multinational company. Nevertheless, she showed up to all our school presentations, volleyball games, and Christmas concerts. She had such a clear understanding of her different roles in life and excelled at all of them. She included us in her work life and brought her work successes into our family life.

These three women, with their inclusive mindsets and behaviors, were my role models from birth. The strength and uniqueness of their personalities, their determination to succeed in all they did, and their defiance of the sexism around them inspired me to build my own career supporting the development of professionals and nurturing inclusive work environments.

create the conditions for high engagement and have a higher likelihood of getting the results they want.

Take Anna Jonen, Business Unit Manager Digital Transformation at Live Reply DE. She was making a sales pitch to a prospective client for a customized package of services. Many around her insisted that she had no chance of winning the new business, but she would not let their pessimism thwart her efforts. She engaged the unique talents of a cross section of coworkers to design a new solution for the client and achieve her sales goal.

> I knew the client and I knew what their pain was. I went out and picked about a dozen people who would have never pictured they belonged together. But the pitch needed this mix of IT architects, solutions managers, sales reps, and customer service specialists. We did have drama in the team due to these differences, but I kept the team focused on the client and the unique ways we could meet their needs. I reminded them how we could bring in everyone's individual talent to create something really unique for the client. As the team came together in sharing this belief, we ended up designing a solution that was perfect for the client, and we won.

DEVELOPS TALENT

> *The mediocre teacher tells. The good teacher explains. The superior teacher demonstrates. The great teacher inspires.*
>
> William Arthur Ward,
> American writer

To *develop talent* requires a turn within the labyrinth of leadership, away from the nexus of control. That is because so much of what is required is not up to the leader who seeks to be inclusive but up to each individual on their team.

First, an inclusive leader must get a handle on a team member's capabilities, which is relatively easy to do. Then come the more difficult tasks of uncovering their motivations (short, medium, and long term), their preferred style of receiving both praise and correction, and their sense of identity as professionals and as unique individuals. A diverse workforce further shrouds these mysteries of what drives people and how we can use that information. A leader seeking to be inclusive can't just operate with a generic sense of human motivational psychology; they must also understand the *sociological* realities of team members.

For example, women, particularly in male-oriented environments, must manage many pressures that the men around them don't even come close to realizing. Whether it's #MeToo incidents, inappropriate jokes, or sexist marginalization that hampers career advancement, these are currents that many women must navigate multiple times each day.

People of color often carry the burden of the news cycles, with headlines about people like them being killed, detained, and deported every day. Three p.m. on a school day can fill a Black parent with dread at the thought that their innocent child could be stopped, harassed, or even unexpectedly shot at by a police officer.

Those who are LGBTQ+ and who don't feel safe coming out must carefully watch their pronouns, even when talking about something as casual as what they did that weekend. They will tell you how exhausting this is.

Sociological challenges also are faced by those with hidden disabilities: the depressed person who can't miss their scheduled medication, the sight-impaired person who needs to find a private office so they can pull up a magnifying glass to read a document, or the hearing-impaired person who comes in early to meetings to get a seat nearest the team leader.

Cultural differences also play a significant role in people's motivation and career aspirations. An Indian woman we spoke to during the research process explained how her parents' expectations that she would give up her job once she got married were impacting her ability to be successful at work—even though she and her husband were both in favor of her pursuing her career. It was only after she addressed the root cause of her internal struggle that she was able to break through the psychological barriers that were holding her back.

Or take this recent example from a Hispanic male who was struggling to identify with the self-promoting people in his organization. In his culture, it was not the norm to talk about oneself or about individual accomplishments, and so he looked down others who talked about themselves and was unwilling to share his personal accomplishments.

Or consider the African American male who grew up in a family that was often distrusting of others and viewed people's attempts to connect with them as inauthentic. This translated into a negative view of networking or developing relationships outside of "getting the work done," impacting his ability to build deeper connections in the workplace to support his career.

These examples illustrate why it's sometimes necessary for people from underrepresented groups to adopt different strategies in order to advance their careers and achieve greater personal success—and why it's key for inclusive leaders to understand their unique motivations and barriers.

Managers and leaders are often unaware of these deep external factors and internal struggles. They see a behavior that seems strange or counterproductive—an employee who keeps repeating the same mistake or a team member who withdraws—and, in their blindness to the deeper realities, these managers arrive at incorrect conclusions about performance and ability.

It's one thing to be a good developer of people in general. It's another to be a good developer of people who are different from oneself. Inclusive leaders realize that to be a developer of underrepresented talent requires another layer of awareness, knowledge, and skill.

"It's very easy to gravitate toward people who are more like you. So if you don't work to get to know people who are not like you, they won't gravitate toward you and you won't be able to offer them much developmental coaching. Therefore, you won't be able to counter the particular barriers that they must face," says Lou Nieto, a former ConAgra executive.

Developing underrepresented talent means helping employees understand that they have the power to take ownership of their own careers and equipping them with the specific insights, strategies, and tools they need to drive their development forward. It means mentoring, sponsorship, and coaching on the part of leaders and managers. It also means advocacy if they are being treated unfairly, and helping them develop greater self-agency—speaking up for oneself—to be heard and to optimize their contributions.

To develop female talent in the male-dominated IT space, Martin Moser from HPE creates job postings that highlight the need for more than just technical experience.

"When women candidates with less IT experience show up, some hesitate about pursuing it further. But if they have a solid technical foundation, plus some of the other strategic and innovation compe-tencies we need more of, we bring them in, leverage the differentiated skills they have, and accelerate giving them some of the additional IT skills they need more of."

Moser's inclusive strategy has increased group representation of women in a meaningful way while still meeting his business goals.

For Anna Jonen at Live Reply DE, the shoe was on the other foot. She needed to develop the talent of men who did not conform to the male stereotypes of being outgoing and direct.

"For me, diversity is also about men who may be a little shy and underutilized because they are less outgoing. I noticed that one of these more introverted men was quietly very good at putting people together in effective teams. So I made him formally responsible for a few people at first, so he could learn from it and get instant feedback. And then I gave him more responsibility. Everyone is special and has potential, and they just need one person to really believe in them and they can grow."

Tram Trinh's story demonstrates that developing talent also requires individual employees' willingness to take risks at doing what needs to be done to rise to the fullness of their potential:

> As one of very few women in my division, and also one of the youngest, despite knowing a lot about the material and being the leader of the group, my lack of confidence kept leading me to second-guess myself. The attitudes of the guys around me who did not value my contributions fed my inferiority complex. It was a boys' club. For some time, I thought maybe I should not talk too much. But as time passed, I felt I was wasting my time being there. In some key areas, I did know more than they did, and I knew the way forward. I got smarter about who I hired, and brought in other innovative thinkers. I worked with subgroups within

the bigger organization to understand what needed to be done, and began to influence in smaller spheres first. I grew fully into my own sense of confidence, and with that came greater respect and influence.

SEEING TALENT: LIFE-ALTERING EXPERIENCE

DEVELOPS TALENT ▪ *Darryl A. Smith, Chicago*

When I was an eager young professional, I landed a job with one of the largest pharmaceutical companies in North America for a territory sales position. I was also one of very few salespeople of color. All my preparation up to that point—my degrees in business and computer science, a handful of interesting internships, and several years of grinding it out in financial services obtaining my Series 6 and 7 licenses—got me my first company-issued car, expense account, and a yearly cash bonus.

Those were the tangible perks, but the most valuable and enduring benefit of the job was being mentored and developed by Bob Hoerdoman.

Bob was one of the most authentically dynamic White male leaders I've ever met. He was responsible for leading national and regional sales teams. He was a strategic leader with a laid-back persona who went out of his way to establish open and trusting relationships with everyone on his team, including me. I had never received such constructive coaching or mentoring to accelerate my career development before.

Bob was committed to my growth. He consistently extended behavioral and developmental feedback to associates across the organization, regardless of gender, ethnicity, race, or tenure. One developmental lesson with Bob became core to how I engage my clients to this day.

We were in a suburb outside of Chicago, part of a newly restructured territory. It had been a stressful multiday field ride. I also had a new product portfolio, a population of physicians, and aggressive growth targets.

Bob posed a question about the interaction with the physician and his office staff we had just completed. He wanted me to precisely

But advocating for someone's development often entails more than just working directly with that person. For Nieto, the former ConAgra executive, it required challenging bigotry:

---

articulate why and how I engaged the physician to prescribe our product to their next five patients. I quickly listed my steps: I had conveyed the unique characteristics of the new portfolio compared to territory marketplace competition, held my ground firmly in the pharmacokinetic discussion when challenged, and provided the features and benefits of the drug.

Bob nodded in agreement and replied, "Those are just the tickets to the dance." There was something more that Bob wanted me to get to. "There's something else you do that will accelerate your ability to drive market share in this new territory. I want you to pay attention to what that extra thing is."

But he was not about to tell me what that was. Instead, he challenged me to chronicle my sales calls over the next few days and look for a pattern. Within that pattern, he reassured me, would reside the answer.

For the next several months, after each office visit, I captured detailed notes of my actions, behaviors, and proposed next steps for each physician or physicians' group. During our field rides, Bob would begin by reading my call notes and then look up and ask, "What behaviors will you focus on today?"

I would answer and he would nod, but it was clear I still was not seeing what he was seeing. Until, one day, I gave a new answer: I would be an active listener.

Eureka! I had uncovered the ability Bob knew I possessed, and now he was ready to share with me his feedback to make me even more effective.

By encouraging me to be an active listener *of myself*, Bob helped me to more consciously and effectively apply a skill I already had. Though Bob knew little about my experiences as a young Black, aspiring corporate professional, he saw me as a whole person and helped me draw more deeply from within myself to enhance my performance. His unique ability to coach and develop me was the gift of a lifetime.

We were reviewing demographic trends in the US and talking about the strategic implications, when a senior R&D person said, "When are they going to assimilate and stop clinging to their cultural practices and stop speaking Spanish?" It was a good opportunity for a learning moment. I turned to him and asked, "If Italy was located south of the Rio Grande, would you be asking me the same questions of the Italians?" The question is not how quickly will Latinos assimilate but how quickly will the world accept their diversity.

For Deena Al-Faris, development of large groups of talent feeling on the margins was about finding group purpose and meaning in an inclusive way.

When we were trying to merge two different companies under one company, we had a problem with the managers who were struggling with the changes. Some of them took it personally that they were not going to retain their previous leadership positions. Others were also worried that their knowledge would not be able to compete with that of others. Everyone was clinging to "their" job, and they did not like the changes or how the others were doing things. I realized that they were clearly lost about the purpose of serving the company and that we needed to figure it out together. I had us locked up in meetings for one month where all we did was to create joint purpose and values statements that we could all share. From that, we developed common goals we could all get aligned to. Once we had that guiding light, the issues of roles and positions resolved themselves a lot more easily.

For Anil Sachdev of the School of Inspired Leadership in India, even the terminology matters in how you develop talent.

"We do not call it a 'talent assessment process' but rather a 'talent appreciation process.' The idea is to learn from people at their best and to find out what their strengths are and not spend a lot of time to focus on their weakness."

COLLABORATES

> *I have been in many teams that have had loads of talent but did*
> *not make it through, and been with teams that did not have that*
> *much talent and ended up being champions.*

Kaká, Brazilian soccer player

It's one of the universal themes of the human experience that shows up everywhere. It's there in children's stories, in epic sports triumphs, in scientific breakthroughs, in exploring new frontiers, in comedy shows, in movies, in city skylines, in mobile apps, in organizations moved by social justice or by profit. It's key to Laurel and Hardy, containing Ebola, landing the first human on the moon, the 2019 US Women's World Cup champion soccer team, Chicago's Magnificent Mile, the telephone, the iPhone, Torvill and Dean, the civil rights movement, global climate strikes, Lady Gaga and Tony Bennett, *Sesame Street,* and *Black Panther.*

The *it? Collaboration.* Over and over and over, it's the catalyst for so much of human achievement, from the practical to the sublime. The art of passion, dedication, and camaraderie, leveraging each member's strengths. The comic and the straight man, the good cop and the bad cop, strategists and operators, goalie–defense–midfield–offense, vocalists–drummers–guitarists, the chief executive and the chief financial officer. . . . You get the idea. Without the interconnected humanity that collaboration brings, there is no attainment, no invention, no collective joy of building something together greater than ourselves.

But it's been more known as an art than a science. That's now changing. Researchers are breaking down the inputs and outputs of "collective intelligence" to better understand why some teams collaborate better than others.

Dr. Thomas Malone writes about the importance of making decisions as a group, forming a consensus, getting ideas from different sources, and motivating people through competition. All are components of collective intelligence. When groups of people with different perspectives come together, collective intelligence comes from it.

In their research, Malone, Dr. Anita Woolley of Carnegie Mellon, Dr. Christopher Chabris of Union College, and Drs. Alex Pentland and Nada Hashmi of MIT Sloan, were able to demonstrate that collective intelligence was greater than the sum of the parts of the various

IMAGINATIVE COLLABORATION AT PIXAR

COLLABORATES ▪ *Brandon Farrugia, Cincinnati*

Through its gorgeous digital animated films, Pixar knows how to touch our hearts. Loss, joy, betrayal, triumph, believing in oneself, embracing one's identity, and destiny are among the various themes in Pixar megahits such as *Up, WALL-E, Toy Story, Finding Nemo,* and *Coco.* There is one other theme, however, that pops up time and again: imaginative collaboration across diversity.

Consider the climax of the first *Toy Story* movie, when a diverse team of toys—Woody, Buzz Lightyear, Bo Beep, Rex, and Mr. Potato Head—escape from Andy's toy-destroying neighbor, Sid Phillips. They made sure no toy was left behind, using their various differentiated skills and perspectives.

In his book *Creativity, Inc.,* Pixar cofounder Ed Catmull captures a few philosophies, strategies, and tactics to induce collaboration. For one, he turned his attention to creating a culture where "anyone should be able to talk to anyone else, at any level, at any time, without fear of reprimand."[3] He changed the physical structure of the office space to draw people out of their offices, with the goal of creating more personal interactions and sharing of ideas. He implemented Notes Day, which shut down the entire company once a week to focus on brainstorming sessions and collaboration at all levels. He focused

individuals in the group.[7] In other words, collaborative teams outperformed individuals working independently. Teams with higher average IQs didn't score much higher on collective intelligence tasks than did teams with lower average IQs. Nor did teams with more extroverted people, or teams whose members reported feeling more motivated to contribute to their group's success.

What the researchers did find were three distinct characteristics that led to greater collaboration, which led to greater collective intelligence:

1. Team members contributed equally to discussions.

2. Team members were adept at tuning in to complex emotional states.

3. Teams were made up of more women.

on removing the fear of failure by allowing employees to share their ideas without negative consequences.

With these approaches and structures in place, he then went to work on getting functionally diverse teams collaborating with each other despite conflict. During a speech in 2019 at MIT's Sloan School of Management, he shared how Pixar's filmmaking success required the very different approaches of both the artistic and technological talent. He noted that there were distinctions that got in the way, as he described that, at Disney, creatives reigned, while at Microsoft, techies were dominant.[4]

Catmull and his management team, however, challenged stereotypes, such as the one that creative people are difficult to work with. "I've got world-class people in technology and art, and their ability to organize and to think are roughly the same," he said. "There are technical people who are disorganized and dysfunctional and argumentative, and there are artists who are crystal clear in their thinking and make great creative leaders."[5]

As a manager, Catmull said, he tolerated a fairly high degree of disagreement between teammates, as long as the conflict didn't turn personal. "We can have people who can argue such that they turn red in the face, but it's about the problem. . . . As long as it's focused on the problem, then we get the best possible outcome."[6]

(Interestingly, the researchers partly explained this last point by the fact that women are better than men at "mind reading"—characteristic 2.)

Not surprisingly, our panel of global inclusive leaders demonstrated these characteristics of collaboration.

Gabor Gonda from HPE developed an inclusive team design that baked collaboration into its processes. His inclusive design served to minimize miscommunication and helped his diverse teams get on the same page:

> We had medium- and small-sized teams spread out across five countries—the Czech Republic, Poland, Hungary, Romania, and Austria—often doing the same thing. We kept facing talent shortages, duplication of

efforts, things falling through the cracks. We had great talent in every location but we weren't getting the job done well.

We collaborated on figuring out the solution and came up with competency centers. It was untried in our organization, and in fact corporate told us it would not work. But we insisted, because the current situation was not the answer. Then we worked hard together to make the competency center come to life. Teams had to be willing to give things up that were going to be done in other centers, they had to trust colleagues from different cultures and languages and whom they did not know as well, and they had to believe that together they could create a better design that met a more comprehensive set of needs. In the end, it all paid off.

Tram Trinh from VITANLINK had to inspire her team to collaborate, by pointing out both the upside of doing so and the downside of not:

For people to collaborate, they need to trust that the resources around will help them to achieve the common interests. As an example, I brought into the team someone who was a very strong scientific person, so much so that other members felt threatened about what this could mean for their positions. I saw they were focused on their individual interests, so I kept reminding them that if the company did not reach a certain milestone, then none of them would succeed. This common goal got them all focused and collaborating.

Back in the United States, Melissa Donaldson, SVP and Chief Diversity Officer at Wintrust, focused on team makeup to ensure inclusive collaboration within her diversity and inclusion center:

I have two members on my team—one is an African American female and other is a Vietnamese female. The African American female has broad depth of experience in EEO [Equal Employment Opportunity] and compliance, and the Vietnamese female has very little D&I

experience. I chose to bring her in because I wanted diversity in different ways. She was a quintessential Millennial, tech savvy, and studying a lot about organization development. She brought things to the table that we didn't have, while those of us who knew D&I well helped increase her knowledge. Together, we put together a better mousetrap for the organization.

At its essence, collaboration is about people of all kinds coming together to get things done and, along the way, devising new ways to do so.

In exploring the first three disciplines, we have seen how much work is required to lead oneself and one's team in an inclusive way. Now it's time to turn from inclusive practices applied one-on-one and with teams to how the entire organization benefits from unleashing the power of diversity and inclusion.

■   ■   ■

DISCIPLINE 4

Applies an Adaptive Mindset

SITUATIONAL ADAPTABILITY
GLOBAL PERSPECTIVE
CULTIVATES INNOVATION

I N 2014, WHEN SATYA NADELLA TOOK THE helm as the third-ever CEO of Microsoft, the digital giant was stumbling. There were new players and new paradigms of mobile and cloud computing successfully challenging the hegemony of Windows. Yet Microsoft had doubled down on its Windows-only course.

"Windows was the god—everything had to work with Windows," said Steve Stone, founder of Microsoft's technology group. But Nadella brought a different perspective.

"Our industry does not respect tradition," Nadella announced in his opening statement as the newly installed CEO. "What it respects is innovation." With this salvo, he began the charge toward what would end up being a winning mobile-first and cloud-first strategy.

Along with this technology strategy, Nadella led a culture transformation within the company, fueling its ability to adapt and learn from its changing environment.

"The day the learn-it-all says, 'I'm done' is when you become a know-it-all," Nadella said in an interview with *Inc.* magazine. "And so to understand that paradox and to be able to confront your fixed mindset each day is that continuous process of renewal."[1]

> **APPLIES AN ADAPTIVE MINDSET:**
>
> *takes a broad worldview; adapts approach to suit situation; innovates by leveraging differences.*

Microsoft's transformation highlights the benefits of inclusive leaders applying an adaptive mindset. Not only did it reenergize employee morale and the sense of purpose at one of the world's most influential companies, it also led to new products enhancing the lives of millions. Not to mention that, within the first five years with Nadella as CEO, Microsoft's stock price nearly tripled and its market cap rose to more than $1 trillion.

Nadella references his different experiences growing up in India and studying and working in the United States as key to his inclusive leadership. They shaped how Nadella adapted to each situation and how he helped others make the necessary changes that personal and business challenges required. From this came his global vision to "empower every person and organization on the planet to achieve more."[2]

When inclusive leaders **apply an adaptive mindset**, their impact broadens from just their individual teams to the wider organization. Their *situational adaptability* and *global perspective* allow them to successfully navigate a wider array of situations and groups of people. As a result, they can begin to leverage the diversity within the entire organization to *cultivate innovation*.

The vast majority of the talent and diversity and inclusion respondents of our Inclusive Leader survey—96%—agreed that the ability to apply an adaptive mindset is extremely or very important for inclusive leaders. Furthermore, the statistical interrelationships among the three competencies that make up this discipline have important implications for the development of inclusive leaders and for the activation of innovation—a key desired outcome of the D&I quest.

With this fourth discipline, the nature of the impact can broaden. Inclusive leaders at senior levels leveraging this discipline may expand from a radius of impact on individuals and teams in the previous disciplines to impact on the wider organization. With their situational adaptability and global perspective, they are now leveraging the diversity within the organization in a way that allows them to navigate and adapt to a vast array of diverse situations and groups of people, anywhere on the planet. By leveraging the organization's diversity, they also begin to have the deeper and material organizational impact to which they have been aspiring, through greater innovation.

SITUATIONAL ADAPTABILITY

> *When dealing with life's many challenges, it is better to be a*
> *Swiss Army knife than a hammer.*
>
> Unknown

Situational adaptability works going forward, sideways, or in reverse. Much as we want to always be proactive, most of the time we don't see things coming. Situational adaptability requires inclusive leaders to deal with whatever comes their way, in whatever shape or form.

"Those skilled at situational adaptability recognize the need to be flexible and act differently because no two situations are exactly alike," writes Heather Barnfield in *FYI*. "They know that using the same approach, tone, and style in a different setting may be consistent but not necessarily effective."

Microsoft CEO Satya Nadella had to quickly adapt after a public misstep in front of 7,500 female engineers. Nadella was being interviewed during a Grace Hopper celebration for women in leadership, taking place at a computing conference. Interviewer Dr. Maria Klawe, a computer scientist who was president of Harvey Mudd College and former Microsoft board member, asked Nadella what advice he would have for women who hesitate about asking for a pay raise. His answer created such an uproar it went viral: "It's not about asking for the raise, but knowing and having faith that the system will actually give you the right raises as you go along. . . . And that, I think, might be one of the additional superpowers that quite frankly women who don't ask for a raise have. Because that's good karma. It'll come back because somebody's going to know 'that's the kind of person that I want to trust. That's the kind of person I want to really give more responsibility to.'"[3]

Nadella's response was not only condescending but also out of touch with the reality of gender pay inequities. Dr. Klawe corrected him on the spot, and he quickly realized his enormous mistake. As he walked off-stage, he discovered his error had already traveled the globe.

Situationally adaptive inclusive leaders like Nadella are able to reflect on the new inputs they are receiving and quickly adjust their words and actions. In this case, Nadella realized his bias and rapidly sought to correct it. A few hours after the event, employees received an email from the CEO, advising them to watch a video of the interview and pointing out his error. An excerpt from that email reads, "Toward the end of the interview, Maria asked me what advice I would offer women who are not comfortable asking for pay raises. I answered that question completely wrong. Without a doubt I wholeheartedly support programs at Microsoft and in the industry that bring more women into technology and close the pay gap. I believe men and women should get equal pay for equal work. And when it comes to career advice on getting a raise when you think it's deserved, Maria's advice was the right advice. If you think you deserve a raise, you should just ask."[4]

One of the first pay gaps Nadella set out to close was at Microsoft itself, where male senior software development engineers earned around $137,000 per year, while senior females in the same role earned $129,000 per year.

Not all incidents requiring situational adaptability are as dramatic and far-reaching as this one. In organizational life, every single day brings challenges that require this competency. And the more culturally diverse the workplace, the more those misunderstandings, missteps, and missed opportunities can multiply. The inclusive leaders we interviewed kept coming back to stories about how they had to adapt to new situations.

Martin Moser from HPE learned the hard way that, in Saudi Arabia, he must take off his shoes before he sits on the floor, and he must not show the bottoms of his feet—even as he awkwardly tries to sit in ways his body is not used to.

"Before someone explained it to me, that showing the bottom of your feet was an insult, I couldn't figure out why they kept staring at my feet. Did they smell? Was it the color?"

Frode Berg of Experian had to adapt his team decision-making to accommodate the Swedes with whom he worked.

"The Swedes are so much more consensus driven, and everyone has to be involved. But with the Norwegians, you just involve a few people in the decision-making. Each context has its pluses and minuses. The approach with the Swedes is quite time consuming and cumbersome, and it takes longer time to get a decision through, but once the decision is made, the foundation to move forward is solid. In Norway, we get a decision through fast, but maybe not all stakeholders are aligned."

Wintrust's Chief Diversity Officer and SVP, Melissa Donaldson, faced a different type of situational adaptability challenge. Surrounded by mostly White males in the finance industry, she adapted to her situation by learning to play golf and being more up to date on the sports headlines. "I figured out that this is where stuff happens, so I said, 'I'm going to learn this game.'"

This kind of approach raises an important question for those in underrepresented groups: At what point does adaptability start to subsume the very differences we aim to celebrate?

It can—and should be—a personal decision. Donaldson decided it was a necessary relationship-building move that would position her well to challenge the status quo—which, as a woman of color in finance, she does often. "Plus, I have ended up liking golf!"

Rita Estevez Luaña of Experian summarizes her approach to how and when to adapt to a situation: "You observe, you see what those who are different from you do in that environment. Listen. Be modest. Learn first—and don't challenge or disrupt until you are informed, trusted, and comfortable. But when you are, then you do."

GLOBAL PERSPECTIVE

A person's feet must be planted in their country, but their eyes should survey the world.

Adapted from George Santayana,
Spanish philosopher and writer

When most leaders hear *"global perspective,"* they assume the concept is about managing cultural differences across different groups of people, whether from different countries or from within a country or region. But in our Inclusive Leader model, this competency is about something much larger.

LEADING A NATION INCLUSIVELY AFTER THE HORROR OF A MASS SHOOTING

SITUATIONAL ADAPTABILITY ▪ *Juliet Warne, Sydney*

After the worst mass shooting in New Zealand's history, Prime Minister Jacinda Ardern faced an unprecedented challenge.

The horror of an armed killer opening fire on worshippers in two mosques, killing fifty people and wounding at least fifty more, plunged the country into uncharted territory. While families and friends were mourning the loss of their loved ones, the country as a whole grieved the tragedy, not only for the loss of lives but also for the hatred toward a particular religious group.

In that moment, the prime minister needed to be a healer who could bring people together around the tragedy. She did so with grace, centeredness, and situational adaptability. Within hours of the attack, she directly addressed the terrorist attacker: "You may have chosen us, but we utterly reject and condemn you."[5]

Wearing a black head scarf, she embraced and opened a dialogue with Muslim leaders that demonstrated respect and care. And when she addressed Parliament for the first time since the attack, she opened with the Arabic greeting of "As-salamu alaykum."

Ardern appeared at ease with the many contexts she was required to confront over the course of this crisis, adjusting her tone, message, and dress as needed. Repeatedly, she countered the Black-and-White, us-versus-them mentality, sensing that a more nuanced and inclusive narrative would help the nation heal and move forward.[6]

In previous centuries, the models for how countries dealt with one another were colonization, peaceful coexistence, or isolationism. In the aftermath of World War II, internationalization was introduced. Then the aptly named World Wide Web connected far-flung parts of the entire planet like never before and gave us globalization.

While we may still not have the same languages, customs, and foods, we now have many more things in common than we ever had before, such as smartphones, social media, search engines, and screen addiction. We also have more shared meta-experiences, such as a

Perhaps her situational adaptability shone most as she addressed a group of schoolchildren. When asked how she was doing, she answered in a way that was deeply personal and yet appropriate.

"How am I? Thank you for asking," she said. "I am very sad." In doing so, she allowed herself to be accessible and relatable to her young audience.[7]

The inclusiveness of her responses cultivated trust, tolerance, and openness, and the impact was profound. She provided an inclusive model for her people to follow; she ensured that diverse voices, particularly those most impacted by the tragedy, contributed to the path forward; and she created the conditions to enact a change in gun laws. Just six days after the mass shooting, Parliament banned the sale of all military-style semiautomatic and assault rifles, with bipartisan support.

Some would say that Ardern responded in a way that is expected of our elected leaders; we expect assuredness in the face of turbulent times, and we expect to be given a path forward when the haze of the current reality grinds us to a halt.

We think what differentiated Ardern's response was her ability to go beyond what might be expected. She responded to the unfolding demands of the crisis with nuance and authenticity, in a way that allowed humanity, empathy, and dignity to be front and center. There is no textbook on how to do this, especially with so many factors in play.

The true test of leadership happens in times of crisis, when the situation throws up something so unimaginable that most leaders, if not all, are left floundering for the right response. To the benefit of New Zealand's peoples, Jacinda Ardern rose to the occasion.

---

global economy, global supply chains, global migration, global terrorism, global pandemics, and global climate change. The hard-and-fast physical and geographic borders are now crossed digitally with ease.

Meta-interconnectivity means that a manager in Buenos Aires can lead a team of people in Gurgaon, Krakow, Riyadh, and London; that Russian bots can infiltrate Facebook accounts and influence elections around the globe; that a lone fourteen-year-old protester camped outside the Swedish Parliament with a handwritten sign can unleash a worldwide climate strike. A global perspective takes into account all these proliferating interdependencies.

"Global perspective is about more than geographic reach. . . . It starts with curiosity—about people, events, problems, ideas, history, and the future," explains Heather Barnfield in *FYI*.

Regardless of one's personal stance on what should be the best world order, those with global perspective are aware of these tidal changes and how they are playing out in different parts of the world, affecting people, markets, and plans for growth. Successfully addressing pandemics, climate change, and other challenges requires inclusive leaders with global mindsets. Hengliang Pan of LiuGong Machinery finds that a global perspective helps him to better understand the markets for his company's products:

> We need to understand the various different markets and how big they are, not just in countries but within regions within these countries. And it's not just about their size but also about how the customers there are different in what they want and how they buy. In the US and Europe, for example, the customer is more demanding about quality and how machines look, and when machines are down, they need to get the machine running again quickly.

Anil Sachdev of SOIL believes that to understand global business, one needs to be aware of geopolitics and how talent and capital flows are taking place across the world. For example, he notes, there are tensions and conflict between the people of Belgium and France that most people are not even aware of. And between Argentina and Brazil. And Chile and Peru. And—Pick any two spots and you will find tensions. An inclusive leader must be aware of how tensions affect commerce and talent decisions.

Massive climate change is also upending what had been givens around the world but that no longer are, or won't be in the near future. Landscapes, boundaries, and lifestyles are changing as islands go underwater, shorelines reconfigure, crops migrate. For example, an increasing number of farmers in Oklahoma are switching from growing wheat to planting what had long been the cash crop of the American South: cotton.[8] Likewise, this cataclysmic climate change is

THE GLOBETROTTER WHO THOUGHT HE HAD A GLOBAL PERSPECTIVE

GLOBAL PERSPECTIVE ■ *Margot Zielinska, London*

He was a senior executive who had it all—excellent education from elite business schools, command of several foreign languages, and a breadth of experience in senior leadership roles across the globe. He considered a global mindset to be one of his key strengths.

Yet, despite this background and experience, he tended to look at problems in an ethnocentric way, pushing for changes that different regions were not ready for. When his regional leaders resisted his ideas, he got visibly frustrated with them, until they reluctantly implemented his directives.

As his executive coach, I not only was aware of his feelings of frustration but also knew from his 360 feedback that the leaders he worked with were frustrated with him. In one of our executive coaching sessions, I asked him what had been one of his key strengths in all his global roles, and without a pause he answered, "My global perspective and my ability to navigate the global environment."

I was silent for a moment, and then I asked him to consider: What if it was the others who were adapting to him more that he was adapting to them? After all, in every continent he traveled to, he was The Boss. Rather than answering me, he got angry. I had challenged him to acknowledge his privilege, and he didn't like it.

However, that session changed everything. Though he didn't like my observation, he reflected on and digested the discomfort my questions had brought up for him. Instead of leading with his ideas grounded in his successes in his home country, he began to listening to the views of his local leaders so that he could better understand their realities.

The results were transformative. With his regional leaders at the table, his teams started solving the big, global problems they were facing at a local level. This change had an immediate positive impact on how he led, engaged his team, and delivered results. It also had a profound impact on him personally. He turned his global exposure into a truly global perspective—a vital skill of the kind of inclusive leader he had always wanted to be.

■

causing unprecedented human migrations around the world as whole communities have fled drought-stricken areas where crops cannot grow and animal populations dwindle. As they move into territories populated with people not like them, civil unrest often ensues.

Geopolitical, geosocial, and geo-environmental disruptions all directly affect organizations, whether they are "global" in nature or not. Inclusive leaders must factor in these complex and quickly changing trends to make the best business and people-management decisions possible.

To back off the big picture for a moment, a global perspective can also lead to new introspection about personal identity. Lou Nieto, formerly of ConAgra, talks about how this competency gets personal and converges with issues of identity within him:

> There is a great line in the movie *Selena* [a biopic of the late Mexican crooner, who was killed at the height of her popularity], when her dad is trying to explain to her, "It's hard being Mexican American, because to the Mexicans you aren't Mexican enough and to the Americans you are not American enough." I talked with my daughters about this and how, my whole life, people have told me that I'm not Latino enough and that I'm not mainstream American enough. I'm a little bit of everything and that's helped me in my career.

CULTIVATES INNOVATION

Diversity drives innovation — when we limit who can contribute, we in turn limit what problems we can solve.

Telle Whitney, computer scientist
executive

Innovation. That elevated promise that inclusive leaders almost always make when extolling the virtues of a diverse workforce.

Yes, greater diversity can lead to greater creativity and innovation, but how?

There is no diversity dust we can sprinkle and *Voilà!*, we have optimized talent, feelings of belonging, and growing markets. It takes an organization fully infused with inclusive leaders skillfully *cultivating innovation* by leveraging deeply running values, beliefs, and motivations to exercise the intricate competencies that unleash the power of diversity throughout an organization.

You can't tap the diverse thinking that innovation requires if a leader has not valued differences on a one-on-one and team basis. Team members will not take the risks that innovative thinking demands if an inclusive leader has not instilled trust or shown they know how to effectively manage conflict across differences. Teams won't lean into the tough work of innovative thinking and solution if inclusive leaders have not fostered an environment of high engagement and collaboration. And talent won't be able to turn their new ideas into actionable steps if they have not been developed into effective contributors with a common purpose.

Microsoft CEO Satya Nadella sees the trait of empathy as a key source of business innovation. For him, this seemingly soft skill is a wellspring for innovation, since innovation comes from one's ability to grasp customers' unmet, unarticulated needs.[9]

"Ideas excite me. Empathy grounds and centers me," he writes in his book, *Hit Refresh: The Quest to Rediscover Microsoft's Soul and Imagine a Better Future for Everyone.*

In the same vein, Tej Singh Hazra, associate client partner at Korn Ferry, believes that "inclusive leaders who are innovative don't see themselves as bystanders, but upstanders. Innovators evolve based on experience—whether successes or failures. They are calculated risk takers, extraordinary listeners, and comfortable enough to share their vulnerabilities. They may not always have the answers, but they set the tone of empowerment at all levels in their organization, to not settle for status quo."

For Gabor Gonda at HPE, the link between diversity and innovation is that "more eyes can see more. We seek different perspectives and create a culture of open debate. Yeah, sometimes those conversations can be more difficult. Sometimes the 'old buffaloes' are agreeing with each other on an idea, and when younger talent says, That's bulls***,' we realize that there is a different POV [point of view] we need to listen to. We like that."

Rita Estevez Luaña of Experian expressed a similar thought: "It's those who are different who help you see what you don't even know you don't know. You tend to think from what you know, but you cannot innovate from what you don't know."

This is why Cristina David at Ericsson ensures Millennials are on her team. And why Tram Trinh of VITANLINK has created a very diverse board for her company, with scientists, physicians, businesspeople, and mathematicians from various geographies and nationalities. And why Johannes Koch of the Global Sales DACH regional team is being reverse-mentored by a twentysomething to learn about blockchain.

Martin Moser, one of Koch's team leaders, explains, "If you can talk or collaborate with diverse environments when diversity is not an inhibitor and inclusion is standard, and every person is equal, innovation will simply happen."

TO THINK DIFFERENT GOES AGAINST MOST OF WHAT WE'VE BEEN TAUGHT

INNOVATION ▪ *Tej Singh Hazra, Toronto*

"If everybody is thinking alike, then somebody isn't thinking." This one quote by General George S. Patton Jr., hanging from the ceiling at IBM Canada's head office, changed my career trajectory forever.

The company's motto, after all, was "THINK." Patton's quote made me reinterpret the meaning of that word in a way that opened a whole new innovative mindset. It was so transformational that it moved me away from the traditional technologist career path I was on, to one of driving organizational capabilities through collaborative thinking and creation.

Since then, I have sought out organizations and leaders who, at their very core, are not about accepting the status quo, and helped them achieve inclusive innovation. Here's one story.

It was the summer of 2014 and Toronto was hosting a global gathering to celebrate WorldPride—a first for Canada. At the time, the global financial institution I worked for was figuring out how to differentiate itself as an employer and client service provider in a highly competitive space.

While the company was forming its marketing, products, attraction, and retention strategy for the LGBTQ+ community, our PRIDE

Melissa Donaldson of Wintrust wants us to understand the value of allowing talent from traditionally underrepresented groups to have an organizational voice, even before they are pressed to be part of innovation.

"In some cases, this could be the first opportunity these individuals have had to really share their point of view or to be creative or to share a line of thinking that didn't have an audience. Innovation comes from that. Had they not been a part of that D&I initiative, they may never have had the opportunity to express themselves in that way. It's about finding those opportunities to demonstrate where differences can make a difference."

Applying an adaptive mindset is how inclusive leaders extend their influence organizationally to produce innovation. But even

employee resource group was already thinking outside the box. Their approach was to combine a commercial differentiation and LGBTQ+ inclusion.

Their idea? To have the bank sponsor a high-end "drag evening."

When the CEO was presented with the idea, she saw the opportunity to step forward as not just an ally but an upstander for the community. And it surely would bring new attention to a bank wanting to establish itself as banking partner, ally, and employer of choice in the LGBTQ+ community.

The evening was a smash hit on so many levels. Guest after guest showed up as their authentic selves, and I very quickly realized this was not an evening to be wearing a tie! Employees, with clients, spouses, and community leaders, showed up, and a new persona for the bank was established.

That single event propelled employee and client engagement to measurable new heights. Seeing the CEO onstage with her entourage of world-class drag performers broke so many stereotypes, and it set the tone for a new spirit and culture at the bank that has carried on to this very day.

Bold and inclusive leadership through innovation can take many forms—including a CEO and a PRIDE group collaborating to enhance a corporate brand through feathers, gowns, glorious makeup, and heels to die for.

———— ■ ————

innovation is not an end in itself. Rather, this discipline sets the stage for the final discipline of *achieves transformation*, working toward the equitable organizations of the future.

■　　■　　■

DISCIPLINE 5

Achieves Transformation

COURAGE
PERSUADES
DRIVES RESULTS

EENA AL-FARIS, COFOUNDER OF CAVIAR COURT AND founder of
Qamrah, a fashion brand, is one of very few female CEOs
of Saudi-owned companies. Her inclusive leadership has helped
achieve transformation at a broader scale on behalf of a workforce of
Saudi women.

In 2000, the Saudi monarchy launched an initiative to reduce the
jobless rate among Saudi citizens. The new mandate stated that all
companies operating in Saudi Arabia with more than twenty employees must employ at least 25% Saudi citizens.[1] This was intended to
reduce the economy's nearly total reliance on skilled and unskilled
foreign workers. Today, there are more than 9 million foreign workers
in an overall workforce of nearly 11 million.[2]

The implications of this policy are multiple and not without
controversy, as they intersect with the heated debates on migrant
labor and its influence on local economies. Plus, much of the Saudi

talent lacked the skills and/or the experience
to handle some of the more specialized new
jobs that opened up.

    "It was a difficult time, because it caused
much disruption we were not ready for," said
Al-Faris. "One of the ways we were creative is
we chose to promote the foreign workers who
stayed, so they could provide guidance to the
less qualified Saudis while we trained them up."

> **ACHIEVES TRANSFORMATION:**
>
> *is willing to confront difficult topics; brings people of all backgrounds along to achieve results.*

    This meant that many people—both foreign and Saudi—had the
opportunity to stretch and grow.

    "That was a beautiful change," reflects Al-Faris.

    But the talent shortages persisted. This led to Al-Faris's other cre-
ative strategy, which was to significantly increase the number of Saudi
women in the workforce and in managerial roles.

    Resistance came from many places. For example, people were
not recruiting women for human resources positions because they
felt women should not be the ones checking on people's behavior.
Furthermore, Al-Faris didn't want to recruit women just for administrative roles. That meant providing greater numbers of women with
the systemic support they needed to succeed. This included providing
some of the female leaders with male assistants, which was essentially
unheard of in Saudi Arabia at the time.

    Al-Faris's inclusive leadership had a transformative impact on
the lives of many women, since new professional opportunities also
meant more influence and higher incomes, which benefited both their
careers and their personal lives.

You might think that Deena Al-Faris's identity would center around
being Saudi, a woman, and a Muslim. She, of course, is all that and
more—and she speaks authentically from those various parts of
her identity. But when she is asked how she describes herself, she
does not use any of those identifiers. Instead, her response is, "The
identity I live is that of someone who drives change."

    In that one line, Al-Faris encapsulates the *So what?* of diversity
and inclusion. When an organization finally becomes more diverse
and inclusive, what difference does it make to its organizational goals
and purpose?

Diversity in itself is beautiful to be around. It can lead to a celebratory environment of belonging and well-being. It can be a reflection of what the world really looks like. But as we have seen throughout this book, left unmanaged, left overlooked, and left unleveraged, diversity does not end up amounting to much. In fact, it can even undermine the optimal performance of an organization.

Inclusive leaders are the ones who can **achieve transformation** at every level of the organization precisely because they have the knowledge and skills to leverage the full range of the enterprise's diversity. And that's what this final discipline is all about.

Achieving transformation is the destination of the proverbial journey. Our talent and D&I professional survey respondents resoundingly agreed. One hundred percent of them said that achieving transformation was either an extremely or a very important characteristic in inclusive leaders.

To be clear, achieving transformation goes beyond achieving change in the narrow sense of just becoming more diverse and inclusive. It's about how leveraging that greater diversity and inclusion transforms the company for a more sustainable and equitable future. It's when greater diversity and inclusion provides an organization with the courage and persuasion to drive results.

COURAGE

You must never be fearful about what you are doing when it is right.

Rosa Parks, American civil rights activist

He was in the CEO succession pool, just one level down from the executive team. Let's call him John, since 5% of CEOs are named John.[3] On the same level was another powerful leader—and let's call him David, since that, too, is a popular executive-level name. David had been around for twenty-five years. He was a rainmaker, a top revenue producer. But he was also verbally abusive to the people around him. He would castigate them in front of others in the most public of places and demean them in private. He would call them stupid and imbeciles. And no one said anything—except John.

In private, John, who had an inclusive leader streak in him and happened to have a smidgen of authority over David, told David that this kind of behavior would not be tolerated.

To reinforce his message, John sought the CEO's backing. "Go ahead if you want," the CEO told him, "but I don't think it's a good idea."

JACKIE ROBINSON'S ADVOCATE

COURAGE ■ *Barry Callender, Atlanta*

The Brooklyn Dodgers part-owner sat in the stands behind home plate, knowing that many of the fans would abuse the player he had hired. Nevertheless, despite the scorn and mistreatment his player received, he knew this was the right thing to do.

The player was Jackie Robinson, the first African American to break the color barrier. While Robinson's story of courage continues to inspire, less is known about the courage of his White male advocate, Branch Rickey, who championed Robinson's skills in the face of all-out opposition.

What made Rickey courageous enough to hire Robinson? At play were a businessman who had a vision to bring the best talent available to the game of baseball and a man who had witnessed up close the prejudices facing African Americans.

While Rickey was a student-coach at Ohio Wesleyan University, a Black catcher named Charles Thomas was denied access to a hotel. Rickey ordered a cot to his own room for Thomas and made it clear to the hotel that the team stayed together or left together. Later, when Rickey played professional football for the Shelby Blues, he was friends with Charles Follis, football's first Black professional player. He witnessed the abusive treatment that Follis endured, as well as the courageous manner in which he endured it.

When Rickey became a baseball executive, he was determined to bring the best baseball players to Major League Baseball. He scouted for talent of color in the Caribbean and in South America as well as in the Negro Leagues in the United States. "I don't know who he is, or where he is," Rickey told Red Barber, the Dodgers' radio announcer, "but he is coming."

While he was looking for an exceptional player, he knew he also needed to find an exceptional person who could withstand all that was going to be thrown at him. At the time, the South was still facing the aftermath of the Civil War, which had killed more than half a million

David did not heed John's warning and did not change his behavior at all. The next time John caught wind of David's verbal abuse, John fired him.

That's *courage*.

Americans in a fight about Black slavery. The baseball commissioner was against desegregating the game, and so were many White players.

In his famous speech at the One Hundred Percent Wrong Club banquet in Atlanta, Georgia, on January 20, 1956, Rickey explained his strategy:

> I had to get the right man off the field. I couldn't come with a man to break down a tradition that had in it centered and concentrated all the prejudices of a great many people north and south unless he was good. He must justify himself upon the positive principle of merit. He must be a great player. I must not risk an excuse of trying to do something in the sociological field, or in the race field, just because of sort of a "holier than thou." I must be sure that the man was good on the field, but more dangerous to me, at that time, and even now, is the wrong man off the field. . . . I wanted a man of exceptional intelligence, a man who was able to grasp and control the responsibilities of himself to his race and could carry that load. That was the greatest danger point of all.[4]

Rickey found his man in Robinson. He liked what he saw him do on the field and how he handled himself off the field. But, knowing what the first Black player in the major leagues would experience, he tested Robinson during his interview by delivering the types of racial slurs that would be hurled Robinson's way.

"'Mr. Rickey, do you want a ballplayer who is afraid to fight back?' Robinson asked. No, came the reply. 'I want a ballplayer with guts enough *not* to fight back.'"[5] Robinson agreed to the challenge.

While Robinson was arguably not the best player in the Negro Leagues, he had the combination that Rickey was looking for. Robinson proved to be stoic in the face of abuse and single-mindedly focused on winning. He took the Dodgers to six league championships and one World Series title. Rickey's courageous bet on diversity and inclusion paid off. He had acted on his belief in getting the best talent, as well as on his belief in equal opportunity.

Courage is a unique kind of competency. It's one that begins to morph, the more the stakes go up.

There are plenty of good leaders who are very good at making good decisions that require a modicum of courage. Many of these decisions are shaped by creative strategy, by effective cost–benefit or return on investment analysis, by anticipation of potential unintended consequences, or by thoughtful reflection about preparing people for the change. This requires hard work, patience, attention to detail, and ensuring that various points of view are considered before stepping out with the decision and action. Along the way is where some courage is needed. Courage to disappoint certain people. Courage to take a calculated risk. Courage to sunset a beloved product.

Then there is the courage that requires digging deeper into one's own inner forces. As the stakes go up and the situations get dicier, it often becomes about ethics and accountability.

"Courageous leaders meet tough situations head-on to constructively resolve," writes Heather Barnfield in *FYI*. "Many times it's not positive. Something went wrong. Something is being covered up or over. Something is not being done right. Someone isn't performing well. Someone is holding something back. Someone is going off on the wrong track. Courage involves letting people know where you stand."

The next level of courage is being willing to address an entrenched status quo that is harmful to those who are underrepresented, to challenge groupthink, and to advocate for the talent that keeps being overlooked. It is also about explicitly leveraging diversity and inclusion to achieve organizational goals such as greater innovation, revenue growth, and brand elevation.

Even leaders who tend to be courageous strategic decision-makers often falter here.

PERSUADES

Don't raise your voice; improve your argument.

Desmond Tutu, South African activist

The ability to *persuade* is another competency that many leaders tend to be good at generically. In fact, people who are not persuasive don't usually make it to leadership. But inclusive leaders up their persuasion skills by seeking to know people in terms of their diverse identities and the formative and experiential journeys that have shaped them. They use this deeper knowledge of others to better package, present, and communicate their cases in ways that speak to those others. They make their persuasive efforts more personal—and effective—by expertly tapping into the profound waters of identity and culture.

The inclusive leaders we interviewed had various daily examples of how they persuaded others around certain diversity issues. Wellington Silverio had to persuade a Deere team in Brazil to accept to their team a very competent woman who did not fit their standards of acceptable weight. Jenny Ni at Dow Chemical had to influence leaders to allow hourly workers the flexibility to attend employee resource group events, because otherwise engagement would go down and turnover would go up. Others had to persuade managers to, for example, extend a job offer to someone seven weeks pregnant, because she was the best candidate, or to promote a person from a racial minority group because they had access to markets they were trying to break into, or to find a way to retain the person with disability by accommodating their need with special software. As is often the case with inclusive leadership, these exhibitions of persuasion had the dual impact of achieving both talent inclusion and broader organizational business goals.

Clearly, in these examples, there also are compliance and ethical reasons to pull from. But in different parts of the world, it's not illegal to avoid offering a woman a job because she's pregnant, for example. The point is this: in contrast to getting people to do things for compliance reasons (that is, through coercion), persuasion is about convincing someone that a certain decision or action is the best thing to do.

Inclusive leaders use persuasion all the time as they advocate on behalf of underrepresented talent. That is because the deck is stacked against underrepresented talent all the time. Inclusive leaders have to muster the courage and use their skills of persuasion to make the cases that not only is D&I the right thing to do from a values and ethics perspective but it is also what organizations need to transform successfully in a world in disruption.

Persuasion in this sense requires us to understand people at a deep level—their formative years; their likes and dislikes; the sources of their strengths, aspirations, and biases—so we can more effectively speak to what matters to them in ways that create bridges between their own interests, the interests of the organization, and the interests of those who have traditionally been left out.

HOW MÓNICA RAMÍREZ PERSUADED MILLIONS TO JOIN THE TIME'S UP MOVEMENT

PERSUADES ▪ *Michael Hyter, Washington, DC*

It was a seemingly mismatched outreach of solidarity in the wake of the Harvey Weinstein scandal. Through an open letter titled "Dear Sisters" in *Time* magazine, seven hundred thousand Latina farmworkers reached out to female actors in Hollywood, seemingly a world away.

Despite their vastly different social status, these two groups of women shared the unfortunate sisterhood of sexual harassment in the workplace.

The letter was authored by Mónica Ramírez on behalf of the Alianza Nacional de Campesinas (National Farmworkers Women's Alliance), an organization she had cofounded. It went viral and was noticed by the Hollywood stars, who reached back in response to join forces.

Out of that collaboration came Time's Up, an organization committed to the protection of women against sexual harassment. From sexual assault allegations against well-known celebrities to the promotion of female creativity, the Time's Up campaign has begun to significantly shift the unequal power dynamics of the film industry. It was a tour de force case study in persuasion.

How was Ramírez able to persuade so many in a way that became a catalyst for far-reaching change?

First, she effectively leveraged who she was, both personally and professionally. Everywhere Ramírez goes, in her talks, writings, and closed-door meetings, she shares her story of being a third-generation American and the daughter and granddaughter of migrant Mexican farmers, and how her parents raised her to be proud of her Latino culture. In a *Forbes* interview, she elaborated, "From a young age, they taught us about social justice issues, including issues affecting migrant farmworkers, and they always stressed the importance of giving back to our community."[6]

She also leveraged her education and credentials. As an attorney who then got her master's in public administration from Harvard University's Kennedy School of Government, Ramírez has been a strong advocate for human rights and fairness for decades. She had both the technical skills and the strategic thinking to get things done well, and also the prestige credentials that make those in power sit up and take notice.

In addition, she was exceptionally effective at making connections across vast differences. Ramírez has a special skill of calling people *in* instead of *out*. She appeals to everyone's common humanity and their desire to be heard and not stand alone.

As Ramírez explained when she appeared on the *Today* show with actress America Ferrara, "While people think that farmworker women are not powerful, farmworker women are very powerful. . . . We have the experience, not just of having suffered from this problem, but we also have the experience of years of organizing that we wanted to bring forward to support the women in Hollywood who are coming forward."[7]

Finally, her persuasion was fueled by inspiration. Ramírez began advocating for farmworkers' rights by writing stories for her local newspaper when she was fourteen. "Any of us, no matter where we come from, no matter our background, have the ability to make a significant impact," she told the *Daily Beast*. "So for little girls who are watching this moment play out, I hope they see they can too."[8]

While very few would have thought Latina farmworkers could have something to offer Hollywood's elite, thanks to Mónica Ramírez's connective influence, they did.

———————— ■ ————————

DRIVES RESULTS

*One never notices what has been done; one can only see what
remains to be done.*

Marie Curie, Polish and
naturalized-French Nobel Prize–
winning physicist and chemist

Just get it done.

Diversity and inclusion is replete with "very interesting" things to
talk, debate, and worry about. But inclusive leaders do more than talk;
ultimately, they *drive results*. They translate the ideas, strategies, business cases, and programs into cohesive cultural transformation that
yields tangible, organizationally valuable results.

What kind of results? Let's start with the most obvious: more
diversity of talent at every level of the organization.

After that, the results should be about how the organization has
effectively leveraged their increased diversity and inclusion to develop
new products and markets, drive better financial results, and build
a stronger corporate reputation. Scientific and field evidence that
greater diversity and inclusion achieves these results is indisputable.

Inclusive leaders and organizations see the connection between
their efforts at work and driving results in their broader communities.
Take Intel. A dearth of women and people of color in the science,
technology, engineering, and math (STEM) pipeline was limiting their
recruitment efforts. Beyond their internal efforts to create a more
inclusive and equitable environment for these underrepresented
groups, they went further, to address a societal root cause: not enough
women and people of color, in general, are entering STEM disciplines.

In January 2015, Intel announced its Diversity in Technology
initiative, with the aim of achieving full representation of women
and underrepresented minorities in Intel's US workforce by 2020.
To support the initiative, Intel committed $300 million to accelerate
diversity and inclusion across the technology industry—from spending
with diverse suppliers and diversifying its venture portfolio to better
serving its markets and communities through innovative programs.
Intel achieved its goal of full representation in its US workforce in
2018, two years ahead of schedule.[9]

Another example is the Eastern Chamber of Commerce in Saudi Arabia, which had an all-male board and did not have women inclusivity on its agenda at all. The chamber did have a women's center with a very limited scope, and the person running that, Hind Al-Zahid (who later became the Saudi Vice Minister of the Women Empowerment Agency), decided it was time to form a council for young women, which would specialize in helping them create their own companies. She approached Deena Al-Faris and three other women to help her form this council.

This women's council is now creating a development program for women to become board members and executive leaders. It has given them a platform to advocate for more civil rights and economic opportunities for women in Saudi Arabia, many of which have come to pass in recent years, including the right to vote, to drive, to attend public sporting events, to travel without a male relative's permission, to receive equal treatment in the workplace, and to obtain family documents from the government.[10] "There were times we thought that women would never have this power, but now we do," says Al-Faris.

"I encourage everyone to go out of their comfort zone," she says. "If you want to do more in this life, you need to believe that if we don't include more diversity we will be limited. Until relatively recently, the concept of inclusive leadership was not important for me. But now I see the motivation it creates in employees and how it leads to results such as greater effectiveness and growth in our company. This benefits us all."

Getting results is what drove Cristina David at Ericsson to shake up the status quo. When she saw how her very talented Indian workers were being dismissed by bigger, more established centers within her company, she started an internal mobility effort that relocated some of her best workers from India to Sweden, with their families. "It's having transformative results," she says.

And so we have completed our deep dive into the five disciplines of inclusive leaders. We have dissected and unpacked the various competencies within each of the disciplines and looked at how the enabling traits weave their way through and through. We have heard the stories and opinions of various global inclusive leaders on how it all comes together.

THE CANADIAN MOUNTED POLICE: HOW WOMEN ON THE FORCE LED TO SAFER COMMUNITIES

DRIVES RESULTS ▪ *David Herrera, Mexico City and Toronto*

In September 1974, for the first time ever, thirty-two women began recruit training at the Royal Canadian Mounted Police (RCMP) academy in Regina.[11]

The academy was not prepared for women and, initially, the physical training requirements for them were not realistic. Eventually, the female standards were changed from "equal" to their male counterparts to "equivalent."

The women also asked for help from Major Doris Toole, who previously had been in charge of female recruit training at Canadian Forces Base Cornwallis, Nova Scotia, requesting that she act as a liaison between the women and the police force. She monitored their training classes and provided advice regarding the visual inequality of their uniforms—having two different dress uniforms for men and women communicated women's subordinate status within the RCMP and called into question their legitimacy as figures of civic authority.[12]

Less than a year later, thirty of the thirty-two women completed their training. Initially, some male officers were protective of their women partners in ways that were paternalistic. But the women just wanted to be treated like equal partners and have each other's backs.

What follows in part 2 are four studies of exemplary organizations at different stages of their Inclusive Leader journey. Some of the stories are driven by the strength of a singular, visionary, charismatic inclusive leader. Others feature institutional behemoths, where inclusive leaders and systems and processes must be part and parcel of a whole systemic approach. Their journeys are as unique to one another as the whole concept of diversity would want them to be.

Go get the popcorn. It's story time.

▪   ▪   ▪

Donna Burns, who was part of the first cohort of women Mounties, explains that it took some time for her to convince her male partners that they should let her do what she was trained to do, but with the understanding that women can tend to handle situations differently than men. Rather than using physical force, for example, female police officers frequently negotiate their way through difficult circumstances.

Other challenges arose. For instance, the RCMP still did not have a policy regarding marriage between two Mounties, and its policies also were unprepared for pregnant Mounties or for sexual harassment on the job. For these reasons, there were many resignations among female Mounties.

Allowing women to join the RCMP didn't just mean being able to draw from a much larger pool of talent (today, women represent 22% of total police officers in Canada). The hiring, development, and advancement of women led to important results in law enforcement itself over time. For example, women's greater likelihood to negotiate before using force led to a new skill set to policing.

And the benefits of representation of women in policing go beyond the RCMP itself, including less use of excessive force, leading to lower financial payouts to victims of police abuse; reduction of unethical behavior; an embrace of diversified skills and leadership styles; and improved investigation of gender-based crimes.[13] By bringing women into law enforcement, these departments not only expanded their skills and motivated the labor pool but also drove results that led to safer communities.[14]

We have explored the depths of what inclusive leadership looks like from a model perspective and through the eyes of inclusive leaders, sharing their opinions and situational examples.

But it all comes back to the *So what?*. So what if we know what inclusive leadership looks like? So what if we have leaders who eloquently share their views on it and who carefully bought into the business case? What difference does it ultimately make in organizations that have embraced the value of equitable organizations and have committed to being the design architects for it? What have they ended up building?

Here, we tell the story of four exemplars, each in a different field and each in a different stage of diversity and inclusion maturity. The stories of what they built are both inspiring and complex in their comprehensive nature—which is the point.

Enjoy!

PART 2

THE EXEMPLARS

6

Barilla: Preserving Tradition While Changing It

FOUNDED IN 1877 IN PARMA, ITALY, BARILLA, the once local, still family-owned company, is now the world's largest pasta manufacturer.

For more than 140 years, the Barilla family brand conveyed openness and acceptance. But as the company continued its global expansion, it began to face new diversity and inclusion challenges. After all, most of the top leadership was Italian—most were even from the Parma area. They had been at the company most of their careers, and so had many of their parents and grandparents. In addition, because it was a family-owned business, the company culture mirrored that of a typical northern Italian family: close knit, paternalistic, and tied to long-standing traditions. These attributes made Barilla a beloved employer for many but left little room for those who did not fit that fairly homogeneous mold.

In the early 2010s, Barilla was a Parma-based company with a presence in different parts of the world. What it wanted to be was a truly global company, and that meant becoming more diverse and inclusive in terms of talent, mindset, and culture. But even as the company's leaders were digesting this realization, changes in the global market were happening at a faster rate than they were ready for, and they were unsure of how to go about making this happen.

Barilla leadership started by hiring a cosmopolitan CEO, Claudio Colzani, former chief customer officer at Unilever. Though Italian by birth and upbringing, Colzani had worked most of his career outside of his home country, including in France, Brazil, and the United States. Under his leadership, Barilla established a road map called the Barilla Lighthouse, which heralded a new, explicitly contemporary and global perspective for the company.

The Lighthouse road map made it clear that the purpose of the company was to be "good for you and good for the planet." It outlined five key points:

1. Be the number one choice of brand and product for people

2. Win in the marketplace

3. Drive continuous improvement

4. Only one way of doing business

5. Proudly be Barilla people

It was this fifth point that invited employees to embrace diversity and inclusion. But early on, its implications were little understood and D&I efforts were limited. Furthermore, despite the Lighthouse commitments, some countries resisted the way the diversity and inclusion process was being conducted; it challenged their traditional way of management.

It became clear that having posters with the Barilla Lighthouse values was not enough to bring about the changes that leadership sought. So Barilla embarked on a deep and far-reaching process that required a full demonstration of inclusive leadership. It led to a remarkable and measurable transformation toward becoming a more diverse and inclusive company.

Barilla became the first Italian company to support the UN standards code of conduct for LGBTQ+ inclusion in the workplace and became a sponsor of the Thomson Reuters Foundation's Openly news platform for unbiased reporting on LGBTQ+ issues around the world. In 2015, Barilla reached a 100% rating in the Human Rights Campaign's annual Corporate Equality Index, which measures how inclusive companies are toward LGBTQ+ employees, and it has kept a perfect score for five consecutive years. It is now recognized as one of the Human Rights Campaign's Best Places to Work for LGBTQ+ Equality. *The Huffington Post* named Barilla a Most Improved Player for D&I, and *Campaign US*, an advertising industry trade magazine, awarded Barilla's digital video series, "While the Water Boils," an I&C [Inclusive & Creative] Disruptor's Award, which celebrates advertising that breaks racial and gender stereotypes.

Internally, employee ratings of management's commitment to promoting diversity and inclusiveness rose from 65% in 2014 to 75% in 2019. Barilla also saw a jump in the number of women in leadership positions *and* in the talent pipeline, going from 32% to 37% for women in leadership and from 37% to 51% for women in the talent pipeline.

But how did Barilla accomplish this kind of turnaround in such a short period of time? And how is it ensuring that these changes continue generating even more progress? Let's go to the tape.

KEY BEST PRACTICES

Barilla leadership quickly put into place several D&I best practices that signaled their commitment to a new vision. The company:

- created new networks, inside and out;
- made public commitments to achieving various equity standards;
- rolled out training;
- established employee resource groups;
- implemented job transparency and new benefits;
- commissioned a comprehensive D&I root cause analysis and diagnosis; and
- put metrics and accountability into place.

NEW NETWORKS, INSIDE AND OUT

Barilla built new internal and external networks to promote inclusiveness. They created a chief diversity officer role, first filled by Talita Ramos Erickson, a Brazilian who had been chief legal counsel for the Americas. Ramos Erickson took the reins when she was six months pregnant.

"They didn't see my pregnancy as a barrier," she says. "They valued my passion for the topic, as well as my background and my work performance, and knew I was the right person for the job."

Barilla also created a global diversity and inclusion board and recruited three external directors: LGBTQ+ civil rights activist David Mixner; Alessandro Zanardi, a Paralympics cycling gold medalist and race car driver; and Patricia Bellinger, Executive Director at the Center for Public Leadership at Harvard's Kennedy School. They joined ten internal employees selected from around the world.

Furthermore, Barilla created collaborative partnerships and relationships with organizations such as Catalyst, which is focused on female advancement, and the LGBTQ+ inclusion organizations GLAAD and the Human Rights Campaign in the United States, and Parks–Liberi e Uguali in Italy.

PUBLIC COMMITMENTS TO EQUITY

In 2016, Barilla's CEO signed on to the United Nations Women's Empowerment Principles. In January 2018, the Barilla Group was the first Italian company to support the Standards of Conduct for Business promoted by the Office of the High Commissioner for Human Rights, aimed at tackling lesbian, gay, bisexual, transgender, and intersex discrimination in business. The announcement was made on January 26, 2018, at the World Economic Forum's annual meeting, during the Free and Equal forum, where one of the speakers was UN High Commissioner for Human Rights Zeid Ra'ad Al Hussein.

These commitments to D&I standards set by outside organizations and the recognition Barilla received for its efforts not only enhanced the company's brand and reputation but also accelerated the maturity of the organization's diversity and inclusion.

TRAINING

In 2014, Barilla launched training on how to recognize and mitigate unconscious bias. It was provided to all office employees in the first year and to the vast majority of sales force and plant employees throughout 2015 and 2016. Feedback training that took into account diversity and inclusion was then launched in 2016 for all managers worldwide and was completed in 2017.

EMPLOYEE RESOURCE GROUPS

To begin making the invisible needs of the minority visible to the majority, Barilla employees started three employee resource groups in America in 2015: VOCE (Italian for "voice") for LGBTQ+ employees and allies, Balance to advance gender equality and work–life balance, and Alleanza for employees of color and their allies. Since then, employees around the world have formed a total of fourteen employee resource groups around gender, LGBTQ+, age and generation demographics, disabilities, different religions and beliefs, and multiculturalism. Harnessing the enthusiasm and motivation of employees across all levels and geographies enabled a faster culture change at all levels of the organization.

JOB TRANSPARENCY AND NEW BENEFITS

In 2016, Barilla created an interactive and widely available job posting system to promote transparency and equity with regard to internal opportunities. Even the diversity and inclusion board member positions are posted internally. Barilla also has launched various work–life programs and expanded its flexible work program, called "smartworking."

COMPREHENSIVE DIVERSITY AND INCLUSION ROOT CAUSE DIAGNOSIS

Barilla partnered with Korn Ferry as an advisory firm to conduct a root cause assessment to identify areas where the company was not living up to its own ambition and self-identity. The findings were then shared with the chief diversity officer and the diversity and inclusion board so they could recommend follow-up actions to the executive team.

Korn Ferry conducted confidential interviews with top executives to assess their inclusive leadership skills and deployed a global D&I survey in the eight main languages used by Barilla employees. These efforts were followed by targeted focus groups in offices and factories around the world.

The survey was developed in collaboration with the D&I board and human resources leaders in all of Barilla's sites around the world. The first of its kind in all of Barilla's history, it was fielded for the first time in 2014 and then roughly every other year thereafter in order to measure longitudinal evolution.

Not surprisingly, the results from the 2014 survey demonstrated that the company was not fully aware of its own internal D&I improvement areas. It also showed the need for Barilla's top leaders to have increased accountability for and more personal involvement in leading the transformation toward greater diversity and inclusion. For this reason, the work also defined accountability metrics for which leaders and the organization could strive.

With findings in hand, Korn Ferry conducted a two-day learning and strategy session with the Barilla D&I board to define the employee value proposition for D&I. The session highlighted the benefits of a diverse workforce within a globally diverse marketplace and the power of all forms of diversity within an inclusive work environment. The session became a catalyst for the leaders to deepen their sense of ownership of the cultural transformation.

METRICS AND ACCOUNTABILITY

Barilla established metrics on four key factors: leadership commitment to D&I, gender balance, flexible work, and inclusion. The biannual survey is one of the primary vehicles for keeping track of results, representation, and talent pipeline demographics.

- Leadership commitment is measured through several D&I survey questions that are combined to form a leadership commitment index. The index rose from 65% in 2014 to 75% in 2019. The goal is to achieve an 85% positive rating by 2025.
- The target for gender balance is 50% women in leadership positions and 50% women in the talent pipeline by 2020. In 2019, 37% of leadership positions were held by women, compared to 32% in 2014, and 51% of the talent pipeline are women.

- The flexible work index has risen from 78% in 2014 to 85% in 2019 and has a target goal of 95% by 2020.
- The inclusion index on the D&I survey has also shown an increase, from 69% in 2014 to 76% in 2019.

There is another very important key metric on the D&I scorecard that has shown positive transformation. In the past six years, the efforts made by Barilla resulted in its highest ever market share in the United States—33% in 2020.

ASSESSING AGAINST THE INCLUSIVE LEADER MODEL

Barilla's story is one of leaders effecting transformational change toward greater diversity and inclusion. But it also is the story of leaders undergoing transformational change themselves to become inclusive leaders.

The advice that Barilla's leaders received, and which they embraced early on, was that the cultural transformation had to touch every employee, from the boardroom to the factory floor. For the evolution to be authentic and sustainable, the changes in mindset and skills had to begin with the most senior leaders. They would be the ones responsible for role modeling, educating, and holding their charges accountable for practicing inclusive behaviors.

In Barilla's case, the intervention could not be addressed merely through an awareness training session. The work had to be individual at first, followed by the collective experience of the global leadership team. Only then could it cascade down to the regional and functional leadership teams and employees around the world.

Let's revisit the five disciplines of inclusive leadership and their enabling traits and see how they manifested in the Barilla leaders' mindsets and actions.

ENABLING TRAITS

There is ample evidence of *authenticity*, as Barilla's leaders were humble and built trust in places where trust had been broken.

They were *emotionally resilient*, maintaining their composure in the face of the struggle to become a truly global organization. After some missteps, they listened to their advisers to be more situationally self-aware of the various diversity issues that they were unfamiliar with, such as LGBTQ+ concerns, globalization, and the various ways the lack of inclusion could manifest. Their self-assurance was evident in their bedrock confidence in the Barilla Lighthouse values, and they faced their future with the optimism that comes from stewarding a 140-year-old trusted brand.

Their *inquisitiveness* was evident from the beginning, as they sought out the differences of their external and internal board members and the consultancy they had hired. They learned to be more curious about differences beyond what many of them knew from their deep-seated and cherished traditional Italian culture. An area of deeper learning that simply took more time, due to its difficult nature, was developing fuller empathy for people unlike themselves.

Finally, *flexibility* ended up being the hardest to master because it requires tolerating ambiguity and being more adaptable to a world that is very different from that of the leaders, who were based in the small agricultural city of Parma in northern Italy.

FIVE DISCIPLINES

Barilla's leaders were motivated and open learners. Throughout the Barilla story, there are plenty of examples of **building interpersonal trust** by *valuing differences* and *instilling trust*.

They had plenty of opportunities to **integrate diverse perspectives** by *managing conflict* and *balancing stakeholders* inside and outside the organization, like never before.

They **optimized talent** by boosting employees' belief that theirs had *become a more engaged* and inclusive culture and by the *talent development* that led to a greater percentage of women in leadership. They began to advocate for *collaboration* as the key to reaping the benefits of being more diverse and inclusive.

As they learned from the D&I evaluation and the D&I board, as well as through the cross-cultural agility training they developed, an **adaptive mindset** allowed them to *think more globally*, *be more situationally adaptable*, and see that increased diversity could be just what they needed to *be more innovative*.

Finally, when it came to leveraging D&I for the bigger goal of **achieving transformation**, *engaging all employees* via employee resource groups accelerated the needed cultural transformation.

Barilla's transformation crystallized the idea that diversity and inclusion was important and vital to the company's health as an employer *and* as a part of its transformation into a truly global company.

SHARING THE TABLE

When Barilla's American headquarters outside of Chicago had a chance to move to a new location, the interior of the building was theirs to redesign. The head of HR, Laura Birk, offered every employee the opportunity to contribute by being part of design teams that would create the ideal workplace—from the main lobby to meeting rooms to the restrooms. The objective was to have a workplace that made everyone feel comfortable.

The new headquarters includes, among other things, accessible gym equipment, gender-neutral bathrooms, and diverse images throughout the building. There is a self-service snack area where employees pay an unmonitored automated cashier. It even includes a celebration of diverse abilities by showcasing a large collective art project made by all employees, inspired by acclaimed American artist Chuck Close, who continued to paint even after he had become severely paralyzed.

While this was happening at the local level, back in the strategic center, D&I has been fully embraced as a business driver. Looking back at the impact across the whole organization, Kristen Anderson, Barilla's second-ever chief diversity officer, reflects, "It took a few years to make the ground fertile for a change. We needed to find the right entry points. We knew that if we started out pushing a message that people couldn't relate to, or a local country culture says is nonexistent, we wouldn't get a lot of engagement."

For Claudio Colzani, Barilla's CEO, one of those key messages was that diversity and inclusion is not just good for the people but also good for the business. "A diverse workforce and an inclusive culture boost engagement and allow for a deeper understanding of society, leading to stronger decision-making. Promoting diversity and inclusion is not just about doing the right thing but also about supporting our growth strategy."

Like managing a diverse gathering of family and friends sharing pasta around the table, Barilla's journey toward greater diversity and inclusion had to balance people and profits, tradition and transformation.

Inclusive leadership is what made it possible.

■　　■　　■

7

John Deere: Inclusive Leadership Feeds the World

DON'T CALL JOHN DEERE—THE COMPANY THAT BROUGHT us the iconic bright green and yellow tractors, harvesters, and plows—a farming company.

"We consider ourselves a technology company," Julian Sanchez, Deere's Director of Technology Innovation, told *Engadget*, in an interview conducted at CES, the annual trade show held by the Consumer Technology Association, where the latest in digital is showcased and unveiled.[1]

Even though the 182-year-old company founded in the American plains did create the first-ever steel plow, Deere's farming equipment today uses GPS systems, 5G LTE modems, satellite imagery, unmanned aerial equipment, and drones, plus it continually sends data to the cloud to be processed by artificial intelligence. Deere's GPS-guided tractors, plows, and harvesters are accurate to within 2.5 centimeters, boosting food yield per acre by planting more on the front end and destroying less food on the back end.

In fact, going digital has been core to Deere's mission to feed the world. "Farmers need to find ways to produce more food, and do it with fewer resources," says J. B. Penn, John Deere's Chief Economist, in a 2015 interview. The United Nations projects that the world's population will reach nearly 10 billion people by 2050, and Penn estimated that global agricultural output will have to increase by as much as 70% over 2015 levels to feed them.[2]

To fulfill its mission, the $30 billion annual revenue company has turned to digitally enabled artificial intelligence as well as collective human intelligence. It aims to optimize the contributions of its sixty-eight thousand employees in more than thirty countries, ranging from Australia and China to South Africa and Latin America. And it's to Latin America—Brazil, specifically—that we go to do a deep dive into how Deere's inclusive leadership is driving its efforts.

TRANSFORMATION IN THE AGRICULTURAL HEARTLAND

In the town of Horizontina, in the grand plains of the Rio Grande region of southern Brazil, nearly 750 miles from São Paulo, John Deere is the biggest employer. Reaching Deere's combine and planter factory takes more than six hours: a commercial flight from Congonhas Airport in São Paulo, another flight aboard Deere's private jet, and a car ride.

Many of Horizontina's twenty thousand inhabitants speak a German dialect dating back to immigrants who founded the city almost a century ago. Approximately 60% of the population consists of German descendants, 20% are Italian and Polish, and 20% are from indigenous populations and African and Portuguese descendants.

The diversity of the town is fully evident as Wellington Silverio, Deere's head of human resources for the Latin American region, Vladimir Alves, Latin American head for D&I, and Cecilia Pinzón, a Korn Ferry senior principal, enter an auditorium with about three hundred factory workers dressed in jeans, T-shirts, and Deere caps.

There is some apprehension among the employees, but also an eager anticipation for what they are going to learn that day about diversity and inclusion.

Silverio walks up on the stage and, without much preamble, describes in compelling ways why this D&I training session is important to all of those in this remote plant. Paulo Herrmann, Vice President, Sales and Marketing for region 3, reinforces the message by saying, "To continue growing, investing in diversity and inclusion is strategic. We need diverse teams to innovate."

Pinzón then comes up to facilitate the session. She asks everyone to write down the names of five people they take care of. Most of the men included themselves, while nearly all of the women left their own names out. Pinzón explains how these answers reinforce engrained gender roles and stereotypes. "For most of the people there, this kind of conversation was totally new," she says.

Over the past decade, Deere has been relentless in creating awareness around diversity and inclusion. All sixty-eight thousand employees, in offices and on factory floors around the world, have gone through foundational D&I training. Deere also has put in place various best practices, such as having a global diversity council as well as regional diversity councils—although the scope of these has now been expanded beyond diversity to what they call "team enrichment." Ten years ago, the company celebrated its first-ever African American woman general manager of a factory in the US.

Starting in 2016, Wellington Silverio sought to deepen the impact in Latin America, launching a comprehensive D&I program across the region's operations. So far, it has involved more than thirteen thousand employees in Brazil, Argentina, and Mexico.

Silverio himself is part of Deere's D&I story. In a country where Afro-Brazilians make up nearly half the population but are nearly invisible in corporate management, Silverio represents an emerging wave of Afro-Brazilians in executive management. For him, it's not just about rising to the fullness of his potential; it's also about leveraging his seat at the table to ensure his story is not the exception at Deere.

"As a Black leader, I have always been part of the minority," says Silverio. "I have experienced firsthand how important inclusion is, because so often I was the one not being included based on my Afro-Brazilian background." As he moved up the ranks, Silverio was able to be more influential—especially as an HR leader—helping those around him develop a greater consciousness and acceptance of those who are different.

In partnership with Alves, the region's first-ever D&I leader (and the first such role outside the United States), Silverio has successfully engaged and enrolled Deere's Latin American business leaders to sponsor and lead the cultural transformation effort. They have made the case not only from a mission-driven imperative of equal opportunity but also from their business-driven imperative to feed the world. For a company like Deere, having a leadership team that promotes— and a workforce that reflects—the global diversity of its consumers is simply smart business.

In Latin America, not only are there vast cultural differences between countries but also farms in the region have been undergoing a generational change, sometimes passing from fathers to daughters instead of to sons. That's a seismic shift for the male-dominated agribusiness industry generally, and in Latin America particularly.

"Agro-biz is very traditional, from a human inclusion perspective," says Silverio. "Deere reflected that tradition." It had a pervasive culture that was not necessarily focused on diversity, with tenures averaging around twenty-five years and deep familial roots. Now, Deere needs a workforce that reflects the diversity of its consumers. This recognition has led to more structural inclusion support, including nurturing the female leadership pipeline. Deere now has a 50% target for women's participation in their young leaders and internship programs.

These efforts have begun to pay off internally. For example, women filled almost a third of production vacancies during a recent selection process in Horizontina. And it has also yielded results externally.

In 2019, Deere's leaders held a meeting in Brazil's southern region to talk about D&I. More than one hundred leaders from Deere's dealers in the region listened in. "Clearly, D&I is now important for them," says Silverio. That same year, in São Paulo, there was a gathering of nearly four thousand women (twice the number from the previous year) at a women in agribusiness conference. While many societal forces drove that high participation, Deere's influence in the space contributed to the surge.

But D&I training at Deere cannot stop at awareness that D&I is a good thing. It needs to also move toward skill building. Back at the factory in Horizontina, for instance, one of the main challenges Deere leaders and managers express is how to conduct sales presentations for a gender-diverse audience, as well as for Millennials.

"They truly were perplexed about how to make deals with women, since many of them never had to before," says Pinzón. "Adjusting to the new styles of the more diverse talent and consumers they are seeking has been a challenge. This is key to being a truly inclusive leader, when you go from merely a supporter of diversity to actually being inclusive."

"The key is for a leader to identify a person's unique characteristics and establish a connection with them on the basis of those characteristics," Alves says. "Understanding someone's point of view not only helps you better understand what they need and how to go about doing something with them; it can also help you be more influential in their thinking."

Deere's inclusive leadership impact is now radiating across the entire organization. For example, when it comes to innovation, various Deere leaders share that the majority of ideas now come from the bottom up. They are generating a greater volume of ideas to address operational, cultural, and customer enhancements than management could ever have conceived.

But encouraging different ideas requires the ability to effectively manage conflict. "To make it work, we need to build the skills to discuss the different ideas, better understand each other, and in the process, also end up constructing a third and new way," Alves says. "Rather than minimizing the differences to resolve the conflict, we have been encouraging everyone to embrace that we can all think differently, and that some of the conflict that comes with that is okay."

Another challenge Silverio and Alves are facing has to do with getting managers at all levels on board. "Sometimes middle management doesn't accept or understand the changes we are proposing at the speed needed," says Silverio. "So we end up with both the grassroots and the senior leaders very engaged but the middle not much at all. This is where we need to invest more and try to win them over in ways that speak to their daily concerns of meeting production metrics."

IMPACT ON DIFFERENT GROUPS

The impact of these various efforts and the shift in mindset has been to generate greater feelings of belonging among employees that come from traditionally underrepresented or marginalized groups.

LGBTQ+

It wasn't too long ago that it was taboo in Brazil to talk about nontraditional gender and sex identities, and it was no different at Deere. But now that Deere Brazil has an LGBT employee resource group and some firsthand experience with helping to support a transgender employee in transition from male to female, attitudes have been shifting.

Getting there, however, was not easy. When this transgender employee shared with her coworkers the change she was undergoing, several made jokes about her clothes, her hair weave, and her makeup. She was on the verge of leaving the company, when a few key leaders at Deere recognized the need to lead inclusively and address the situation head-on.

These inclusive leaders asked team members to empathize by thinking about what it would be like for them if their heterosexuality were judged and ridiculed in the same way. Then the transitioning individual shared the kinds of challenges she wrestled with all the time. The anti currents began to shift, and eventually she was accepted for who she said she was.

One simple but powerful measure that change has happened is that people now talk openly and affirmatively about LGBT. And through focus groups, LGBT employees have shared the positive and healing impact this has had on them.

RACE

In commemoration of Black Awareness Day, which had been created to provoke a reflection on the legacy of discrimination and inequality passed down from the slavery period in Brazil, the Black Employee Resource Group was launched. An external speaker brought a historical perspective to the group's Black Awareness Day event, helping listeners understand how and under which pillars racism is structured in Brazil. The goal of the event was to seek everyone's commitment to building a society where racism is no longer an issue. Deere in Brazil is now striving toward meeting their 30% representation target for Black male and female talent.

WOMEN

Deere has three different employee resource groups focused on women's development: WomenREACH, Women in Operation, and the Society of Women Engineers. Deere's talent acquisition is now fully committed to ensuring that female candidates are included in short-lists, and they have developed mentoring programs and leadership training specifically for up-and-coming women within the company.

These actions have helped to increase the number of women hired. In 2019, there was a 13% increase in the number of women hired or promoted to close vacancies by the talent acquisition team, and 22% of leadership positions are held by women.

DISABILITY

For more than twenty-five years, Brazil has had one of the longest-standing workforce quotas for employing people with disabilities: 3% to 5%, depending on company size. Despite the quotas, however, people with disabilities have had a difficult time being accepted by their coworkers in Brazil and other Latin American countries.

In addition to the broad diversity and inclusion training initiative, a parallel development program focusing on people with disabilities was rolled out. Deere is now beginning to see more people with disabilities in management. These are people who had the skills all along but needed a bit more support. For example, in the Horizontina plant, a hearing-impaired leader can now fully participate in D&I training because he is provided with a sign language interpreter.

AGE

About 60% of Deere's Latin American employees are Millennials, and there are daily frictions between them and older employees. Deere in Latin America has instituted reverse mentoring and has helped build skills for members of different generations to adapt their styles to one another and to promote increased understanding and collaboration among them.

BRINGING IT ALL TOGETHER

To **build interpersonal trust,** Silverio, Alves, and business leaders throughout the region have leaned in hard to the *valuing of differences* in a region of the world where machismo has created so many barriers for women and LGBTQ+ individuals, and where there are other problematic societal legacies toward those of a lower economic class, those with darker skin, or those with disabilities. Declaring the value of differences and celebrating them has gone a long way in helping these leaders to *instill trust*.

In unpacking the **optimizing talent** discipline, we can see that building interpersonal trust has had a positive effect on *driving engagement*, *developing talent*, and *encouraging collaboration* among Deere's factory and office employees.

This puts Deere Latin America on the path toward becoming stronger at the other Inclusive Leader disciplines. They are in the beginning stages of **integrating diverse perspectives** as they become more knowledgeable and skilled at *balancing diverse stakeholders* and effectively *managing the inevitable conflict* that starts to surface when people from different groups that have not mixed much in society are brought together.

This maturing in inclusive leadership is also starting to play itself out in the discipline of **applying an adaptive mindset.** The competencies associated with this discipline—*situational adaptability*, *global perspective*, and *cultivating innovation*—require an in-depth experience with greater diversity, knowledge of how the differences manifest, and skill at extracting the most from the diversity, in an inclusive way, to get to these types of outcomes. Deere Latin America is at the beginning stages of this inclusive leader capability.

Finally, with regard to the **achieves transformation** discipline, becoming more diverse and inclusive not only strengthens Deere financially but also makes it more attractive to new generations of talent who might not have considered a career in agribusiness. Adding to this the message that it is a technology company with an ambitious mission to feed the world illustrates Silverio's stated objective to "modernize the company in such a way that it is seen as a place new generations want to work." Reaching these various business and talent goals would be the full manifestation of *driving results*.

"When I think about what I am doing now, and how it is important to me and my purpose in life, I'm so content to be a part of all of this," says Alves. "I want to change the world with what I can do with my hands and see people happy and engaged—this is my life's purpose."

Just as Deere's GPSs are precise to within 2.5 centimeters, Deere recognizes that inclusive leadership also has to be a highly honed skill. Not only will their employees experience a greater sense of belonging, feeling valued and being engaged, but also these inclusive outcomes will benefit us all as they continue to do their part in feeding the world.

■   ■   ■

8

Marriott: Where Everyone Belongs

IT'S A RED CARPET NIGHT IN A huge hotel ballroom for the world's largest hospitality company, Marriott International. The ceremony on this particular night is for the J. Willard Marriott Award of Excellence, honoring company associates who exemplify Marriott's core values.

The house lights come down, the screens go up. On video, images of Marriott employees doing their daily jobs scroll past as the voiceover is heard: "I grew up in poverty. We had nothing. Marriott gave me a chance to lift myself out of it. This job changed my life and the lives of my children. Whole generations in my family will never be the same."

Since the company's beginnings in 1927, long before inclusive leadership was a thing, Marriott's number one priority has been putting people first. From the outset, they understood that every human being wants an opportunity to build a rewarding and meaningful life, to be respected and valued. Take care of the associates, they will take care of the customers, and the customers will return, as the founder for whom the award is named would say.

That bass line of reciprocity—associates being taken care of and they, in turn, taking care of guests—is the foundation of Marriott's inclusive culture and the driving force behind its extraordinary growth into a company valued in excess of $20 billion.

Like musicians laying down different musical tracks on top of the bass line, Marriott has laid down various culture-shaping tracks over their people-first value to make the associate and guest experiences deeper, richer, and more meaningful. One of those culture-shaping tracks is based on commonalities, another on differences.

The commonality track focuses on the core longings that people have, despite their differences. "At Marriott, we want *everyone* to feel that they belong, that they are family," says Executive Vice President and Global Chief Human Resources Officer David Rodriguez. "It's about a sense of unity that better enables us to love the unique qualities that make each of us special."

In the differences track, Marriott has zeroed in on celebrating those unique qualities of its employees and guests. Exemplified by its groundbreaking #LoveTravels campaign, Marriott strives to inspire those who share its commitment to and support of acceptance and inclusion of all.

INCLUSION BY SURFACING COMMONALITIES

David Rodriguez is also a PhD in industrial/organizational psychology. From his informed perspective, the key to inclusion is a culture of shared values. Much of his leadership energy is rooted in the enabling traits of our Inclusive Leader model. For him, the outcome-based five disciplines are the natural outgrowth of being grounded in the more values-based traits.

"A sound corporate culture is vital to business success," he says. "But it can't be imposed on a company or defined retroactively. Debating the kind of culture you should have is likely the wrong discussion. The real discussion should be about how you champion your core values. The culture will follow." Rodriguez develops strategies based on his and the company's belief that "everyone wants community, purpose, and opportunity." Here's how.

COMMUNITY

Rodriguez points to research indicating two keys to happiness: personal relationships and social networks. "Since we spend so much of our waking hours at work, the ability to build meaningful relationships on the job is vital to our well-being," he explains. "This in turn will strengthen organizations as workforces channel their increased commitment and enthusiasm to tackling the many challenges businesses invariably face."

The holistic well-being program TakeCare, launched in 2010, is one way in which Marriott fosters community among its more than 730,000 people worldwide who wear a Marriott badge of some kind. It offers a spectrum of enrichment programs worldwide, including programs focused on stress management, exercise and fitness, nutrition and weight management, financial well-being, career advancement, engagement, team building, and inclusion. In 2019, Marriott "gamified" the program with TakeCare Level30, an app-based well-being challenge available for associates and guests. Players can partner up and compete to help build positive, rewarding behaviors like meditation, reading, and movement into a daily routine. Marriott also established a Healthy Hotel Certification program to publicly recognize hotels for creating a healthy work environment for their associates.

PURPOSE

Marriott celebrates associates who go above and beyond to meet the needs of their guests and to serve the communities in which they operate. To provide access to opportunities to serve, Serve 360 was rolled out as a social impact platform addressing some of the world's most pressing social, environmental, and economic issues. For example, Marriott International trained more than six hundred thousand hotel workers in human trafficking awareness and is on the forefront of multiple sustainability initiatives.

OPPORTUNITY

While we usually see the opposite in our own Korn Ferry D&I diagnostics database, Rodriguez reports that Marriott's workforce data doesn't show significant differences in job satisfaction based on race, ethnicity, age, or gender. This is in many ways a reflection of how Marriott is able to offer tens of thousands of opportunities, many with low barriers to entry, which can transform the trajectory of an individual's life and their ability to provide for their families—as in the case of the employees featured on the ballroom screen in the opening story.

The Emerging Leader Program, a signature inclusive leadership development program, identifies high-performing associates at varying career points and puts them through a yearlong development and sponsorship program. More than 1,500 associates have completed or are enrolled in the program; more than half of the participants are women, and more than a third are racial/ethnic minorities. Nearly 100% of participants have been promoted or selected for strategic developmental roles after going through the program.

The Women's Leadership Development Initiative, launched more than twenty years ago, seeks to develop a strong pipeline of women leaders and provides networking and mentoring. Today, 92% of women at Marriott feel they are treated fairly, regardless of their gender, and 82% say everyone has the opportunity to get special recognition—roughly the same percentage as men—according to the latest Great Places to Work survey.[1]

Today, more than 40% of the top one thousand Marriott leaders are women—and that includes the C-suite, at 44%. Marriott has established a goal to achieve parity in gender representation for global leadership by 2025, and the proportion of people of color among their senior leadership is 78% higher than the average for hotel companies that are Great Place to Work–certified.

With a multitude of high-impact approaches based on commonality, however, there are still differences that make a difference. How do Marriott's inclusive leaders address this reality?

INCLUSION BY SURFACING DIFFERENCES

One of the most explicit ways in which Marriott surfaced the beauty and power of differences was through its recognition of the breadth of its guests' diversity.

Since 2014, #LoveTravels—the cornerstone of Marriott's purpose-driven marketing program—has represented the celebration and support of inclusion, equality, human rights, and peace. #LoveTravels launched with a message of acceptance through the telling of stories from diverse travelers.

Marriott says of the campaign, "When #LoveTravels, the world is a more inclusive and peaceful place." This sentiment informs the work the company does, because as a hospitality company, it views providing a safe and comfortable environment for guests and associates—regardless of age, race, gender, sexual orientation, or ability—as a core responsibility. It also illustrates that love is a universal language, and when it travels, it has the power to bridge cultures and inspire discovery around the world.

The campaign broke more barriers than many realized at first glance. Marriott's #LoveTravels outreach revealed a sophisticated and nuanced understanding of diversity, particularly with regard to intersectionality. For example, it showcased the full spectrum of the LGBTQ+ community: a couple getting married on one of Marriott's properties, a Gen X lesbian couple, LGBTQ+ couples with and without kids, single gays and lesbians, older gay Baby Boomers, and so on.

Understanding of diversity within the traditional diversity labels also was apparent. There were stories of Blacks and Latinos and Latinas in different stages of life looking for a range of experiences—everything from adventure to glamour and from sports to pampering. In some instances, Latinos were English dominant, while others were Spanish dominant or even Spanglish dominant. Marriott also zeroed in on long-standing and popular traditions in various demographics, including large family reunions and multigenerational travel.

This cultural sensibility continues to be reflected in a multitude of ways. For instance, Marriott has become known in certain regions, such as the Washington, DC–Baltimore area, for example, as a go-to place for Indian weddings.[2]

When it came to structural inclusion, in 2013 Marriott debuted brands with particular Millennial appeal (AC Hotels and Moxy), and in 2015 Marriott opened a new hotel in Indiana called Courtyard Muncie. The hotel is the first teaching hotel in the United States for people with disabilities; 20% of its 219 staffers have intellectual and/or developmental disabilities.[3]

BRINGING IT ALL TOGETHER

Let's look at Marriott's D&I outcomes through the lens of the five disciplines. CEO Sorenson's approachability and continual efforts to visit and engage with associates at properties around the world, whether

LABOR DAY REFLECTION: ISMETA'S STORY

Arne Sorenson, Marriott CEO, Bethesda

The subject line of the email was just two words: Customer Feedback. I probably hesitated for a second before opening it. . . .

I was prepared for a problem. What I got instead was praise.

Praise for Ismeta. Ismeta works as a food and beverage attendant at one of our franchised hotels in downtown Chicago. In her role, she is on the front line with weary business travelers, anxious families with patients receiving care at local hospitals, exuberant sightseers looking to enjoy Chicago. Her job is to help ensure that the breakfast goes off without a hitch at a hotel that often serves one thousand guests in a morning.

One email like this to the CEO about an associate in the course of her career would be extraordinary. I've received nearly a dozen about Ismeta.

"She truly is a lovely, lovely person with a rare quality for being able to connect with people in such a way that brings out the best in all of us and has a way of making you feel so welcome," said one fan. Another noted, "I really appreciated her cheerful attitude and the demonstrating the 'Marriott spirit to serve!'" One had a suggestion for me: "You should video her and use it as a training video on how to treat guests."

Behind the smile and extraordinary customer care is a woman who has experienced unthinkable sadness. Ismeta left Bosnia nineteen years ago

it's a morning run or via a provocative video or thoughtful post, have gone a long way in perpetuating the Marriott family feel that generates a great deal of **interpersonal trust.**

Marriott's original international growth strategy was to provide US businessmen with a feeling of home when they traveled abroad; however, it has since evolved its US-centric focus. Sorenson gave significantly more autonomy to the leaders in other parts of the world by creating four regions and empowering them to make their own growth decisions, anchored in meeting guests' expectations.

"I can't make all those decisions," Sorensen sagely said as he **integrated diverse perspectives,** *balanced stakeholders* through after losing members of her family in that country's brutal genocide. Picking up the pieces, she made her way first to Germany and then to Chicago and began working for White Lodging, which franchises a Residence Inn and more than one hundred other Marriott properties. . . . Ismeta's journey is an example of individual resilience and the powerful impact of a good job where both you and your work are valued.

At a time when the debate in Washington is focused on building walls and reducing legal immigration, my thoughts turn to Ismeta. Our economy and our society benefit from immigration done right. But the conversation on immigration seems to be one of extremes—from blocking the entrances out of fear to flouting the law in sanctuary cities. We need to make sure our borders are secured as well as our airports. But we also must recognize that immigration is essential to numerous industries—including hospitality—and that so many immigrants are contributing to the greater good of our country. . . Finding a solution that benefits American citizens, our economy, as well as the immigrants themselves should be the priority in Washington.

Ismeta's life is now an American story, an expression of this country's ability to provide opportunity to those willing to embrace it. She is making the experiences of our guests better, she is making Marriott better, and she is making our country better. And I can't think of better feedback than that.

From Arne Sorenson, "Labor Day Reflection: Ismeta's Story," LinkedIn, September 4, 2017, https://www.linkedin.com/pulse/labor-day-reflection-ismetas-story-arne -sorenson. Used with permission.

■

decentralization, and found a very effective way to *manage the inevitable conflict* that diversity brings.[4]

Marriott has consistently earned best-in-class category engagement scores for two decades, showing up on best employer lists time and again. And visitors to their more than 7,300 properties around the world consistently experience staff who are welcoming, helpful, and attentive as a result of strong training and feeling valued by their employer. This is the epitome of **optimizing talent** by *driving engagement*, *developing talent*, and *encouraging collaboration*.

Moreover, Marriott's #LoveTravels campaign was the result of an **adaptive mindset** that *cultivated innovation* and was *situationally adaptive*.

Marriott's financial success and status as an employer of choice is proof it knows how to leverage diversity and inclusion to **achieve transformation** by *driving results*.

Marriott, like the other exemplars here, celebrates its accomplishments; however, it realizes it still has a long way to go. Inclusive leadership is needed to further the advancement of people of color, of women, of people with disabilities, of veterans, and of younger generations. And while there has been skillful situational adaptability to manage conflict, overall, the company has a conflict-averse culture that has at times led to unintended consequences, such as team members not always being sure of how well they are performing.

END SCENE

After a day of juggling budget meetings, strategic sessions, and vendor selection, Rodriguez and Maruiel Perkins-Chavis, Vice President of Workforce Engagement and Global Diversity and Inclusion, are at the modernized Marriott cafeteria during a Chinese New Year dragon dance. The cafeteria is packed and the mood is celebratory. As the dragon slithers throughout the audience, I (Andrés) think back to something I heard Rodriguez say in one of our many conversations over the years: "Diversity and inclusion has been the number one factor of success in our ninety years."

The dragon bobs his enormous head up and down. The musicians bang their cymbals. The dancers leap.

It's taken generations of inclusive leadership at Marriott to create a culture of family and belonging, where all are treated with dignity and respect.

It's what happens when leaders and organizations put people first.

■　　■　　■

9

Ravinia Festival: Setting the Stage from the Stage

NSTITUTIONS UNWILLING TO ADAPT TO THE WORLD'S hyperdiversity are increasingly vulnerable to extinction.

At 128 years old, the venerable Chicago Symphony Orchestra (CSO) could have been a case in point—along with its summer home, the Ravinia Festival, which, at 112 years of age, is the oldest outdoor music festival in the United States.

According to the League of American Orchestras, classical music audiences are declining 2% per year globally, and in the United States they have dropped by 30% since 1982. These audiences are also aging. Between 1982 and 2002, the portion of concertgoers under thirty fell from 27% to 9%. The continuation of this trend could shrink the audience for classical music to minuscule.

Yet the Ravinia Festival holds steadfast to its mission: "To develop broader and more diverse audiences for classical music through education and outreach programs and by maintaining affordable ticket prices." It recently added a key new sentence: "And where everyone feels welcome."

Well-intentioned but naive? Or realistic and sustainable?

The Ravinia Festival and the Chicago Symphony Orchestra face many of the same existential threats as retailers, makers of carbon-fueled automobiles, movie theaters, restaurants, taxi dispatchers, and other for-profit enterprises. Digital transformation combined with demographic changes is yielding a new marketplace looking for very different kinds of products, services, and experiences.

Despite the cautionary tales of Kodak, which ignored the importance of digital, and Blockbuster, which miscalculated the power of streaming content, there are plenty of hundred-plus-year-old organizations that have leveraged diversity and inclusion to revamp their tried-and-true models and attract new audiences. John Deere did it. Procter and Gamble did it. Northern Trust did it. And this is what Ravinia set out to do under the leadership of CEO Welz Kauffman, an inclusive leader who, over a twenty-year period, has anticipated and addressed the implications of changing demographics with great success.

Inclusive leaders like Kauffman recognize that diversity and inclusion is not just a good people thing to do; it is also a good business thing to do. In a time of massive disruption, focusing in on diversity and inclusion can be the very thing that saves organizations.

"To help save classical music, we needed to attract audiences that were younger and from all colors and backgrounds while retaining our core traditional audiences by still delivering the same quantity and quality of the programming they loved," says Kauffman. "But we also needed to create additional revenue streams with other forms of music that appealed to these audiences we were not yet reaching."

Ravinia Park, where the festival is held each year, is an idyllic setting. A majestic fountain plays water-themed music selections, such as Handel's *Water Music* and Debussy's *La Mer*, as the water, colored by the hues of changing lights, sprays in various patterns. Concertgoers pulling red Radio Flyer wagons weighed down by all the trappings of a fancy outdoor picnic file into the landscaped lawn, which is graced by genteel lightscaping and awe-inspiring sculptures, including a Botero, a Chadwick, a Hunt, and a Plensa. To accompany their foodie-pleasing spreads, many port candelabras, white linen tablecloths, and champagne buckets, while others arrive with Kentucky Fried Chicken buckets in tow. On sold-out nights, fifteen thousand gather to listen to music while having a one-of-a-kind under-the-stars experience.

Unfortunately, these idyllic scenes are not enough to create a financially sustainable structure for Ravinia and the Chicago Symphony Orchestra. Even the performances of classical music greats, such as Yo-Yo Ma, Kathleen Battle, Christopher Parkening, Marin Alsop, and Itzhak Perlman, who all draw large audiences, cannot make this art form economically viable on their own. Corporate sponsorship and generous benefactors from the traditional classical concert demographic help narrow the financial gap, but their contributions are still not enough by a long shot.

To provide sustainable support for Ravinia's mission, Kauffman was particularly adept at two of the five disciplines of inclusive leaders: *applying an adaptive mindset* (comprising *situational adaptability*, *global perspective*, and *cultivating innovation*) and **achieving transformation** (comprising *courage*, *persuasion*, and *driving results*).

Kauffman first needed to get the Ravinia trustees on board with diversifying their offerings to attract a wider audience. He engaged them in an exercise to hammer out an explicit mission statement, and as it turns out, there was consensus in wanting everybody to feel welcome and included. This was defined as everybody having a right to belong, which meant affordable pricing, meaningful programming, diverse cuisine, great toilets, and a beautiful park—what we call "inclusive design."

With the board's advice and endorsement, Kauffman executed five key inclusive strategies:

1. Develop new audiences through pop concerts.

2. Create special classical music events that attract new audiences.

3. Diversify the classical musicians onstage with the CSO.

4. Create a low-cost and attractive pricing structure for classical music performances.

5. Go through the kids.

KAUFFMAN'S FIVE STRATEGIES

DEVELOP NEW AUDIENCES THROUGH POP CONCERTS

"Programming, programming, programming," says Kauffman. "It's about casting the widest net and having the very biggest tent possible. In addition to the ability to attract a classical audience, which had always skewed older and White, it was about creating programs that would attract all sorts of different people—from different age, race, cultural, and sexual orientation demographics. It's about saying you will be providing something for everyone, and living up to that."

Kauffman set out to stage shows that appeal to various diverse audiences. Across hundreds of pop acts, there are now African American draws like Wyclef Jean, Lauryn Hill, the Temptations, 50 Cent, and Common; LGBTQ+ favorites such as the B-52s, the Indigo Girls, Culture Club, and Dolly Parton; Latino and Latinx acts like

LISTENING HAS BEEN A KEY PART OF MY BEING MORE INCLUSIVE

Welz Kauffman, Ravinia CEO, Chicago

I am child of the sixties. Growing up, my parents took me to every march in San Fran. I thought that every kid spent Saturdays marching. When my parents threw a big party for Democratic politician George McGovern at our home, no one came because everybody around us was a Republican.

I am proud that my parents, who were striving to be middle class, were public school teachers and were in the union. My parents' values were also influenced by their spiritual beliefs. We were raised as Christian Scientists, and they didn't want me to be a Boy Scout since they thought it was too militaristic. We also couldn't watch *Hogan's Heroes* because my parents didn't think the Nazis were funny.

When I was growing up, it was not only about Vietnam and Black rights; it was also the heyday of Leonard Bernstein, who, with his commitment to immigrant rights, celebrated Puerto Rican culture in New York through *West Side Story*. With his own gay identity, he couldn't be a better poster child for the world that shaped me. As a fan and as a musician, I too embrace diversity in my love of all forms

Lila Downs, Tigres del Norte, and Rodrigo y Gabriela; and Millennial favorites like OneRepublic, Feist, and Kesha; not to mention crossover artists such as Santana, John Legend, and Lenny Kravitz.

American Idol finalist Jennifer Hudson belted out gospel as the headliner of the annual Ravinia gala. There was a collaboration between contemporary dance company Luna Negra Dance Theater and Tiempo Libre, a Miami-based salsa band, for one of Ravinia's opening night performances, while a Latin dance contest was held under a tent in the middle of Ravinia's fabled lawn. Conspirare performed their oratorio "Considering Matthew Shepherd," in homage to the twenty-year-old who was the victim of an antigay hate crime.

"That's how we're going to get Black or Latino or gay or Millennial and Gen Z audiences," says Kauffman. "Unless we had people onstage that represented the diversity we wanted to attract, it would have never happened."

---

of music. While I played in a garage band in high school and college, I also loved classical music and trained as a classical musician. My playlists today include Jerry Herman, Brahms, Drake, Troye Sivan, Brad Paisley, Carrie Underwood, Little Nas, Chopin . . .

I can't divorce these formative experiences from who I am today. They're in my DNA. When I think of diversity, I think of normalness. I think, *Isn't this the way that things should really be?* Because it has felt so natural to me, part of my learning to be inclusive was learning to be a better listener to those for whom diversity was not normal. From an influencing change perspective, I learned that if I jumped in too fast, I put them off. I needed to acknowledge that they were having a hard time letting go of the way things had always been. Listening, therefore, really has been a key piece of my being more inclusive, even as I was advocating for a more inclusive approach on the part of others.

When I got challenged about changing the programming, my answer was always, "I'm actually not changing it. I'm expanding it."

This is good business. Look at the world around us. Whites will be a minority fairly soon, if not already, in certain parts of the country. This has implications for the bottom line. It was both right from a values and a financial viability perspective.

■

And it happened beyond expectations. In the first years, crowds showed up with a scouting mentality; they were scoping out the place. After several years of Ravinia showcasing increasing diversity onstage, the crowds got bigger and more diverse, and their sense of ownership grew.

But the journey toward greater musical diversity was not without its setbacks. Some argued that contemporary music concerts would diminish Ravinia's classical music mission and significantly alter the Ravinia experience. Plus, the staff were not prepared for the vast demographic changes in attendees, and neither was the city of Highland Park, where the festival is located. Cross-cultural and unconscious bias training had to be provided for the staff.

As an inclusive leader, Kauffman was adept at listening to the different priorities of various constituents and then *balancing stakeholders* who had fundamentally different understandings of Ravinia's place in the world. For the traditionalists bucking nonclassical music entertainment, he reminded them that Ravinia was not originally built as a classical music venue but as an amusement park. For those focused on the bottom line, he showed them how Ravinia has been able to invest nearly $65 million in improvements throughout the park, using the extra revenue generated through the pop concerts.

Kauffman's inclusive leader competencies of *situational adaptability* and his ability to be cross-culturally agile — knowing the discourse of both classical and nonclassical music — also served the cause well. His training as a classical pianist and his work for the New York and Los Angeles philharmonics, the Atlanta Symphony, and the Los Angeles and Saint Paul chamber orchestras convinced traditionalists that he was as committed as they were to preserving classical music.

"When things got difficult on the nonclassical show side, the conversation always went back to Bach and Beethoven, because that's a safe place to talk. It's true that if I didn't have some modicum of classical music credibility, none of this would have been possible," he explained.

For Kauffman, the culture transformation tipping point occurred the night that Los Tigres del Norte, the ranchera big band from the northern part of Mexico, made its Ravinia debut. As the all-Spanish-language concert blared from the stage, several long-serving Ravinia trustees — all White and older — made their way to a restaurant on the grounds for a separate event. As they waded through the sold-out all-Latino crowd wearing cowboy hats and boots, they heard the staccato of myriad Spanish conversations all around them, all the while mariachi trumpets, strings, and vocals blasted from the stage.

"I had some of the Whitest people in the Ravinia family—and I count myself as one of those—asking me, 'So who are Tigres del Norte?'" recounts Kauffman. "I answered, 'They are this great band with great entertainers from the north of Mexico—hugely popular, and they are antidrug and have a political bent.'

"They looked at me and they looked all around them again and big smiles unfolded on their faces. 'The complexion of the audience changed tonight,' one of them said. 'And it's a great thing.'"

Tapping into these new contemporary audiences has meant growth. Since Ravinia began aggressively mixing its summer lineup between nonclassical acts and CSO performances, revenues—earned and contributed—are up. The number of donors has doubled!

But what about making classical music more appealing and accessible to these audiences that CSO had not been reaching: young people and those of color? That brings us to Ravinia's four other inclusive strategies.

CREATE SPECIAL CLASSICAL MUSIC EVENTS THAT ATTRACT NEW AUDIENCES

Understanding what kind of experiences nontraditional audiences want has been the secret to driving up the number of concertgoers to CSO performances.

In focus groups and surveys, the Gen Xers' greatest complaint about the Ravinia experience on a classical music night has been the "shushers"—staff with librarian scowls carrying placards that read "Quiet Please." The Gen Xers have been frustrated and surprised by their presence. Their many comments can be synthesized in the following way: "I can't think of a better way to expose my children to classical music than at an outdoor venue in the middle of a beautiful summer night. The conditions are perfect to bring them—be with family, let the kids run around, listen to gorgeous music. But the shushers just put a damper on the whole thing. Why would we want to come again?"

So Kids Lawn was born. Sensibly placed at the back end of the park, with oversize play musical instruments to interact with pre-concert . . . and no shushers. Kids Lawn has become a very popular feature, though it is still too early to have a true measure of whether this has led to greater attendance on a sustained basis.

For the Millennials and the Gen Xers without kids, there are the not-to-be-missed social events such as Beer, Brats, and Beethoven and Classical Strings and Chicken Wings. Sponsored by Ravinia's associate board of young professionals committed to helping raise funds for the park, these events feature all classical music, but the social context is different, including an allowance for chitchat-level noise.

Finally, there are the movie nights. Imagine being out on the lawn, surrounded by friends and family, participating in a picnic feast while watching *Titanic*, *Lord of the Rings*, *Gladiator*, *Star Trek*, *Fantasia*, or *Coco* on huge screens, with the CSO performing the musical score live. It's not without controversy: some classical musicians feel the events trivialize the classical music listening experience. But these movie nights are the CSO's biggest nights of the summer by far.

DIVERSIFY THE CLASSICAL MUSICIANS ONSTAGE

CSO performances now regularly feature guest conductors and solo artists who reflect the full diversity of available artists. These have included conductors from Mexico and Venezuela as well as Latinos, Latinas, and African Americans such as Carlos Miguel Prieto, Rafael Payare, Gabriela Montero, and Bobby McFerrin, and singers such as Audra McDonald, Jennifer Hudson, and Cynthia Erivo.

CREATE A LOW-COST AND ATTRACTIVE PRICING STRUCTURE FOR CLASSICAL MUSIC PERFORMANCES

Ravinia's new pricing strategy is simple and compelling: lower prices in an easy-to-remember sound-bite format. "25/10/Free" is shorthand for twenty-five-dollar pavilion seats, ten dollars for lawn, and no charge for lawn tickets for kids and students through college. While it's still too early to understand the full impact of the new pricing structure on cultivating new audiences, it has been easy to market and has definitely created stickiness in the minds of new classical concert goers.

GO THROUGH THE KIDS

For more than fifty years, Ravinia has provided extensive music education to kids in Chicago public schools forty miles away. Its Reach Teach Play program touches around seventy-five thousand kids annually, primarily from traditionally underserved communities. Based on the innovative music education program Sistema, which originated in Venezuela, the program revolves around *nucleos* (nexuses or meeting groups). Each child experiences being an asset within her or his nucleo, meeting several times a week. Then each nucleo joins other nucleos for a weekly multi-nucleo class. Recitals throughout the year showcase the students' progress. Along the way, there are myriad field trips to Ravinia classical music concerts for these Chicago students and their parents.

But before 2016, Ravinia had not reached out to the underserved communities in its own backyard, largely due to the belief that Lake County, where Ravinia is located, was wealthy and not in need of youth music education. In reality, there is a large low-income and even homeless population in the area.

Within Ravinia's vital twenty-five-mile radius, where the bulk of its classical music audiences reside, there are hundreds of thousands of Latinos, many of whom, though not all, are working class. Their exposure to classical music is limited, and most do not know about Ravinia. If they do, it has not traditionally felt like a place where they would be welcomed. Ravinia's manicured lawns, fenced perimeter, and high hedges, and the lack of diversity of its audiences on classical nights, no doubt contributed to this feeling.

Then, in 2016, breakthrough.

Sistema Ravinia was inaugurated for Lake County that year, but this time, due to proximity, the after-school, four-times-a-week, two-hours-a-day coming together was able to happen at Ravinia itself. It turned out to be a game changer. In its first year, the program involved an impressive five schools, two hundred children, and twenty teachers and principals.

For the kickoff, there was a half day of activities on the Ravinia grounds, including a tour and a concert and Q&A with fourteen-year-old Mexican American piano prodigy Daniela Liebman Martínez. When the kids heard her speak in her native Spanish, the demeanor in the auditorium changed. Here was someone like them who was a *virtuosa.*

THE SALSA DANCING THAT MADE IT HOME

As we wrap this up, I (Andrés) have a confession to make as a Ravinia trustee. As a Latinx tail-end Boomer, I am a member of those newly targeted audiences who, for most of my life, has not been a classical music fan. While I superficially enjoyed having it as background music, I did not understand the music. I found myself fidgeting in my seat during long, slow movements, and I chafed judgmentally at not being able to burst into exuberant cheering after an explosive final note that, inconveniently, was placed between movements.

But today I consider myself a new fan, slowly deepening my knowledge about the art form, its history, its evolution, and the long-standing and up-and-coming virtuosos. I now listen to recorded classical music and attend live concerts more than I ever have in my life. And this is directly due to my having been seduced by Ravinia's efforts to reach new audience members like me.

Tellingly, the turning point for me was a Latin concert at Ravinia. As a Peruvian who grew up in the sprawling and chaotic metropolis of Lima, I had come to the United States for college. Once I married, an opportunity had presented itself to rent a wonderful starter house in Highland Park, on Pleasant Avenue, a five-minute walk from Ravinia's main entrance. Highland Park has many attractive amenities that make it a great place to live, but I was not so sure my Latinx self really fit in this new community. After a few years as renters, we had the opportunity to buy the house, which we did, even as I had mixed feelings about this being a place where I would feel welcome enough to plant my roots.

But then, on the evening of the day we closed on the sale of the house, we heard syncopated rhythms emanating from the Ravinia Festival, rising up over the trees and filling the air as we stood on the front yard of our newly bought home. And then and there, in the city of Highland Park, Illinois, my wife, Lori, and I danced salsa.

And I knew then that I could call this place my new home.

The students were also given instruments for permanent ownership; for most, it was their first time even touching a classical music instrument. Faces lit up and voices squealed with delight as they coaxed their first musical note from their instruments.

In addition to the obvious impact of Sistema Ravinia on these kids' musical experiences, Ravinia has suddenly become accessible to hundreds of Latinx families. Not only are the children coming to Ravinia weekly but also their recitals will be taking place on Ravinia stages. And now, when a classical or nonclassical concert is publicized, rather than ignoring the marketing as irrelevant to their families, the thought is *Tigres del Norte at Ravinia? Ah, that's where my kid plays*.

DIVERSITY AND INCLUSION ACROSS THE BOARD

Diversifying the board of trustees beyond tokenism has also been a priority. In 2020, a board that just six years ago had only three racial minorities (out of nearly seventy members) now has fifteen. This, of course, is changing board dynamics and its ability to add wise counsel on D&I to its positive impact. On the formal side, there is now a project-based D&I working group that, for the next few years, is charged with ensuring that Kauffman's legacy of bringing more equity, diversity, and inclusion to Ravinia continues to deepen and widen even after his retirement.

Then there are the spontaneous interactions that take place that would not have happened without greater diversity. A few years ago, when Kauffman was announcing the upcoming season's lineup, he listed Mary J. Blige on the roster. In what is usually a staid environment, cries of "Woo-hoo!" and yelps of joy burst out from the African American trustees. It was infectious.

"On the way home," says Kauffman, "we had a bunch of curious trustees googling 'Blige.'"

That's the power of diversity.

■　　■　　■

Part 3 lays out the mega diversity and inclusion

challenges that inclusive leaders are going to have to tackle—the intractables that have continued to elude solution and the emerging issues for which there are no established best practices.

We will explore these topics through the lenses of structural inclusion, identity inclusion, and sociopolitical inclusion.

Structural inclusion is about unearthing the biases that have been codified into the processes, structures, and policies that are used to manage talent. If structures are not made more inclusive, it won't matter how much training or pay incentives leaders are given; addressing their behavior won't be enough to bring about equity.

Identity inclusion is about how to be fully welcoming of the full range of human diversity. It requires inclusive leaders to understand how people manifest their identity in the workplace, and how this can affect their performance and engagement.

Sociopolitical inclusion is about helping organizations rise to the new challenges of these times, particularly the increased polarization between people on the basis of who they are and what they believe. Every day sociopolitical divisions on the outside walk inside. In addition, an ever-vigilant global audience is ready to hold companies to high standards of inclusion and diversity—through protests, boycotts, and shaming. Much as most organizations would like to stay out of the fray, they can't if exclusion happens in their stores, their products, their ads, and their workforces.

Inclusive leaders must tackle these tough issues if they are to have credibility and impact. See this as a primer to get you ready.

PART 3

TACKLING THE MEGA DIVERSITY AND INCLUSION CHALLENGES

10

Structural Inclusion: Confronting the Reference Man Norms That Leave Most of Us Out

EET THE REFERENCE MAN. THIS PERSON, OR rather this concept, has influenced our lives in more ways than we realize. Inclusive leaders must confront the Reference Man's legacy of creating default structures, processes, and norms designed for a very narrow range of humanity.

First introduced in 1975, the Reference Man concept was devised to simplify calculations of radiation exposure. It went on to be used in research models of nutrition, pharmacology, population, and toxicology. Intended to personify all of humanity, the Reference Man was in fact defined in very specific terms: male, twenty-five to thirty years old, 154 pounds, five feet six inches tall, Caucasian, with a Western European or North American lifestyle.

The bias toward young, able-bodied White men can be found in every corner of the designed world. Ever wondered why the line for the women's toilet is always longer than for the men's? It's because the design of women's restrooms does not take into account their specific needs.

The same biases can be seen in thermostat settings in office buildings, the height of top shelves, the position of light switches, the

THE WORLD IS STILL BUILT FOR MEN

VOICE RECOGNITION DEVICES

Many voice recognition systems fail to work for female users. Why? It appears that they have been designed to recognize a male voice. This was exemplified by one user's report that after five failed attempts of trying (and failing) to get her voice recognition system to call her sister, she lowered the pitch of her voice. And it worked the first time.

APPLE'S SIRI

When Apple launched its artificial intelligence system, Siri, it could help you if you'd had a heart attack, but if you told it you'd been raped, it replied, "I don't know what you mean by 'I was raped.'"

MAP APPS

Map apps fail to account for women who may want to know the safest, in addition to the fastest, routes.

HEALTH MONITORING SYSTEMS

When Apple launched its health monitoring system in 2014, it boasted a "comprehensive" health tracker. It could track blood pressure, steps taken, blood alcohol level, even molybdenum and copper intake. But Apple forgot one crucial detail: a period tracker.

size of safety masks, the shape of body armor, and the dimensions of crash-test dummies, not to mention clinical drug trials and chronic disease research, where 80% of the cells used are from males. They have even made their way into many elements of digital hardware and software design, from smartphone grips and keyboard key size to voice recognition algorithms.

Talent systems have been as susceptible to design biases as any of these other examples. In the past, many human resource leaders embraced a one-size-fits-all approach, convinced that it was the most

FITNESS MONITORS

One study of twelve of the most common fitness monitors found that they underestimated steps during housework by up to 74% and underestimated calories burned during housework by as much as 34%. Today, women still do the majority of the housework, so this really matters.

CAR SEATS AND SAFETY

Modern car seats are designed based on male crash-test dummies and are too firm to protect women in accidents. The seats throw women forward faster than men because the back of the seat doesn't give way for women, who average lighter and smaller bodies.

Women also tend to sit farther forward when driving, making their legs more vulnerable in an accident (given the angle that their knees and hips sit). And they have less muscle in their necks and upper torso, making them up to three times more vulnerable to whiplash. So while more men than women are involved in car crashes, women are 17% more likely to die in one.[1]

Adapted from Caroline Criado Perez, *Invisible Women: Data Bias in a World Designed for Men* (New York: Abrams Press, 2019). Used with permission.

efficient and effective way to manage hiring, performance, advancement, and reward, particularly as organizations grew and became more global. And indeed, they also believed it would create equality.

Perhaps inevitably, the "one size" in question turned out to be HR's equivalent of the Reference Man. In this way, unconscious biases were built into talent systems and have served to preserve glass ceilings and to perpetuate unequal outcomes in access, opportunities, support, and rewards.

UNCONSCIOUS BIAS TRAINING IS NOT ENOUGH

Unconscious bias training has been dominating D&I efforts in almost all major corporations—and with good reason, as we've seen. This scientifically grounded approach has improved self-awareness and has helped many to admit their biases without feeling judged. But the evidence suggests that unconscious bias training in and of itself has not done much to break down the barriers holding back traditionally underrepresented talent. Glass ceilings remain firmly in place—even in companies that have invested heavily in unconscious bias training—especially for people from racially and ethnically underrepresented groups.

Perhaps this should come as no surprise. Unconscious bias is only one small piece of the puzzle. For organizations to ensure that their D&I investments deliver results, they must take a more comprehensive approach to diversity and inclusion. This starts with driving personal transformation in their leaders and employees by enabling individuals not only to recognize unconscious bias but also to counter and mitigate it. We call this *behavioral inclusion*.

In addition, organizations need to transform themselves at a systemic level, reexamining and reshaping their talent processes to ensure they are fair and equitable. We call this *structural inclusion*. Behavioral inclusion optimizes performance through social sensitivity and psychological safety; structural inclusion does it through a process that allows for equal contribution of all team members. Both are critical to enhancing the collective intelligence, decision-making and problem-solving abilities, and creativity of diverse teams working on complex tasks.

Behavioral inclusion training leads individuals on a journey of self-discovery, alerting them to the biases that hamper their decision-making and equipping them to act on this newfound self-awareness by behaving in a more consciously inclusive way.

Typical behavioral inclusion exercises draw on powerful neuroscience research to expose our difficult-to-deny biases in dimensions such as race, gender, age, culture, sexual orientation, and physical and mental abilities. These exercises are highly effective at inducing aha moments in participants, enabling them to recognize unconscious biases that have been influencing their attitudes, actions, and decisions about others.

Many behavioral inclusion programs stop at this point in the process, but individuals can only benefit from their self-awareness journey if they work on building counterbias capabilities as well. This means acquiring the skills, competencies, tools, and techniques that turn awareness into moment-to-moment actions, that help people go from micro rejections to micro affirmations and from micro inequities to micro equities, and to make judgments on a deep understanding and appreciation of difference.

Such a shift in behaviors can be achieved by designing a learning journey that allows participants to practice counterintuitive and consciously inclusive ways of dealing with familiar work situations such as interviewing, mentoring, performance management, and conflict resolution. As you'll read in the upcoming section on "fit," these work experiences tend to be rife with culturally reinforced, unconsciously biased responses and can lead to decisions and actions that prevent all talent from reaching its full potential.

Currently, unconscious bias tends to be the focus of behavioral inclusion efforts. But it is by no means the only issue at play. Organizations serious about behavioral inclusion must also address power structures, privilege dynamics, and diversity of social networks. Research conducted by the internationally recognized Dr. Sukhvinder S. Obhi, Professor of Psychology, Neuroscience, and Behavior at McMaster University in Canada, has shown how power interferes with inclusive behaviors and produces negative effects on leaders' brains.

His work, along with that of other researchers around the world, has shown that power can increase stereotyping, reduce the tendency of the brain to simulate the experiences and behaviors of others, reduce empathy, and impair risk perception. In Dr. Obhi's words, "It is

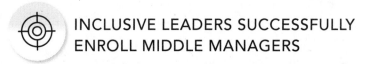

INCLUSIVE LEADERS SUCCESSFULLY ENROLL MIDDLE MANAGERS

STRUCTURAL INCLUSION AT WORK ▪ *Barry Callender, Atlanta*

One of the most debilitating realities in companies who declare they are fully committed to diversity and inclusion, and who have invested many resources in it, is the lack of middle management proactively engaged in the D&I efforts. This is a root cause gap, because middle managers are the ones who have the most direct impact on the experience of underrepresented talent. As a result, some people are not fully supported or developed, their talents aren't fully utilized, and their career expectations aren't met.

Senior management cannot sit back, admire its visionary enterprise-level D&I strategy, and assume that middle managers will make it happen automatically. Instead, senior leaders must demonstrate inclusive leadership with their managers to enroll them as inclusive managers. Here are three common reasons why middle managers resist such enrollment, and what inclusive senior leaders can do to address them.

Middle managers have difficulty understanding the connection between their objectives and the organization's D&I objectives.

Typically, many middle managers will complain, "My evaluation is based on productivity, quality, and safety, not D&I. Of course, we should hire more women and minorities and treat everyone fairly, but I can't focus on everything." This is a challenge senior leadership must address, ideally before launching the D&I strategy.

First, senior leaders can articulate how D&I is good for the organization, and the critical role of middle managers in achieving and making D&I successful. This is because middle managers are responsible for motivating employees to serve, process, build, and design on a daily basis. Next, explain precisely how success will be measured—for example, by on-time performance, employee engagement scores, customer satisfaction, or rework. Research has proven that all of these can be improved when diverse teams are managed inclusively.

Middle managers are often promoted for their technical proficiencies, not leadership skills.

Creating an inclusive workplace for a diverse workforce brings a level of complexity to management that most middle managers have never considered. Diversity can be even more daunting because, unlike many other aspects of leadership, managers can't figure it out on the job. If they make a mistake, they understandably feel they have risked offending someone or, worse yet, are actually accused of inappropriate behavior, harassment, or discrimination.

The first step is to provide middle managers with basic talent management skills, including how to manage the careers of the employees who report to them. Diversity and inclusion then needs to be integrated into these fundamental managerial tasks. This kind of integrated training goes a long way in increasing manager effectiveness as well as trust levels between managers and their employees.

Middle managers sometimes believe that diversity does not apply to them because their teams are homogeneous.

To many middle managers, the initial goals and communication around D&I often sound like a new spin on affirmative action—a focus on gender and race—leading to responses like "We have a great team and everyone gets along. What's wrong with that? The junior person has been here ten years; we all grew up in the same area, have similar cultural backgrounds, love sports, and we're all family guys. I don't want to mess around with a formula that works by complicating things with '*diversity*.'"

Combine this mentality with a limited understanding of the less obvious elements of diversity and you have a middle manager who doesn't see the need to become an active participant.

It's critical to help middle managers focus on the business and performance benefits of diversity. Are they aware of and can they articulate the different thinking, communication, and work styles of their direct reports? How effective are they at leveraging those differences to foster innovation, creativity, and productivity? Can they identify how unconscious biases show up on their teams and how it affects worker engagement and productivity?

Senior leaders can also emphasize that the ability to successfully manage a diverse workforce is a prerequisite for senior leaders of the company. To that end, managing different teams in different areas should be a part of the company's leadership development program, increasing the chances that potential senior managers will have led teams with all ranges of diversity.

———— ■ ————

imperative that leaders fully understand how power can affect them if they don't use it mindfully. Once such understanding is gained, strategies for the more effective use of power—to create positive change—can be leveraged to move the organization toward better outcomes."[2]

Behavioral inclusion does indeed help individuals to internalize inclusive behaviors. But what if the organizational structures in which they operate are preventing them from acting in a truly inclusive way?

This is why this other element of structural inclusion is essential for transformation.

Many of the talent systems and processes supposedly designed to optimize human performance are in fact riddled with built-in biases. And while those biases may have been introduced unintentionally, that hasn't stopped them from undermining the progress of traditionally underrepresented talent at a deep and systemic level.

How do we know this? Just look at the absurdly skewed demographics of the world's C-suites and boards. Consider the fact that only 7% of current Fortune 500 CEOs are women (and 7%, astonishingly, represents an all-time high). Whenever Korn Ferry conducts disparity assessments of performance ratings or promotability, our findings are very consistent. No matter the industry, the pattern is almost always the same: everything else being equal, women are promoted at a lower rate and paid less than men, and members of racially and ethnically underrepresented groups are promoted less, paid less, and rated lower on performance than White people.

The presence of these exclusionary forces means that it is not enough simply to equip people with counterbias capabilities. Without also addressing the biases of the systems in which individuals operate, you are, so to speak, jogging in a smog-choked city. Addressing systemic biases is what structural inclusion is designed to do.

THE THREE PILLARS OF STRUCTURAL INCLUSION

If you want to build a truly diverse and inclusive organization, you need to transform the organization as a whole—the people, through behavioral inclusion, and the processes, through structural inclusion. We often use a traffic analogy to describe how behavioral and structural inclusion work together. Behavioral inclusion is about everyone learning to be good drivers, cyclists, and pedestrians who abide by the rules and exercise good judgment as they encounter unexpected traffic situations. Structural inclusion is about ensuring that there is proper signage and that there are traffic stoplights, well-marked lanes, speed bumps, and law enforcement to channel people toward desirable actions and decisions. Both are essential for a safe and efficient road system.

While behavioral inclusion focuses on the mindset and capabilities of individuals, structural inclusion requires an organization-wide approach leveraging the three pillars of equality, equity, and inclusive design (figure 6).

Equality is the promise that no one will be favored or disfavored because of who they are or because of any dimension of diversity. It ensures fairness for everyone and represents a deeply held belief in meritocracy. Organizations can pursue this aspiration through their values and codes of ethics and by instituting nondiscriminatory policies and practices in hiring, assessment, promotion, and rewards.

Equity is about answering the question of whether the promise of equality was fulfilled. When not, and this is usually the case, equity then becomes about righting past wrongs. It recognizes that not everyone has had equal opportunity to compete in and benefit from the dominant system. People from certain backgrounds start off with

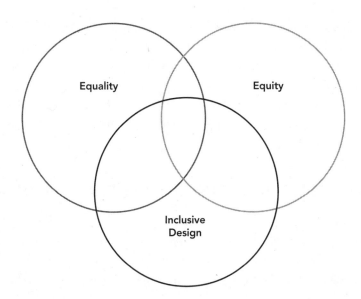

Figure 6. The three pillars of structural inclusion.

unearned advantages or disadvantages that perpetuate inequities in access, rewards, opportunity, and support.

To go back to our traffic analogy, equality is about all road users being largely governed by the same rules (stop at red traffic lights, indicate when turning, and so on), whether they're driving a car, a truck, a motorcycle, or a bus. The rules have been created to ensure efficiency and safety for all, and nobody wants to see the law favoring one person or group over another.

Equity, meanwhile, is about rectifying the reality that not everyone is able to take equal advantage of the traffic system. This will involve countering the disadvantages faced by certain types of road users by introducing measures such as special parking areas for cyclists, beeping crosswalk signs for people with impaired sight, special lanes for carpoolers, and elevators in subway stations for those with mobility limitations.

If companies are serious about achieving fairness for all, they must first explore every aspect of their talent processes to identify potential inequities and their historical root causes. They can then be eliminated, or at least significantly reduced. To make the outcomes of, and the interplay between, equality and equity possible, organizations need to apply *inclusive design*.

To pull it all together, real transformation requires a broader set of behavioral inclusion interventions to address barriers to inclusion, including helping individuals to develop counterbias capabilities, or conscious inclusion. Structural inclusion also is needed to ensure that behavioral inclusion sticks—and that means a focused effort to right legacy inequities and, through inclusive design, to establish systems and processes that prevent unconscious bias from happening in the first place.

THERE IS NO SUCH THING AS A DEFAULT PERSON

Concerns about the ethical and commercial perils of the Reference Man are not new. Early pioneers include Jutta Treviranus, the founder and Director of the Inclusive Design Research Centre at OCAD University in Toronto, who began exploring the dynamics of exclusionary design in digital products way back in 1993. Focusing initially on disability inclusion, the center developed a set of inclusive design principles that went on to influence thinking at companies such as Microsoft, where it ultimately led to the formation of the Microsoft Inclusive Design team, whose own set of best practice standards are now available open source.

Inclusive design rejects the Reference Man paradigm and recognizes instead this simple truth: there is no such thing as a default person. As the Microsoft Inclusive Design team explains in its manual: "The interactions we design with technology depend heavily on what we can see, hear, say, and touch. Assuming all those senses and abilities are fully enabled all the time creates the potential to ignore much of the range of humanity."[3]

Whether you're designing a workplace, a transport system, or a virtual reality headset, the goal should be to address the needs of all potential users, starting with the most marginalized and excluded populations. This allows you to produce more elegant and streamlined designs that benefit a wider range of humanity. From the Microsoft team again: "Everyone has abilities, and limits to those abilities. Designing for people with permanent disabilities actually results in designs that benefit people universally."

Think about how those curb ramps for people with disabilities have also made life better for joggers, cyclists, and parents with strollers. Closed captioning, which was created for the hard-of-hearing community, now enables everyone to follow the action in loud sports bars or crowded airports. The high-contrast screen settings that make it possible to read a Kindle in bright sunlight were originally made for people with vision impairments. And what do you think inspired remote controls?

Inclusive design is the antidote to exclusion. As Kat Holmes, one of the leading thinkers on inclusive design, writes in *Mismatch*, "Ask a hundred people what inclusion means and you get a hundred different answers. Ask then what it means to be excluded and the answer will be uniformly clear: 'It's when you're left out.'"[4]

It is for this reason talent systems must stop being designed for the default user and instead home in on finding and designing for the overlooked user.

Here are our four core principles of inclusive design for talent systems, inspired by the original inclusive design principles developed by the Inclusive Design Research Centre.

1. DEFINE EQUALITY

The value of equality is enshrined in most vision statements, codes of ethics, and nondiscrimination policies. But what does equality actually mean? The answer will vary from organization to organization. Inclusive design journeys should therefore begin with an explicit, self-reflective exploration and declaration of what kind of equality the organization stands for and how equality manifests itself in talent management practices and processes. The organization must then ensure that its aspirational statements, guidelines, and policies all support this declaration. They must be clear about the nonnegotiables that are expected of every leader, manager, and employee, and about the rules, standards, and guidelines that will ensure that no one is favored or disfavored on the basis of who they are.

2. UNEARTH INEQUITIES

Many of today's organizations are inadvertently creating and perpetuating disparities through their talent systems. Our second inclusive design principle is to unearth those inequities and discover whether there is "fault in the default." This can be achieved by examining the data and by exploring the experiences of overlooked talent groups—experiences that can be difficult and even painful. Is the organization living up to its commitments on equality? Do all have the same opportunities, access, support, and rewards? Is all talent being paid equally for equal work?

- **Access**. Do employees have equal access to resources, leaders, programs, and other tools they can leverage to achieve their full potential?
- **Opportunity**. Do employees have equal opportunity to experience short-term, high-visibility developmental projects or job postings?
- **Support**. Do employees get equal support in learning new skills, receiving constructive and honest feedback, and being mentored, sponsored, and advocated for?
- **Rewards**. Do employees enjoy equal rewards for comparable impact, and are contributions to the organization always fairly recognized?

3. LEARN FROM DIVERSITY

The only way to break away from the Reference Man and ensure that inequities are not perpetuated is to modify or create systems using input from all users—from the mainstream to the overlooked. This requires a humancentric and empathetic approach. Designers must be curious about people's vast differences and consider the needs, wants, and aspirations of the most excluded user rather than simply assuming similarity and building their solutions around the lowest common denominator.

4. SOLVE FOR ONE, BENEFIT ALL

Science and experience are showing us that if we can make something work for the exception, then we will end up with a better design for all. Similar successes can be achieved in talent system designs if we specifically address the needs of overlooked users, those whose experiences, mindsets, and visibility are in the minority. But addressing their more intensive needs due to legacies of unfairness and marginalization actually yields a better design for all.

By applying these four inclusive design principles, organizations can develop talent systems and processes that are free from legacy inequities and inclusive of all human differences. The ultimate aim, of course, is to create equality for everyone.

Inclusive leaders understand why these levers are essential and also hold their organizations accountable to inclusive designs that support structural inclusion.

HOW FIT DESTROYS DIVERSITY

As an example of structural exclusion let's look at one prevalent outcome of the Reference Man's legacy on talent systems: the unchallenged concept of "fit" when it comes to assessing, hiring, and promoting candidates. How often have we heard the dreaded deal breaker: "She just was not the right fit"?

"What made them not a fit?" is something inclusive leaders are asking more frequently. The answers arise from any number of subjective impressions, such as "the way they talk"—whether they have a non-American accent or because they use more or different words than

KAPOR CAPITAL: FUNDING THE POWER OF TRANSFORMATIVE IDEAS AND DIVERSE TEAMS

One example of a structural inclusion mindset that defies the Reference Man concept comes from the social venture capital investment firm Kapor Capital, which has $350 million in assets under management.

In an investment world where very little capital in the United States goes to start-ups owned by women and people of color (in 2017 and 2018, women received a mere 2.2% of venture capital funding),[5] Kapor Capital is committed to countering this inequity. The investment firm puts its money on the powerful combination of transformative ideas and diverse teams to solve real-world problems for millions.

"Our entrepreneurs come from all walks of life. We believe that the lived experiences of founding teams from underrepresented backgrounds provide a competitive edge. Their experiences inform the questions they ask and the problems they identify that give rise to profitable, tech-driven solutions," says Freada Kapor Klein, partner at Kapor Capital and founder/Board Chair of SMASH.

Their portfolio tells a story of Kapor Capital achieving its mission. According to their website:

- 60 out of 102 investments (59%) have a founder who identifies as a woman and/or an underrepresented person of color

- 38% of their first-time investments have a founder who identifies as a woman

- 34% of their first-time investments have a founder of a racially underrepresented background and

- 25% of their first-time investments have a founder of Asian ancestry[6]

Kapor Klein—who is one of four cofounders of a multiracial, multiethnic investment team—describes a consistent philosophy that permeates the various entities and nonprofits housed in the Kapor Center in Oakland, California. In addition to Kapor Capital, the center also houses its signature program, SMASH, a three-year STEM-intensive residential college prep program that empowers students, most of whom are Black and Latinx, to deepen their talents and pursue STEM careers.[7] Half of their graduates go to the top 1% colleges and universities.

Also at the center are various of the incubating start-ups Kapor Capital is funding or that need a place to set up shop. These various streams form a "beehive" that is precisely intended to provide access, opportunity, support, and reward to those who have been overlooked by the systems currently in place.

Kapor Klein explains some of the key methods that have led them to defy standard practice:

> I've been a champion of linking stories and data, because neither one works alone. Stories are anecdotes, not data, and data can be soulless or faceless and intellectual. We have full-time researchers who have put out various landmark studies, one of which is on inequity in access to education in science, technology, engineering, and math in California. Is it a pipe-line problem or a bias problem? It turns out that, through a combination of stories and data, the answer is that it's both. In the entire state, there was a total of only thirty-nine African American girls who took AP classes in STEM. Then we look at big places like Google and say that, yes, there is a pipeline problem that reflects racism by requiring certain credentials, which only perpetuates the biases.

So Kapor Capital invested in a company called interviewing.io, with a platform for anonymous technical interviews, where applicants can do practice interviews with big companies like Uber. When they are comfortable, applicants can unmask themselves. When they do, they show that they are qualified candidates who had previously been rejected at the résumé level without even receiving a phone screening interview.

The Kapor Center's beehive of structural inclusion has become self-replicating; in helping individuals gain the skills and opportunities they need, they also are infusing those individuals with the same sense of mission to innovate to create products and services that will benefit the many.

For Kapor Klein, inclusive leadership means tying together social justice, human need, and economic prosperity for all: "I have a visceral and historic sense that none of us are free until all of us are free."

the typical young, able-bodied White male. These subjective impressions often represent the Greatest Hits of unconscious bias excuses.

As organizations seek to hire stellar talent, much emphasis is placed on the required qualifications for success in the role, but come interview and selection time, cultural fit or a lack thereof begins to weigh heavily. The intangibles of personality, educational influences, and personal interests become part of the compare-and-contrast of the various candidates.

Even when interviewers use behavior-based interviews and objective competencies designed to mitigate bias, various studies prove that subjectivity has a much greater influence on who gets selected than most want to admit. One such study of management consultancies and law firms, by Kellogg School of Business Associate Professor of Management and Organizations Dr. Lauren Rivera, demonstrated that interpersonal affinity, such as liking the candidate, sharing interests with them, or being able to picture socializing with them, weighed heavily in the hiring manager's final decisions. It's what Rivera refers to as the stuck-in-the-airport test (*Can I picture hanging out with this person?*), and it becomes just as vital as qualifications and experience.[8]

Additional studies provide hard data showing the influence of other biases in hiring.[9] The National Bureau of Economic Research, for instance, sent identical résumés to the same organizations, changing only the names. They found that résumés that had Anglo-Saxon names had a 50% higher callback rate than those with "ethnic sounding" names.

The results underscore how overemphasizing fit can have business consequences that extend beyond optics. Organizations' investment of millions of dollars to achieve greater diversity and inclusion end up suboptimized as homogeneous hiring continues. The result? More groupthink at a time when businesses need new ideas and innovation.

But there are some understandable reasons for the prevalence of hiring for cultural fit. Korn Ferry Institute research in 2019 found that 40% of new senior executive hires typically leave after eighteen months, so the risk of hiring someone who is different is high. And, to be sure, cultural fit still has an important place in the criteria used in hiring decisions. So let's not throw the baby out with the bathwater but instead apply inclusive design to try to resolve the dilemma.

Fundamentally, the "hiring for fit" concept needs to be redefined. What counts as a real requirement for success must be separated from what is tradition, a preference, or even bias. Is being a great addition to a golf foursome a genuine requirement for success? What about the ability to socialize outside the office? Does the candidate really need to have a degree from the University X (where others on the team attended), or could a candidate from a different program bring a fresh perspective?

The key question to ask is, "If we hire this person, what will they be adding to the mix?" Think of it as akin to financial portfolio theory, where diversification is a key to maximizing returns.

In a collaborative effort with Tim Vigue, now D&I Director at Pixar, we identified different types of fit worth considering: business imperative fit, complementary fit, and future fit.

- **Business imperative fit** is when new types of leaders with new skills make a better fit for organizations undergoing business model shifts, such as a financial institution expanding from commercial to retail banking. In these cases, there is less of a need for new talent that fits the current mold of leadership. In fact, those very leaders who had fit so well must now adapt.

- **Complementary fit** is when candidates possess a key difference from the existing team that could stimulate new ideas. A culture that has been dominated by type A personalities maybe needs the counterweight of more reflective types. A tight command-and-control hierarchy at a beer manufacturer may require more facilitative leaders to better manage a younger generation that is more egalitarian and collaborative. A hospitality chain that has primarily catered to middle-aged male executives probably needs more female marketing leaders and design specialists. A car company that has negligible penetration in fast-growing racially and ethnically diverse communities would benefit from diversifying its line managers and product designers.

- **Future fit** reflects the need for candidates who possess new skills, experiences, and approaches that will enable the organization and its teams to meet emerging challenges as the business environment evolves. For a team that is shifting from being measured on its efficiency to its ability to solve for customer needs, future fit may be about being curious and collaborative instead of structured and directive, for example.

Cultural fit will always be important. It's natural for people to want to be around those they feel are easy to work with. There is a very real human, even biological, basis for being attracted to people just like ourselves. Plus, the risk of creating disruption in senior leadership by hiring a nontraditional candidate is real.

In a previous era, this logic served companies well enough. But no longer. In today's hyperdiverse world, the Reference Man simply does not fit anymore—if it ever did.

Inclusive leaders must do the work to dismantle his legacy.

※　※　※

11

Identity Inclusion: The Perennial Unfinished Business of Race and Gender

For all the attention that race and gender have received over the past two generations, progress has not yet achieved breakthrough status. The advancement of women—White women, specifically—has been the most marked, and this is the major focus of diversity efforts, globally and across industries. The advancement of those who are non-White, however, has been shamefully marginal, and is more worrisome, because it is a goal that has been pursued with limited conviction and commitment until very recently in the overwhelming public's and corporate antiracism response in the wake of George Floyd's killing by police in Minneapolis in May of 2020.

While each form of diversity deserves full attention in organizations, we will be focusing here on the unfinished business of race and gender inequity as well as on the newly emergent dynamics of intersectional identities.

PART 1: RACE—SKIN TONE, RACISM, AND PRIVILEGE

Despite race and skin color being the original diversity sin that corporations sought to expunge, as the definition of diversity has expanded, race has, to the dismay of many, become among the most fraught issues to discuss.

Inclusive leaders do not flinch from ensuring that colorism and racism do not get sidelined, or that discrimination on the basis of skin color stops exacting such a heavy price for the advancement of people of color.

But given what has been a deep polarization on this topic in corporations that had made racism taboo in many places, the mainstreaming of antiracism in the US and elsewhere has now accelerated the need for understanding by those who seek to make up for lost time. It's key that leaders seeking to be inclusive get grounded and savvy on the realities of melanin discrimination. Colorism is discrimination based on skin color *within* the same racial or ethnic group, whereas racism is discrimination based on skin color *across* different racial groups.

Let's look at each of these and then explore the role of inclusive leaders in addressing both types of exclusion based on skin color.

COLORISM: SHADES THAT MAKE A DIFFERENCE

There is a reason for grouping the non-White groups of Black, Asian, Latino, and Native American under the sometimes awkward umbrella of "people of color." It's because color does make a difference. Race and skin color were the original diversity issue for corporations, and to the dismay of many, they still remain some of the most fraught dimensions of diversity.[1] Against a backdrop of increased White nationalism propagated by influential leaders in society, media, and government, 55% of Americans believe there is discrimination against *White* people in the United States, according to an NPR poll, though a much smaller percentage said they had actually experienced it.[2]

Given the deep polarization on this topic, it's key that leaders seeking to be inclusive get grounded on the realities of melanin discrimination. For example, while most people are aware that racism is discrimination based on the skin color across different racial groups, colorism — discrimination based on skin color within the same racial or ethnic group — is much less discussed and understood.

The longing for Whiteness in different cultures around the world takes different forms for different historical and demographic reasons. In Latin America, India, the Middle East, Africa, and all across Asia, there exists within the same racial/ethnic groups a favoring of those who are lighter-skinned. In India, it is called the Snow White syndrome.[3] In Asia, the preference for Whiteness is revealed in the Chinese and Japanese proverb that says "One White covers three ugliness."

The most visible sign of the obsession with lighter skin can be seen in the $23 billion global market for skin whiteners. India's skin-whitening market alone was estimated at $432 million in 2009 and is expanding at a rate of 18% per year. There, the sales of whitening creams outstrip those of Coca-Cola and tea. In one advertisement for bleaching cream brand Fair and Handsome, the male model points a strong finger with the caption, "Hey you! Stop being so dark." Meanwhile, 50% of women in Taiwan whiten their skin, as do four out of ten women in Hong Kong, Malaysia, the Philippines, and South Korea.[4]

Colorism is also at play within distinct racial groups in countries with racial diversity, such as the United States, the United Kingdom, and South Africa. It is a well-understood reality that those with fairer skin within the Latino and Black communities either are favored or are perceived to have an advantage in the broader society. Some Black celebrities, like singers Beyoncé and India.Arie, have even been accused of lightening their skin, based on a difference in skin tone across a variety of photographs. In these cases, the difference was likely due to photographic lighting and postproduction manipulations. However, the fact that the performers approved these altered representations seems to reinforce society's preference for those who are lighter-skinned.

This bias for Whiteness has economic and status implications. The further a group gets from being White, the less positive are the outcomes within a country, in terms of educational opportunities, health outcomes, and workplace experiences. Brazil, for instance, has

134 different terms to capture different skin color gradations. If skin color does not matter, why this obsession with a Crayola-like color scheme? But these gradations don't just make for interesting conversation; they make an economic difference. On average, White and Asian Brazilians earned twice as much as Black or mixed-race Brazilians. Black Brazilians also are much more likely to be poor and rarely reach the top levels of business or politics.[5]

Inclusive leaders must be aware of the damaging tentacles of colorism in order to counter its impact on diversity and inclusion efforts. However, racism remains the much more insidious and destructive force. Let's explore why, by looking at the United States as a case study.

RACISM AND DEHUMANIZATION

There cannot be an honest reckoning of the lack of progress of people of color in leadership without a willingness to look at America's insidious legacy of institutional and systemic racism. More than 250 years ago, the original US Constitution enshrined the dehumanization of Black slaves by declaring that one slave was equal to three-fifths of a person. When the horrific system of slavery was abolished, it was replaced by a succession of laws and practices that continued to do lasting damage to African Americans — even after they were outlawed. Segregationist Jim Crow laws and lynching have now been replaced by mass incarceration and police killings of unarmed Blacks through a variety of methods: chokeholds, shootings of innocents, being left unattended in a prison cell while sick. It's been racism at work as long as the US history. Then came the killings of Floyd, Arbery, and Breonna Taylor in rapid succession, indicating to mainstream society how pervasive and even how much worse racism was becoming again.

The evidence of this damage in corporate America is the continual reality of White privilege in the workplace today. People still tend to be evaluated more positively, the closer they are to Whiteness.

In a study by University of Chicago Economics Professors Marianne Bertrand and Sendhil Mullainathan, résumés with White-sounding names were 50% more likely than those with Black-sounding names to receive callbacks from employers (9.7% compared to 6.5%).[6] A New York City hiring discrimination study conducted by Princeton University Sociology Professor Devah Pager and her colleagues concluded that, "A Black applicant has to search twice as long as an equally qualified White applicant before receiving a callback or job offer from an employer."

White applicants for employment with known and serious criminal convictions are more likely to be given a chance than are Black men who share common positive characteristics, such as a high school education, clean-cut appearance, or verbal aptitude, even if the Black man has no criminal record.[7]

Likewise, when it comes to style of dress, hair, clothing, skin tone, and all manner of appearances, White standards prevail. For instance, Black women have repeatedly shared in focus groups that we have conducted over the years that, when it comes to hair style, they feel forced to straighten what is for many their naturally curly hair.

Despite being labeled as the "model minority," Asian Americans, in particular East Asian Americans, have been seen as best suited for technical and competence positions, but not for leadership or management. Researchers at the University of Toronto found that East Asian Americans were stereotyped as high in competence and low in warmth and dominance.[8]

Let's take a look at the three main groups that make up the "people of color" demographic in the US—Blacks, Asians, and Latinos. While these groups share the experience of melanin exclusion, how that exclusion manifests for each group can vary quite a bit, and unique headwinds each group faces require interventions that address their unique root causes.

BLACKS MUST OVERACHIEVE TO GET AHEAD

"If you were to ask an organization how many of their top African American leaders are thinking about leaving, the answer would likely be more than they realize," says William F. Busch III, a Managing Director at FMG Leading, who specializes in organizational strategy and transformation.[9] And much of this talent is leaving to become entrepreneurs, further thinning the Black talent pool for corporations.

It's easy to understand the exodus.

"Many African American professionals are losing faith that the corporate sector values them," said Jesse Tyson, President and CEO of the National Black MBA Association, in a recent interview with the Korn Ferry Institute. In addition to nurturing an environment of greater acceptance of Blacks, there needs to be a better understanding of not only the challenges Black talent faces but also the truly extraordinary benefits they offer corporations.

To find out what these challenges are, the Korn Ferry Institute conducted a research project in partnership with the Executive Leadership Council (ELC), a by-invitation organization of Black leaders no more than two levels down from the CEO. Researchers interviewed twenty-eight senior Black profit-and-loss (P&L) leaders at Fortune 500 companies who are considered to be in the pipeline for a CEO role; three-quarters of them also underwent Korn Ferry's Four Dimensions of Leadership psychometric leadership assessment. Here are the key findings:

- **A need to overperform**. "Being Black in corporate America means confronting misperceptions about skills and performance," says project coordinator J. T. Saunders. The executives in the study shared that, despite their success, they had to repeatedly prove themselves in tough assignments before they were given the chance to advance. Unlike many of their White counterparts, who were more often promoted on the basis of potential, these Black leaders had to wait until they had a more proven track record to be given the chance to go to the next level. "Nearly 60% of the Black P&L leaders we interviewed reported having to work twice as hard—and accomplish twice as much—to be seen on the same level as their colleagues."

- **Willing to risk it all**. Given how much this need to do more slowed down their advancement, many of these successful executives chose to take on riskier assignments, more frequently, than their White counterparts. Fifty percent of the executives said they intentionally sought out tough projects that would give them greater visibility within their organizations. And organizations had a similar mindset: 36% of the executives said they were assigned extremely tough projects that no one else wanted to handle and that had a high risk of failure. "Many of these Black P&L leaders weren't afraid to put everything on the line, even if it meant possible failure," says the report's colead, senior client partner Audra Bohannon.

■ **Masters of their own destiny.** "Leaving their careers to chance was never in the cards for 60% of these Black P&L leaders," says Michael Hyter, Korn Ferry senior client partner and coleader for the research project. Knowing they faced more resistance than their White counterparts, they held themselves accountable for their career progress, taking extra care to develop highly strategic, analytical, and planful approaches to their professional development.

All in all, to be Black in corporate America means overcoming more obstacles, meeting more requirements, taking more risks, and having greater resilience to put up with the unfair treatment in terms of access, opportunity, and reward. And this experience is even more pronounced for Black women (see sidebars, pages 168 and 172).

ASIAN AMERICAN WOMEN AS LEADERS ABOLISH SO MANY STEREOTYPES

Stereotypes lead people to judge Asian American women as less fit for leadership than identically qualified White women, White men, and Asian American men, according to a recent study conducted by researchers at Stanford University and the University of Georgia.

In the study, eight groups of respondents were asked to read a letter of recommendation for an American candidate seeking promotion to a full professorship in comparative literature at the University of Virginia.[10] The candidate was named variously Emily Yang, Eric Yang, Emily Mullen, or Eric Mullen and was described as being either "brutally honest . . . in order to maintain the high standards of the field" (dominant personality) or "overly polite . . . in order to protect authors' fragile egos" (overly nice personality). In all instances, the letter of recommendation described the candidate as highly competent, with a PhD from the University of North Carolina at Chapel Hill, more than forty publications, five well-received books, and a MacArthur genius grant.

After reading the letter of recommendation, respondents rated the candidate's leadership suitability on a scale of 1 to 6. Of the eight candidates, "dominant" Emily Yang and "too nice" Emily Yang received the lowest leadership ratings.

The researchers wrote, "The Asian woman is perceived as less fit for leadership regardless of behavioral style . . . [even] when competence is firmly established."

AFRICAN AMERICAN WOMEN: REFUELING OUR SPIRITS

Audra Bohannon, Boston

I often attend Black female gatherings where I join other accomplished Black women in a variety of different fields. These gatherings are an oasis, a space of coming together that feeds the soul and fuels the spirit. For us, they are essential to manage the unique headwinds we face, being Black and female in corporate America.

At one of these occasions, in Napa Valley, I was sitting at the table enjoying a meal with dear friends. All are extremely powerful in their area of expertise and have built very successful careers. The discussion focused on two competing realities for us: how we very much enjoy what we have gained through our accomplishments, and how heavy has been the toll that comes with it. We have had to expend so much energy to break down these barriers to success, such as isolation, the perception that we lack potential and leadership ability, and the affront of White male direct reports asking for transfers because they refused to work for a Black woman. Story after story was shared, validating the unique challenges Black women face. Even with huge budgets, staff, and areas of responsibility, the reality of being on the receiving end of negative treatment is part and parcel of being Black and female. It feels unfair and, if I am honest, it hurts.

One colleague, from a consumer products company, shared how she was overlooked for a critical assignment that she was actively seeking.

At first glance, one might think this is because, as another study found, Asian American women experience being stereotyped as docile, subservient, and unable to stand up for themselves. But no, the researchers found that Asian women cannot not avoid questions about their leadership by being more assertive.[11]

"Even if an Asian American woman is competent *and* shows dominant behaviors associated with traditional hierarchical leadership, the stereotype of Asian American women as subservient and invisible may still result in people judging her as relatively unsuitable for leadership," explains our colleague Karen Huang, PhD, a clinical psychologist in the Korn Ferry executive search practice. It's a can't-win situation. That's why these negative stereotypes of Asian American women need to change.

She was told that they didn't know she really wanted it—even though she brought it up several times. Another friend, in a tech company, was excited to receive a promotion that she rightly deserved. But then one of her colleagues invalidated all her hard work, telling her, "You know you got the job because you are Black and female, right? Diversity is a hot topic right now. I don't know where it leaves us White guys."

The shared experiences of discrimination made us wonder how we managed through them all. We persevered, for sure, but we have been left profoundly exhausted in ways we did not imagine. That is why we needed this time to come together. These gatherings serve as refueling stations. These are places where, as Black women, we can exhale. We can just be.

We can also uplift each other. A heightened level of clarity about our reality leaves us energized and excited about continuing to drive toward our next level of achievement. By recognizing and talking about it, we are better able to manage the headwinds—individually and collectively. We will not be overwhelmed.

This is the hand we have been dealt, and we will play it hard and well. We will not let it kill our spirit. We have prevailed and excelled, and we will continue to do so.

I can't help but wonder, though, how much more we could accomplish—for ourselves, our families, and our organizations—if the energy we expend managing being overlooked, undervalued, and resisted was redirected toward driving our businesses, our careers, and our lives.

Title IX, which radically transformed girls' access to educational and athletic opportunities, was cowritten and championed by a Japanese American legislator, Patsy Mink. *Pitchfork*, the "most trusted voice in music," is led by Puja Patel, daughter of a mother from India and a father from Zimbabwe. Stitch Fix, the $2 billion company that has upended the traditional clothes shopping experience, is led by Katrina Lake, granddaughter of a Japanese immigrant. These wildly successful Asian American women are not subservient worker bees.

"They demonstrate that Asian American women can leverage creativity, courage, entrepreneurship, and leadership to build great companies, make an enduring cultural footprint, and profoundly enhance people's daily lives," says Huang. "It is time for a revision of the prevailing stereotype of Asian Americans as passive nerds who lack leadership qualities."

LATINX IDENTITY PRESSURES: ASSIMILATE, OPT OUT, OR DOUBLE DOWN?

Charlie Garcia, former CEO of Sterling Financial Group and of the Association of Latino Professionals for America, grew up in Panama. He tells this story:

"My first roommate at the US Air Force Academy was trying to break the ice by telling me a joke about the popular American TV series *Mork and Mindy*. I innocently asked, 'Who's Mork and Mindy?' He replied, 'What planet did you get off of?' Later, I would put my salsa music on and people would knock on the door, yelling, 'Turn that sh** off. We're in the United States.' Then somebody changed my name tag from Garcia to O'Garcia, and they started calling me Ogarsha because they said I looked Irish."

Garcia's experience represents just the tip of the iceberg of differences between those of Latin American descent and White Americans, in terms of cultural values and assumptions.

"For too long, the full burden has been put on Latinos to assimilate into the dominant culture," says Dr. Robert Rodriguez, founder and President of DRR Advisors and coauthor (with Andrés) of *Auténtico: The Definitive Guide to Latino Career Success*, from which several findings in this section come. "Doing so can be detrimental to Latinos' own sense of personal identity and empowerment. Plus, corporations lose the benefits of the differences in perspectives and backgrounds that Latinos bring to the workplace."

Depending on the cultural gap, resisting adaptation to the majority culture could be a losing battle. At the same time, standing one's ground—and in fact, influencing the adaptation to one's own cultural preference—may be the healthiest way to optimize personal and organizational performance.

It is important to note that, in contrast to other people of color, non-Afro-Latino leaders actually have a choice about how much their heritage will be part of their leadership identity. This is because Latinos are not one racial group but rather an ethnic group that is a combination of races, including Caucasian, indigenous, Asian, and

Black. For some, this makes it possible to "pass" as a member of the majority culture if they choose to do so. Therefore, for many, their Latino identity relies heavily on when they choose to assimilate and when they stand their cultural ground, whatever that ground may be. This "to be or not to be" decision for Latino executives was at the heart of the professional journey of many of the leaders interviewed.

How Latino leaders deal with these crosscurrents of cultural pride and stinging discrimination is further complicated because there is little uniformity in the formative years of many Latino and Latina individuals. For some, their early years were fully immersed in Latino culture, while others were the minority, sometimes the only Latino or Latina, in a mostly European American culture. Moreover, some grew up in racially mixed environments. There are multiple variations in how the executives interviewed dealt with their cultural identities when confronted with stark choices about whether to assimilate, opt out, or double down as they pursued their ambitions. But the one thing they almost all had in common was that, at some point in their educational and work journeys, each was confronted with the need to choose.

The messages that Latino receive about their group can be positive, negative, or neutral, depending on the identity lens they choose to use. Taken from the book, these are the broad categories of identities Latino leaders have assumed: unapologetic, equivocal, retro, or invisible.

- **Unapologetic Latinos** have fully embraced their Latino identity and have chosen not to hide it, even in the most non-Latino of environments.
- **Equivocal Latinos** have some boundaries about their Latino identity because of European American values to which they were heavily exposed in their formative years and during their educational and career pursuits.
- **Retro Latinos** may have grown up as equivocal Latinos but, for a variety of reasons, in adulthood have gone back to their Latino roots to discover or rediscover elements of a distant or submerged heritage and culture.
- **Invisible Latinos** have fully and deliberately denied and disowned any connection to Latino culture, whether they grew up in a Latino environment or not.

AS WHITE WOMEN, WE NEED TO ADMIT WE HAVE NOT BEEN FULLY INCLUSIVE OF WOMEN OF COLOR

Shannon Hassler, Atlanta

As a White woman deeply committed to the advancement of women through Korn Ferry's work researching the success traits of women CEOs and our Advancing Women Worldwide solutions, I have learned that my own blind spots are far bigger than I thought. When you're in the dominant group, it's still too easy to miss things that are right in front of you.

Women's advancement efforts commonly have been and continue to be led by White women, with the benefits mostly realized by White women. It has taken those of us pushing for equality too long to realize this and its deep implications.

I've been challenged by women and men of color to expand my vision, deepen my understanding, acknowledge my privilege in work and society, and leverage it for greater equality for the sake of racial/ethnic inclusion. The painful irony is that I spend a lot of time in my role challenging White men to do the same thing when it comes to women.

This choice that many Latinos and Latinas have of how they will identify creates a very different dynamic than for those who—because of the darkness of their skin or certain facial features—don't have the same choice. So while accent, surname, and cultural behaviors are reasons why people are discriminated against, inclusive leaders are tuned empathetically into the striking reality that how close one is to Whiteness matters. When leaders don't acknowledge this racism and/or colorism, they will fail to achieve true inclusion of all. Inclusive leaders are needed to reduce the personal toll on this talent and the opportunity cost to organizations that are not benefiting from talent that feels like they fully belong.

PART 2: GENDER—WHERE ARE THE WOMEN CEOS?

It's the 2020s and we are still having this conversation: Why are there so few women in leadership?

This turning of the tables has been a powerful call-out. For example, while we were quick to call attention to all-male conference speaker and panel lineups, once we were in a position to influence and own agendas, we've made the same type of mistake by too often putting forward all White speakers and panelists.

Although we still have a long way to go for parity, women have risen in leadership ranks. Even so, the gains have not been equal for all women. Women of color continue to be left behind.

Women of all races face common challenges, such as the double bind (be nice but also be tough), the imbalanced home and/or caregiving load, deep-rooted gender-based assumptions, harassment, and less access to sponsors and influential networks, but women of color face them at a heightened level—plus they must carry the additional burden of racism.

The compounding impact of race and gender on the advancement of women of color continues to be among the most intractable and the most overlooked issues. That means the growing number of White women in influential positions have an additional responsibility: to address the equity gaps of *all women*.

------------------------ ■ ------------------------

Women in this century have achieved fifty-fifty parity in the overall workforce, they account for half or even up to two-thirds of college undergraduates and graduates, and they have been entering the workforce with as much intent to grow and advance in their careers as men. Yet the number of women CEOs stubbornly hovers between just 4% and 6%, and only 22% of C-suite executives are women. Furthermore, of those C-suite roles, most are heavily skewed toward staff roles versus CEO-feeder roles with profit-and-loss or direct client responsibility.

"Where are Wall Street's women CEOs?" asks Claire Zillman, coauthor of *Fortune's Broadsheet* newsletter. She writes, "At a congressional hearing in April [2019], Rep. Al Green (D–Texas) put a finer point on what was already known. He asked the seven White, male megabank CEOs sitting before him to raise their hand if they thought a woman or person of color would be their successor. Not a single hand went up, reiterating that the tip-tops of US bank elite are all White, all male and, perhaps, going to stay that way."[12]

These dismal statistics reflect the top of the house, but the crystallization of the glass ceiling begins early in women's careers. A 2019 McKinsey report revealed that as early as at the first manager level, for every one hundred men promoted or hired, only seventy-two women were hired or promoted to manager.[13] While there was some variation by industry, none were spared from this indictment—the trend lines were consistent, no matter where we looked. This is why the World Economic Forum projects that the global gender gap will take 108 years to close and that it will take 202 years to achieve economic gender parity.[14]

When we at Korn Ferry asked HR executives at the Conference Board roundtable in 2019 why progress has been so slow, they shared what they believe are the top barriers, including:

- hiring manager mindset and bias, whether conscious or unconscious

- more positive expectations for men, who are more likely to be promoted based on future potential, whereas women tend to be promoted on past performance

- fewer early opportunities for women to advance in business line, profit-and-loss, operational, and international roles

- insufficient practices and cultures to support the integration of work and life demands, which tend to more often affect women

- less candid feedback for women, or clear engagement with them on career trajectory

- cultures that are less forgiving of failures by women than by men, making it more difficult for women to rebound after a misstep

- less access to influential mentors, sponsors, and champions

- weak leader accountability for results[15]

"There's no good reason why so many more men than women are being tapped for promotions, only a bad one—bias," Facebook Chief Operating Officer Sheryl Sandberg and Rachel Thomas, President of Lean In, write in the *Wall Street Journal*.[16]

Furthermore, it is possible that "women's advancement" has narrowly and unconsciously focused on White women. The rising tide has not lifted all women. Within senior leadership positions in the United States, Asian women represent 1.7%, African American women represent 1.2%, and Latinas represent 1%, for a total of just 3.9%.

No wonder women in the prime of their careers are opting out of corporate to start their own businesses. These barriers lead to organizations being unable to retain high-performing, talented women, or to accelerate their careers, resulting in a further depleted pipeline. The number of women-owned businesses increased nearly 3,000% since 1972, according to the *2018 State of Women-Owned Businesses Report* commissioned by American Express. Not only that, but between 2017 and 2018, women started an average of 1,821 new businesses per day in the United States, making up 40% of all new entrepreneurs.[17]

While these numbers mean more options for women, what is the cost to corporations who are losing so much talent? What will it take to change this state of affairs and to begin to advance women exponentially?

To find out, the Korn Ferry Institute, funded by the Rockefeller Foundation, studied fifty-seven former and current women CEOs at Fortune 1,000 and similar-size companies. "We didn't want to just focus on why more women are not CEOs; we wanted to focus on their common success factors," says Jane Stevenson, global leader for CEO succession at Korn Ferry, who coauthored the study along with Evelyn Orr, the Korn Ferry Institute's chief operating officer.

One of the most eye-popping findings was that the female CEOs consistently rated in or above the ninety-ninth percentile on seventeen of twenty key leadership traits.

"These traits are indicators of potential by the time women are in their early thirties," explains Beatrice Grech-Cumbo, who coleads Korn Ferry's Advancing Women Worldwide solution. "If we can create opportunities to uncover this hidden talent early, engage them effectively, and ensure they are linked with the critical experiences and exposure necessary to progress, we will meaningfully improve gender diversity throughout the senior leadership pipeline."

HOW MANY WOMEN ARE ENOUGH?

What is "adequate" representation? In a survey of HR executives conducted by Korn Ferry and the Conference Board, respondents indicated that the answer is 46% of women in vice president roles and higher, on average. The Paradigm for Parity, a coalition of business leaders dedicated to addressing the leadership gender gap in corporate America, advocates for fifty-fifty candidate slates; however, they caution, targets must be created on the basis of a true understanding of the "available force" as a starting point.

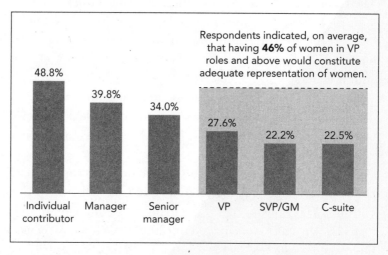

Percentage of women at every level of leadership. *Sources:* Korn Ferry; and The Conference Board, 2019.

In some areas, availability can be more challenging. Let's take engineering as a case study.

Currently there is *not* fifty-fifty gender parity in the number of women getting engineering degrees, and so goals must take into account this talent supply. Still, a careful look at the entire female talent pipeline in engineering reveals plenty of behavioral and structural inclusion inequities that lead to a depleted leadership supply of women engineers.

First, girls are still being tracked away from science, technology, engineering, and math courses in primary and secondary schools. By the time young women apply to college, there are far fewer women than men even declaring an engineering major. One study unearthed key findings about what further reduces the pool of women.

- Of those who enter university declaring an engineering major, a higher percentage of women compared to men were siphoned away from the pool by changing majors away from engineering.

- There was another hit when 15% of women who graduated with the degree chose not to pursue engineering.

- Another 21% entered the field but left. And here's the clincher: while 20% of these made the choice to leave to tend to family full time, the other 80% went to other full-time career roles, busting the myth that women are only leaving the workforce for full-time stay-at-home parenting.

- A hostile work or college environment was the number one reason for dropping engineering.[18]

When we talk about "available" labor force, inclusive leaders can take action in a variety of ways, the first of which is helping their organizations to *not* use the small current labor pool as an excuse. Inclusive leaders need to be advocates for their organizations to actually do something to increase the labor pool by, for example, inspiring more girls and young women to pursue engineering and to give them an attractive and helpful path into the profession. They need to engage in an honest discussion about the overall engineering culture that is contributing to hostile work environments. And they need to double down on ensuring that the women doing engineering work in their midst remain engaged and valued, and are advancing to the fullness of their potential.

Multibillion-dollar corporations have the resources and sway to influence young women to consider engineering as an attractive career. Companies such as IBM, Johnson Controls, John Deere, and others are doing just this by sending women engineers to speak at myriad career and higher education fairs, and are going further by providing internships, apprenticeships, and job promises for those who complete their degrees.

Equity targets, then, should be set not just to the current supply reality. They also should consider the increase in talent as more women enter these corporate-sponsored engineering programs.

There were some other key findings as well.

- **Few set out to be CEO**. Only 12% of the women always knew they wanted to be a CEO. More than half gave no thought to being CEO until someone explicitly told them they had it in them. Therefore, the women CEOs were, on average, four or more years older than men at the time of appointment and had held at least one additional senior leadership role.

- **Many started out in STEM**. More than 40% of the CEOs started out with college degrees in science, engineering, or math—twice as many as those with a background in the arts and humanities (21%). About 19% studied business-related subjects like economics and finance.

- **There was no single career path**. The Korn Ferry Institute discerned that the women took four distinct career approaches. While some zigzagged, eager to learn new things, and some focused on driving innovation and growth, only a few concentrated primarily on strategic career experiences aimed at becoming CEO.

- **They sought out challenge**. These women didn't just excel in difficult and unpredictable work assignments; they sought them out.

- **They were motivated by purpose and culture**. The CEOs interviewed said they were motivated by a sense of purpose—the thought that one's company could have a positive impact on its employees, community, or the world at large. "So, appealing to women with money and power is not the most compelling," says Orr. "We need to articulate roles in terms of impact and outcomes that make women feel good about the trade-offs they will be making."

- **They had a different mindset as CEO**. The women CEOs were much more likely than their male counterparts to credit their team, which showed up in their assessment scores related to humility and confidence. This is important to note, because it means that women will likely to have to be drafted into CEO roles, as they are less likely to aggressively pursue them.

In addition to a moral imperative to provide equal opportunities to women to rise to the fullness of their potential, the economic impact when they do is stunning. A Peterson Institute study found that, for profitable firms, a move from no female leaders to 30% representation led to a 15% increase in net revenue margin. Or, to aggregate that across entire economies, the World Bank estimates that nations leave $160 trillion on the table by keeping women from fully participating in national economies. Further, S&P Global estimates that an increase of women in the labor force would add a "staggering $5.87 trillion to the global stock market in ten years."[19]

So here we are. The case for gender diversity is clear. The pipeline is full of talented women. The glass ceilings are inexcusable. "The question is no longer 'Why is it difficult to have women in key roles?'" challenges Stevenson. "Rather it is now 'How can we afford *not* to have women in key roles?'"

Inclusive leaders are needed to answer this call.

PART 3: INTERSECTIONALITY—DIVERSITY OF ONE

Gina's birthday surprise one year was unearthing her family tree by spitting into a tube. The 23andMe kit was attractive and easy to use. A few weeks later, her results came back, revealing a mixture of racial and nationality lineages, including Nigerian, Asian, and Norwegian. As someone who had grown up White in a mostly White suburb outside Columbus, Ohio, Gina was thrilled to see that, in some ways, she too is a person of color. Or is she?

Elizabeth Warren ran into this dilemma when she claimed Native American ancestry. Her diversity credentials were questioned, and she set out to prove it was true by taking a DNA test. The results vindicated her. Or did they?

Rachel Dolezal, the former president of the Spokane, Washington, chapter of the National Association for the Advancement of Colored People, had claimed to be Black for years. While she is light-skinned, it was her curly hair, her studies at Howard, her Black family members, and her position as a professor of Africana studies that bolstered her identity as African American. Or did it?

Today, there are waves of people thrilled by the prospect of increased diversity and inclusion, but there is also a counter wave of deep polarization driven by racism and xenophobia. In this context, the quest for cultural identity is hot.

WHAT KOREAN BARBECUE TACOS TELL US ABOUT ASIAN–LATINX CROSSOVER

Andrés T. Tapia, Chicago; and Karen Huang, Philadelphia

Rarely do people talk about Latinxs and Asians in the same breath. Yet, every day, millions bite into and dance to Latinx–Asian fusion.

Kogi BBQ's Korean tacos meld Korean and Mexican gastronomy—what the *Freakonomics* blog refers to as "two of L.A.'s favorite cuisines"[20]— into something so popular that it redefined the food truck industry, won a Best New Chef award from *Food & Wine*, and inspired a movie, *Chef*, and a reality TV show, *The Great Food Truck Race*.

Samuel Arredondo Kim, one of South Korea's biggest up-and-coming heartthrobs, was born in Bakersfield, California, to a Korean mother and Mexican father. On the other side of the equator, Korean K-pop artists, with their upbeat messages, boyish sex appeal, and ultraprecise dance moves, have found great popularity in Central and South America. Meanwhile, Latino culture has influenced K-pop in songs such as KARD's "Hola Hola," SF9's "O Sole Mio," and BTS's tango-inspired "Airplane pt. 2."

Bruno Mars, one of the world's bestselling musical artists, is Latinx Asian; his father is Puerto Rican and Jewish and his mother is Filipino. Olympic medalist Arthur Nory Oyakawa Mariano is a brilliant Japanese Brazilian gymnast. And Franklin Chang Díaz, the first

What really determines one's cultural identity? Is it something in our blood, as many like to say, or is it a choice? Or a combination?

Rachel Dolezal's claim to be Black was undone by the fact that her two parents are White. Dolezal based her claim on a desire to be Black, but without any Black DNA—at least as evidenced by her two White parents.

In the case of Elizabeth Warren, the public's incredulity that this Massachusetts Senator had Native American blood was squashed by the confirmation that she is indeed one-twentieth Cherokee. Yet there is nothing in her lifestyle, her circle of friends and family, or her worldview that demonstrates a Native American identity. Hers was not a lie like Dolezal's, but was it the truth?

Asian–Latino American immigrant in space and a NASA Astronaut Hall of Famer, is Costa Rican Chinese.

These contemporary intersections actually reflect a long history of Latino and Asian cultural contact. Japanese immigrants began coming to South America in the late 1800s as indentured laborers for the cotton and sugar plantations. Their influence has been so great that São Paulo has the largest urban Japanese population outside of Tokyo. The former president of Peru, Alberto Fujimori, was the son of first-generation Japanese immigrants.

Spanish colonization also led to Asian–Latino intersections. Many Filipinos, for instance, consider themselves the "Latinos of Asia" because the Spanish colonization of the Philippines over three centuries imbued Filipino culture with Latino norms. In the Philippines, Roman Catholicism is the most common expression of faith, and Filipinos share many everyday Spanish words, such as *mesa*, *tenedor*, and *cuchara*. And now, full circle, many of the 3 million Filipinos who immigrated to the United States ended up in southern California, where the Latinos of Asia are connecting with the Latinos of the Americas.

These intersections have great implications for organizational diversity and inclusion strategies and programs as people embrace multidimensional identities such as "Mexipino" and "ChinaLatina."

This is why we now can munch on a couple of Kogi BBQ tacos while streaming K-pop's "Hola Hola" on Spotify and have it all feel so congruent.

For Gina the stakes were low, without the glare of the press, social media, or political enemies. But her DNA results did not end up giving her any insight into her identity beyond what she already knew. She was still a Methodist Midwestern American from the suburbs. However, her knowledge of what's in her blood did begin to open her up to new experiences. For instance, she began to travel to meet people with a shared DNA heritage, experiencing the Nigerian tribe from which she had traces of descent.

Now take Camila, a successful professional who grew up in Buenos Aires with an Argentinian mom and a Guatemalan dad. Her native language is Spanish, she dances tango, and she sips yerba mate. But when she is asked about her cultural identity, "Latinx" is not her first answer.

"Because my grandparents are European Jews who migrated to South America and I grew up celebrating Jewish traditions and learning Hebrew, I feel more connected to Israel than Argentina," she says. "I am a Latina, but I'm other identities, too, that mean as much to me."

Meanwhile, Susana, a colleague of Camila's, is a fluent Spanish speaker with dark brown hair. She studied, worked, and lived in Mexico for many years, even dancing and singing backup in a *grupo versátil* band. Most of her closest friends, romantic partners, and godchildren are Mexican. For decades, many people have assumed that Susana is Latina, but she is racially White. While Latina multiracial heritage includes White Europeans, Susana has no Latin American DNA. Can she declare she is culturally Latina?

In an era when diversity goals categorize people into simple identity boxes, neither Camila's nor Susana's story is unique. What makes someone Latinx or Latina? Is it DNA? Parents from Latin America? Who has the right to claim a Latino identity?

DNA tests reveal the secrets of our blood, but not of what is in our hearts. That, instead, comes from the choices we make in response to what we were born with or into, and who we want to become. And it unfortunately is still the case in today's America that the closer you are to Whiteness, the more choices you have.

"This DNA/heart conundrum is further complicated by skin color. The darker one's skin color, the fewer options arise for self-proclamation," writes Andrea Johnson, Executive Director at the Courageous Conversation Global Foundation, in response to a LinkedIn blog on this topic of identity. "Darker-hued folks can feel connected to cultural attributes outside of the race category they are 'perceived' to be; however, unless they have the opportunity to express their connection, they are treated as members of the race/culture connected to their outward appearance—no matter what is in their heart. The advances in the home DNA market lends additional confusion and sometimes validation to the mix."[21]

While diversity is more relevant than ever, sweeping demographic changes in the past generation have made the way we think about it obsolete. The stalwart paradigms of group identity based on race, gender, age, sexual orientation, or disability no longer cover the scope of our multidimensional identities. No one is just Black. Or Latinx. Or female. Or gay. Or sight impaired.

We are much more complex than that. We have entered the age of ultradiversity, where every person is a diversity of one: GayVeteranXer. ElderlyPersonWithaDisability. MillennialIntroverted. LatinxFemaleManager. BoomerAfricanAmericanGeneralManager. WhiteMaleWithAdultKids. LesbianSingleMother. Instead of thinking about the diversity of groups in simplistic ways, we must begin to think about the diversity within each individual.

MAJORITY MINORITIES

What does *minority* mean when "minorities" are actually the majority in number?

In fifty US cities, "minorities" make up the majority of the population. In ten US states, Whites are a minority group. In California, Latinos are the largest ethnic group of all. In the United Kingdom, ethnic Britons are expected to be a minority by 2060. In Latin America, the new economic majorities of the emerging middle class are of indigenous descent and are darker-skinned. It was so much easier to discriminate against them when they earned two dollars a day. Now, with their newly earned financial resources, their children are competing with those from old-money families for scarce seats in private schools.

Miami is now the unofficial capital of Latin America, and the United States is the second-largest Spanish-speaking country in the world. São Paulo, Brazil, has the second-largest Japanese population after Tokyo. Chicago has the second-largest Polish population after Warsaw. Toronto has the highest percentage of foreign-born residents of any city in the world.

Even these new majority minorities defy traditional labels and categories. Just ask the "Blaxican" or the "Mexipino." Or the biracial household names Barack Obama or Soledad O'Brien.

Even when talking about Latinos, what kind of Latino are we talking about? The Spanish dominant? The English dominant? The Spanglish dominant? The one who grew up in the United States or the one who grew up outside of it? The Mexican, the Puerto Rican, the Cuban, or the ones from twenty-plus other Latin American nationalities?

The "diversity of one" concept challenges us to see race and ethnicity as single threads interwoven into the fabric of a person's identity and to recognize that the cloth contains many other "fibers."

Current diversity strategies are not set up to address this complexity. For example, we have affinity groups structured unidimensionally. There is a Latinx group, a Black group, an Asian group. But for those individuals who fit all three categories, which group do they join to have their needs met?

Multidimensional identities also affect diversity strategies in talent acquisition. Take sourcing and recruiting of Latinxs, for example. A major US-based wealth management and insurance company has set out to attract Latinx talent and build up a larger Latinx clientele. Korn Ferry is helping this company with learning and strategies that are multifold and based on a foundation of building cross-cultural agility. These skills involve helping members of the majority culture to realize that there is vast diversity among Latinxs and the talent and customer-attraction strategies have to be nuanced to appeal to the different Latinx and Latino groups. Likewise, Latinxs within the organization need to become more attuned to their own biographies and to understand the forces that shaped them into the unique diversity-of-one Latinxs that they are. Their self-awareness, which they can share with their non-Latinx counterparts for mutual learning, is just as important.

YES, BUT WHICH WOMAN?

It is a Decade for Women—not because the United Nations declared it so, as it did during the years of 1976 to 1985, but because women are truly advancing today at an accelerated clip. In most developed countries, women are better educated, participate to a greater extent in the workplace, and are more ambitious than in any previous generation.

Gender is one of the most common diversity issues around the world, but that does not mean it can be addressed the same way everywhere. Chinese, French, Afghan, and American women face circumstances and attitudes quite unique to their countries. Also, women of different ethnic groups or socioeconomic classes within the same country face varied challenges. Likewise, a Baby Boomer professional woman with adult children may have little in common with her Gen Y counterpart who is just starting a family and is dealing with issues of child care and balance, or with a Gen Xer without children, or with the growing number of women who are choosing not to have any children, ever.

"It was ten years ago that I was contemplating both motherhood and my career, and how I could potentially balance both," said Jeanine Amilowski, formerly a director of research at Korn Ferry. "I grew up living in a very close extended family with a strong belief in the African proverb 'It takes a village to raise a child.' When the career choices of my husband and I took us nine hundred miles away from our family, the village I grew up in didn't appear. Access to child care and workplace flexibility were not openly discussed in the work environment, and it influenced my personal decision not to have children. And even when women's affinity group programs emerged, they are mostly designed around work–life balance, maternity issues, and breast-feeding."

This also upends gender dynamics between men and women. More professional women in developed and emerging economies postpone marriage and children, while in certain societies men are sharing more household duties and an increasing number of women earn more than their partners. Male identity—for centuries associated with "breadwin-ner," "protector," and "leader"—is shifting. Men, particularly Gen Xers and Gen Yers, are assuming identities such as "nurturer," "supporter," and "primary parent."

What this tells us is that it is no longer enough to talk about "wom-en's issues" broadly. Intersectionality demands seeing the diversity within the diversity.

DISABILITY DIVERSITY: WHO IS TRULY DISABLED?

What does "disability" mean when there are plentiful examples of people with disabilities outperforming those who are supposedly able-bodied? We now have athletes with prosthetic legs competing for gold in the Olympics—not the Paralympics. We know a proofreader who is sight impaired and outperforms her seeing peers in accuracy, an industry-shaping chief diversity officer who is four feet tall, and leaders of social change movements who use wheelchairs for mobility.

Yet, when you walk into the corridors of most company campuses, it is rare to see employees with a visible disability. Given the types of skills and talents that can be found among people with disabilities, we should be seeing them by the dozens or even hundreds. But while few will say it aloud, many still believe that people with disabilities are not viable employees; in addition, most also worry about the potential costs of accommodation.

But not all. When it comes to hard-core business operations, the Danish software quality check company Specialisterne (the Specialists) hires for the competence—not "disability"—of autism, seeking those with photographic memories and obsessive attention to detail who can spot an error in millions of lines of code.

A few years ago, Walgreens decided to build its new distribution center in Anderson, South Carolina, using "universal design," an architectural approach that takes into account the vast diversity of needs across the whole ability/disability spectrum. They also provided disability inclusion training to all, including employees with disabilities, who could learn about disabilities different from their own. The results were stunning. With 40% of employees having some form of physical or cognitive disability, the center benefited not only from the positive feelings of authentic inclusion but also financially. Of all the distribution centers in the Walgreens system, Anderson is the top performer by 20% or more.[22]

In both of these companies, disabilities are not detriments—rather, they are drivers of high-impact effectiveness. For them, disability inclusion has led to higher engagement, lower absenteeism, increased loyalty, and continuous improvement. Other companies now are emulating the Walgreens model, including Brazilian cosmetics multinational Natura at its new distribution center outside São Paulo.

Don't we all need chairs to give us stamina, lights to see, amplification systems to hear, climate control for comfort, and weekends to unwind? Our "normal" physical and mental limitations are being accommodated every moment of every day, at great cost—a cost that no one questions. And yet when it comes to access and opportunity for the disabled, nearly everywhere around the world, we hear business leaders balk and resist because it's deemed too costly and too difficult.

Who is really disabled? It is, indeed, each and every one of us.

BUILDING AN EFFECTIVE AND FLEXIBLE PLATFORM FOR DIVERSITY OF ONE

Contemporary diversity is laying waste to Diversity 1.0's simplistic categorizations. But how do we affordably design human performance systems that allow for the diversity of one, ultraflexibility to meet the needs of ultradiversity?

For innovative help, we need look no further than our smartphones. Music streaming platforms such as Spotify and Pandora provide the inspiration. In the days of mass-produced compact discs, music industry executives had the final say on the set list. But, as we have all experienced via music streaming services, that limitation has been obliterated. Fans can now create their own highly personalized, multi-dimensional genre mixes that make us groove, bop, and thrive. Human capital management must find its equivalent.

We need platforms that all talent can access and that are tailored to meet their career ambitions and needs. These tools also need to churn out customized assessments, profiles, and developmental plans that both talent and their leaders can mold into "set lists" that capture their diversity of one.

There is one major caution before we charge up this hill of ultra-diversity: the rethinking of diversity does not release us from the obligation of tending to the unfinished business of Diversity 1.0. There is still room for programs and approaches that address the needs of groups that have been stigmatized and marginalized by society. While ultradiversity is the new game in town, it is undeniable that the social constructs that lead to racism, sexism, homophobia, and ableism are still deeply entrenched in our societies.

Race still matters for the young Black male driving or walking down the street, who can run into racists whether they are wearing a uniform or not. Gender still matters as long as women are earning eighty cents to the men's dollar in the United States—and even less in other countries. Disability still matters when those who need access face the lack of wheelchair ramps or braille signs or closed captioning. Homophobia still matters as long as there are laws that allow some who are LGBTQ+ to be fired, refused services, fined, jailed, or even put to death.

But even here, we must get past the unidimensional labels.

The past's simpler notions of how to increase the inclusion of Blacks and other minorities (such as by eliminating segregated lunch counters, protecting their right to vote, and outlawing workplace discrimination on the basis of race and gender) are no longer enough. Today, the processes of talent assessment, high-potential identification, leadership development, advancement, and onboarding must avoid not only "old-fashioned," explicit discrimination but also the invisible forces of unconscious bias and structural exclusion and systemic discrimination.

Because when all is said and done, in a diversity-of-one world, we must ensure that everyone counts.

■　■　■

12

Sociopolitical Inclusion: When the Outside Comes Inside

L EADERS SEEKING TO BE INCLUSIVE ARE BEING confronted with the outside coming inside from all angles.

Chick-fil-A, Fisher Investments, Google, H&M, Hallmark, SoulCycle, Uber, Unilever, United Airlines . . . all got hit with it. Some exclusionary act took place with one of their products or within their places of business, which activated a trip wire of controversy touching deep diversity and inclusion issues. Fierce tweet storms triggered boycotts, dropped advertisers, and tarnished brands.

Meanwhile, government policies around immigration, speech, guns, police, climate, LGBTQ+, race, and reproductive rights in numerous countries are going against the D&I values that many corporations have espoused.

Then there are events such as killings of Blacks going about their daily business in broad daylight, family separations due to mass deportations, a global pandemic, terrorist acts, mass shootings, and climate catastrophes that are leaving whole societies shaken. Dazed and scared employees are longing for spaces to talk about what happened and how it has affected them, but these often are not available. What employees experience outside the company's walls is not left behind as they arrive at work and swipe their ID badges. The sense of threat and insecurity is an underlying tension that saps productivity—and things only get worse when leaders ignore this reality.

Organizations' ability to lead inclusively in this sociopolitical climate has been mixed. Most have been uncertain and confused about how best to respond. But some have been bold. Surprisingly, the most compellingly moral, reassuring, and helpful voices in these threatening times are arising not from elected officials or faith-based organizations but from corporate leaders who have chosen to use their brand reputation and interpretation of their values to take a stand.

After the killings of George Floyd, Ahmaud Arbery, and Breonna Taylor ignited massive rage in the US, hundreds of CEOs issued bold statements against racism within days. After various mass shootings in 2019, Dick's Sporting Goods decided to stop selling guns. Marriott issued a statement against the Muslim travel ban in 2017. Nike doubled down on its long-standing support of Black athletes by signing on Colin Kaepernick at the height of the take-a-knee protest against police violence toward Blacks—even as the star quarterback was being marginalized by the National Football League. After the White supremacy marches in Charlottesville, North Carolina, the CEOs of Apple, Intel, Merck, Visa, and Walmart were among at least eighteen who made unequivocal statements against racism and discrimination. Even in the conservative world of finance, Blackrock's CEO has declared the investment company will "make investment decisions with environmental sustainability as a core goal," and Goldman Sachs stated that it will not invest in any initial public offerings for companies that don't have any women or non-White members on their boards.[1]

Many other companies, however, have made the deliberate decision not to venture into handling these political hot potatoes. In choosing disengagement, some took hits to their corporate reputation in terms of disappointed consumers and employees; others did not.

As the outside comes inside, there are no easy answers for how best to respond, and leaders need the most honed of inclusive leadership skills to navigate these treacherous waters. It is important, however, for organizations to conduct proactive risk assessments regarding each of their stakeholders, to look deeply into how these external events align or misalign with their organizational values, and to think long and hard about those most likely to be overlooked in whatever the organization decides to do.

RESPONDING TO EXCLUSIONARY EVENTS

When policies and events hurt the most vulnerable among us, how can organizations offer hope and support?

Much as corporate leaders would rather stay on the sidelines, there is a strong case to be made that a head-in-the-sand approach doesn't work for employees. There also is the moral imperative to consider. As Nobel Peace Prize awardee Desmond Tutu stated, "If you are neutral in situations of injustice, you have chosen the side of the oppressor."

Fortunately, support can come in different forms. For one, it can be directly aimed at the exclusionary policy. Take United Airlines, which has partnered with the National Immigrant Justice Center to allow frequent flyers to donate their miles to the organization so that more lawyers can travel to immigrants and asylum seekers who need representation and legal education. Those miles also can support the justice center staff in traveling to lawmakers to create humane immigration policies.[2]

Some companies show their support through less public acts, focusing instead on internal efforts to provide their employees with empathy and support. After yet another police killing of an unarmed Black man through a chokehold, or of a Black woman playing with her nephew in her own home, the feelings are raw and the fears intensified for employees of color going to work the next morning. At three p.m., Black and Brown parents are anxiously waiting for that text that their teenage son has arrived safely home.

Publicis rolled out a series of courageous conversations after the Charlottesville neo-Nazi rally and killings. Aware that the polarized moment could stir more blaming than bridge building, leaders asked for an approach that helped all sides listen to one another. No one

CAN HUMOR HELP DEAL WITH THE OUTSIDE COMING IN?

Pamela O'Leary, San Francisco

Before the live taping of *The Daily Show* begins, a video mocks the safety demo that airlines play before a flight takes off. The live audience is warned that jokes might be made about Black people. They calmly instruct us to see whether our Black friend is laughing first, before we start laughing. The show hasn't even begun yet, but we've already chuckled together through a conversation about race and have been primed for the diversity lessons we are about to receive.

American society is a tinderbox right now, due to its inability to reconcile its differences across political ideologies, race and ethnicity, gender, religion, sexual orientation, and immigrant status. As I sat in the middle of an audience reflective of this vast diversity, I thought about how we could all use a good laugh together, how in an ideal inclusive society, people from different backgrounds wouldn't laugh at each other; we'd laugh together.

Then I wonder: Can *Daily Show* host Trevor Noah, and comedians like him, help us bridge the divides? Just as food has been one of the most prevailing ways to bring people together, can laughter do the same?

This is an urgent question for me, personally and professionally. My work in diversity and inclusion in Silicon Valley is fraught with many pitfalls. But there I was, in that TV studio, laughing at the very discomforts I lean into so seriously as a corporate consultant.

Unlike the audience of *The Daily Show*, most of the people in my diversity classes don't choose to be there; they are informally mandated or strongly encouraged by their employer. As you can imagine, these circumstances don't put them in the best mood to learn. But the goals of *The Daily Show* and of the work I and many others like me do in D&I are the same: getting people to rise above their daily suspicions and antagonisms, to see their own blind spots, and to be more empathetic toward others.

I use reason, business cases, and the shared goals of employees working for the same company to help expand people's understanding of why D&I is important. It actually works quite well. But it's often all so serious, and we don't laugh much at all.

During a *Daily Show* interview, Miss Universe Zozibini Tunzi expressed her concern about gender-based violence and how she feels "women are an endangered species these days. I feel like one day we're just going to wake up and there's no women anymore." Noah replied, "That would be horrible! That's why I am an ally!"

Bam! While we are doubled over with laughter, he slips in past our weakened defenses and raises awareness of serious diversity and inclusion issues that reveal the painful realities of people from underrepresented communities.

Noah also tells jokes about living under apartheid. In his book *Born a Crime*, he writes, "The hood made me realize that crime succeeds because crime does the one thing the government doesn't do: crime cares. Crime is grassroots. Crime looks for the young kids who need support and a lifting hand. Crime offers internship programs and summer jobs and opportunities for advancement. Crime gets involved in the community. Crime doesn't discriminate."[3]

Issa Rae navigates the challenges of Black womanhood through personal coming-of-age stories. In the book *The Misadventures of Awkward Black Girl*, she states, "When I was a teenager, . . . others questioned my blackness because some of the life choices I made weren't considered to be 'black' choices: joining the swim team when it is a known fact that 'black people don't swim,' or choosing to become a vegetarian when blacks clearly love chicken."[4]

Mindy Kaling and Arturo Castro demonstrate the challenges of growing up in immigrant families. On *The Mindy Project*, Kaling's character proudly explains her choice to have a Hindu head-shaving ceremony for her child: "I just don't want my kid to learn how to be an Indian from a Bombay Palace menu on my fridge." In an episode of *Alternatino with Arturo Castro*, Castro describes how some White women he has dated reduced him to a stereotype. They wanted him to speak Spanish with a strong accent and salsa dance, even though he really doesn't like to dance. I hate to admit it, but I have been that White woman.

Of course, we must handle charged issues related to race, gender, sexual orientation, and disability with care and in ways that don't lead to cruel jokes and an unsafe environment. On the other hand, we need to be less afraid to call things out as they are. Humor, when done right, can take enough of the edge off.

---

could devalue others on the basis of who they were, and participants were encouraged to acknowledge and own their part in forging new solutions.

The reason this worked is that the aim was *not* to get to full agreement across our many different ways of being, thinking, or doing. As with wider D&I efforts, the goal is to understand and actually leverage those differences for a more engaging, productive, and innovative environment. To do this, we need to better understand how others experience life and work.

While incendiary headlines, tweets, and memes amplify the voices of the extreme fringes, the majority of citizens and employees hunger for a way to bridge divides rather than to widen them. The dilemma is that they don't know how to accomplish this. Inclusive leaders can provide the playbook for how to have constructive conversations across differences.

INCLUSIVE LEADERS GET PERSONAL

When leaders encourage teams to take time out to talk about what is going on, it creates integration between the societal, the personal, and the workplace. To be an inclusive leader in this context, it is also helpful to pause and reflect on exactly what makes these events feel personal to you. These insights make it easier to listen with genuine empathy to those who may have been more directly impacted.

Inclusive leaders can also use their position of privilege to stand up for their workforce. We have perhaps the most diverse workforce ever in history, so an attack on any underrepresented group is an attack on vital members of your organization. Apple CEO Tim Cook is a great example of standing up for workers. In a memo to Apple employees about the attempted repeal of the immigration policy called Deferred Action for Childhood Arrivals, or DACA, he wrote, "I am deeply dismayed that 800,000 Americans—including more than 250 of our Apple coworkers—may soon find themselves cast out of the only country they've ever called home."

"Inclusive leaders enhance their leadership capabilities when they publicly support human right initiatives," says Korn Ferry's Tej Singh Hazra, an associate client partner. "A domain once considered too risky by the general counsel."

"It seems inclusive leadership is the most difficult for leaders," comments Heather Holland, a management and human capital consultant and an expert in mediation and arbitration, in a LinkedIn post about these types of issues. "Not because of lack of skill but because at some point it will likely require one to go against the status quo."[5]

*   *   *

CONCLUSION

Creating Inclusive Organizations—Who Has the Last Word?

WE HAVE JUST PERFORMED A BOOK-LENGTH DISSECTION of what an inclusive leader looks like. We have shared the five disciplines and then deconstructed them into the various detailed traits and competencies required to deploy them. We have learned from exemplary individuals and organizations. We have delved into various new trends and hopefully have presented new insights into the issues we face in designing the equitable and inclusive organizations of the future.

But . . .

While we used what we know about leadership and derived new insights with new research, a new and younger generation of inclusive leaders is emerging, with a radical perspective that is already defying our understanding of how transformation will happen.

Our research has been very influenced by the existing hierarchical organizational and leadership paradigm. Therefore, our model serves to activate and develop leaders that are inclusive, up and down the organization. This is a good, powerful, and necessary thing right now. There is much work to do here that will yield very good results in the near and medium term.

Note how we wrote "up and down the organization." That is simply not how Millennials, and Gen Z right behind them, see things. They are upending this twentieth-century downstream model with a horizontal, crowdsourced, inclusive leadership approach.

And so via focus groups we tested how our assumptions and findings would play out with people in those generational groups—male and female and from a range of countries in Africa, Europe, and Latin America, plus India and the United States.[1] These younger generations will make up more than 70% of the workforce in 2025,[2] and while most are not yet fully in positions of power and do not have broad influence in critical mass numbers, they will—soon.

We examined how they choose to be inclusive, and here's what we found. First, like the inclusive leaders we interviewed for the study, they see inclusiveness as about empathy, accepting others for who they are, and seeking out and valuing others' points of view. One statement by a Ghanaian in our Africa virtual focus group demonstrates their alignment with current diversity and inclusion aspirations: "Being in an inclusive environment makes me feel alive and where I don't have to act. I can be my authentic self. Where I will not be second-guessed and am invited to contribute. That would feel like home." In addition, they had an alternate view of how leadership works to achieve inclusive transformation.

CROWDSOURCED INCLUSIVE LEADERSHIP

Can you name the leaders of Black Lives Matter, #MeToo, the student climate strikes, Occupy Wall Street, the Hong Kong resistance, or March for Our Lives? Other than Greta Thunberg, the Swedish environmental activist, probably not. Yet each of these youth-led movements has had a massive impact on awareness raising and societal change.

Inclusive leadership that seeks equity today and for the future is a major driver behind these movements, so much so that they are redefining the locus of control of leadership. Rather than residing in individuals, leadership resides in the collective. That's because these movements arose out of a distaste for existing leaders who allowed so much to go wrong: police brutality, climate change, student debt, socioeconomic inequality, pandemics, and the deep-seated systemic racism evidenced by the disproportionate number of incarcerations and killings of young people of color by those who are supposed to protect them, for example.

In corporate organizations, the youth are also dismayed by limited opportunities to advance, minimal investment in their growth and development, and the wide and growing pay gap between those at the bottom and those at the top. Rather than waiting around for their elders to model inclusion in action—since they often see so little of it—the next generation is doing it themselves.

We witnessed this in their spontaneous response after the Marjory Stoneman Douglas school shooting in Parkland, Florida, which felled seventeen students. Just five weeks after the tragedy, students mobilized more than eight hundred marches for stricter gun control measures across the United States and in multiple other countries, including several hundred thousand marchers in Washington, DC, alone.

At the DC march, 100% of the speakers were teens and preteens, though they were diverse in many other ways. They were focused, determined, eloquent, politically savvy, and consistent in their messaging. They expressed a combination of mourning and defiance, with commitments to action and to inclusion.

"We recognize that Parkland received more attention because of its affluence," said Jaclyn Corin, a White female survivor of the Parkland shooting. "But we share this stage today and forever with those communities who have always stared down the barrel of a gun."

After meeting with a group of teens in Chicago on the topic of gun violence, Parkland shooting survivor Emma González tweeted, "The platform us Parkland Students have established is to be shared with every person, black or white, gay or straight, religious or not, who has experienced gun violence, and hand in hand, side by side, We Will Make This Change Together."

This self-awareness has led to the embrace of their message by youth in urban areas strafed by gunfire, such as Chicago and Washington, DC.

Also consider the difference made by one lone protesting sixteen-year-old sitting outside the Swedish parliament building with a three-word sign reading "Skolstrejk För Klimatet" (School Strike for Climate). Within a year, Greta Thunberg inspired more than 4 million students to stage their own climate strike walkouts in 163 countries.[3] But she did not lead the effort; she was merely its catalytic conscience. It was the collective who then crowdsourced to mobilize millions.

Now take the recent demonstrations in Hong Kong to protest China's encroaching control of the territory. While many young people ended up in jail, there was no leader. In fact, most faces were covered by bandannas, gas masks, and even the mask of Anonymous. And they succeeded in getting parliament to rescind extradition to mainland China, and other policies.

The Black Lives Matter demonstrations in the Summer of 2020 and ongoing have been led by young people as well. Some of the largest marches in various cities were organized by teens.

These events happened on the street, far from the hallways of corporations and other organizations. But the same marchers and protesters are also working inside those organizational walls. They want to like their organizations, they want them to do better, and they are expecting more as their leaders say they seek to be more inclusive. Their expectations are high. And every year they move into more influential leadership roles.

The next generations are questioning inclusion at a meta level. They are saying that the system is not just flawed *within* the organizations (organizational structural inclusion) but also within society (societal structural inclusion). Wherever they look, they see institutions that have failed to deliver inclusion. No wonder the children of capitalists are embracing socialism in massive numbers. They are questioning a world run on fossil fuels that are leading to the warming of the planet. They are questioning education that puts many of them in lifelong debt. They are even questioning how we measure economic success.

In fact, the prime minister of New Zealand, Jacinda Ardern, announced in 2020 that the country is going to use a new measure of economic growth, the genuine progress indicator (GPI), to measure how well the economy is working for all groups, not just the dominant ones.

According to *Investopedia*, "The GPI indicator takes everything the GDP [gross domestic product] uses into account, but adds other figures that represent the cost of the negative effects related to economic activity (such as the cost of crime, cost of ozone depletion and cost of resource depletion, among others). The GPI nets the positive and negative results of economic growth to examine whether or not it has benefited people overall."[4]

THE HEAD AND HEART INCLUSIVE LEADERS

Transformational leadership guru Brené Brown, PhD, has had a particularly strong influence on Millennials and Gen Z. Her TED Talk on vulnerability was one of the most watched of all time, with more than 5 million views in 2020. Brown, who also authored *Daring Greatly: How the Courage to Be Vulnerable Transforms the Way We Live, Love, Parent, and Lead*, believes that the times demand that courage be demonstrated by being vulnerable.

While a growing number of inclusive leaders today, including those interviewed for this book, have succeeded in modeling vulnerability, Brown and her followers take it to a whole new level. This more vulnerable, psychologically present, and heart-centered perspective is what the next generations are craving. This is where they are taking the discourse of inclusive leadership—and don't expect them to make it easy for those of us who are uncomfortable with this approach.

Which leads us to one last key finding of our inclusive leadership research: this work is about marrying the head with the heart. In our sampling of twenty-four thousand broad-based leader assessments taken between 2015 and 2019, we unearthed a clustering of traits and disciplines around two types of inclusive leaders: those who led with the heart and those who led with the head.

The heart-led cluster stood out for its high average scores on the people-related traits of *authenticity* and *emotional resilience* and the disciplines of *optimizes talent, integrates diverse perspectives*, and *builds interpersonal trust*. The other cluster had high average scores on the enabling traits of *flexibility* and *inquisitiveness* and the disciplines *applies an adaptive mindset* and *achieves transformation*. This more mindset- and action-oriented cluster exemplifies leading with the head.

Even those who are inclusive have to learn new ways of leading. Heart-centered leaders must develop an approach to D&I that leads to organizational impact, while head-centered leaders must work on not only achieving greater diversity and inclusion but also leveraging it for business and organizational results. Their impact will be limited if they are not emotionally connected with the diversity of people they are leading.

These findings around head and heart reinforce what Millennials and Gen Z are telling us.

Millennials and Gen Zers all over the world are setting a higher bar for their leaders and themselves. Without the need of any research of their own but rather from their values and lived experiences, they told us in no uncertain terms what they already knew: to be truly inclusive, they must lead with head and heart.

In the Latin American focus group of Millennials and Gen Z professionals, participants told us how different their lives and societal experiences are compared to their bosses and their parents. Their parents don't understand why a straight woman would join the gay pride parade in Santiago. Their bosses wonder why people need to be "valued," since they are getting paid to do what they are supposed to do. Or why corporations need to be mindful of being inclusive of indigenous or Afro-Latin talent. Or why it's wrong to think—and say out loud—that they don't want their children to have female or Black teachers.

A focus group participant said, "We have gay friends, and women are going to college and getting jobs to get ahead, and not just get married. We are also not accepting the growing economic inequality our parents grew up with and did not question."

In this focus group, one young professional said, "I wouldn't be able to work at a place for very long if I don't see the upper-level people adhere to the value they preach." But others added that they expect everyone around them to exercise inclusive behaviors; they do not see it as being just the domain of a handful of leaders. Cecilia Pinzón, Korn Ferry's diversity and inclusion leader in Latin America, agrees. "When we first started in D&I in Latin America, many of us were observers. D&I was seen as being about others. Now it's about all of us. We just can't only be observers anymore," she says.

Another person in the same focus group declared that, given his generation's values, it was only a matter of time before the new norms would kick in: "As more Millennials come into leadership, it means more people supporting diversity, so it will change."

In the Indian focus group, several participants gravitated toward the areas of socioeconomic inclusion. "It is the lowest level of workforce that does the cleaning work, but it belongs to the largest population. They do this work because they want to make sure that their children will not have to. Organizations need to create a level of equality among their employees by washing the plates after you eat and not having different areas for them to sit, or cutlery to use."

They agreed that even in India's highly traditional and hierarchical culture, dynamics are changing. "If you join an organization at a midmanager level and contribute good, innovative ideas, the leaders are open to these types of suggestions, creating a better place to work."

Both the Indian and African focus groups mentioned technology as an enabler of inclusion. A member of the India group said, "[With digital,] the systems are getting more decentralized and more horizontal. This will lead to more inclusion." Someone in the Africa group noted, "Due to AI [artificial intelligence] and technology, people will be asking for much more transparency, because they will already have a lot of information available to them. And leaders will need to follow the needs of the people."

For the African professionals, respect for the environment is an important aspect of inclusion. "An inclusive society doesn't just talk about inequality, race, et cetera, but is also a society that respects the environment. Climate change is a new trigger which will make us go back to fighting among humans, so we will need to talk about climate change in a way that is inclusive of all."

The group also explained how much their view of leadership has changed from that of past generations. "It used to be that when a military leader came into town, everyone would be excited by his very presence," said one. "But today, you don't see this reaction. Their leadership will be defined by whether they are doing the right thing."

Another stated, "With our generation of young leaders, there is the need of understanding that a position doesn't make a leader; the leader makes the position."

The need for heart-and-head leaders is strong and will only grow as these younger generations step into greater positions of influence in the workplace. But we have a long way to go.

In our quantitative look at nineteen industries in our global database, we found that only 1% to 10% of leaders are skilled inclusive leaders. Furthermore, no leader had scores in the top 25% of all the disciplines and trait clusters. This staggering data pushed us to think bigger than just developing individual leaders. We must develop whole organizations.

While helping leaders fill their individual gaps, organizations need to approach inclusive leadership in a collective manner—as teams, groups, and the organization as a whole. Together, everyone in the organization needs to practice the head *and* heart of inclusive leadership if they want to reap its benefits. It's going to require a systemic approach.

COURAGE AND WILL

We know what the issues are around diversity and inclusion, and in many ways we know what needs to be done. We know the root causes, and that addressing them requires addressing legacy inequities through structural inclusion, behavioral inclusion, and inclusive design principles.

Yet, as with climate change, we remain paralyzed in truly creating equitable organizations. Why? What's missing? What does it take to achieve the deeply desired yet elusive transformation toward greater diversity and inclusion?

At a profound and human level, it requires more courage and will.

Courage to even ask the question "Do inequities exist?" and, when they are confirmed, to confront the past wrongs and make them right. Courage to walk in the shoes of those who are different from oneself. Courage to go to their environments, to see things from their perspective. Courage to sit in the crucible of conflict and listen deeply to what is not being said. Courage to be curious and exploratory about what makes those unlike us different in how they think, feel, and act. Courage to share stories of our own journeys and how they have shaped our view of the world.

And the will to see the changes through, since transformation takes more than one cool training experience or high-profile initiative. It's a long journey to get to sustained cultural change. It is not for the faint of heart.

Do you have the courage and will to unleash the power of all us?

■　　■　　■

Appendix A

BONUS TRACKS: SPOTLIGHTS ON THE ENABLING TRAITS AND STRUCTURAL INCLUSION

AVA DUVERNAY: SEEING THE REAL US

AUTHENTICITY ▪ *Johné Battle, Miami*

When They See Us is not just the title of Ava DuVernay's powerful four-part Netflix series about how the Central Park Five teenagers were falsely accused of rape and how long it took to prove their innocence. (They lost five to twelve years of their lives in prison.) It is also her clarion call for inclusion through authenticity, which has driven her mission-driven filmmaking.

DuVernay's work as a writer, director, producer, and film distributor has included the historical civil rights drama *Selma*, the criminal justice documentary *13th*, and blockbuster hits such as Disney's *A Wrinkle in Time*, which grossed more than $100 million at the box office with its norm-breaking diverse cast.

These hits have made DuVernay the highest-grossing Black woman director in box office history, and the most decorated. She has garnered the Academy's Best Picture nomination for *Selma*, and the film won the award for Best Original Song; sixteen Emmy nominations and two Emmy Awards; a British Academy of Film and Television Arts award; and a Peabody Award. When she's not working on her projects, DuVernay is inspiring the work of other people of color and of women through her nonprofit film collective, ARRAY, which was named one of *Fast Company*'s Most Innovative Companies. She also sits on the advisory board of the Academy of Television Arts and Sciences and chairs the Prada Diversity Council.

DuVernay has created a movement grounded in being authentic to what matters most *to* her, what matters most *about* her, yet all in the cinematic frame of *us*.[1] She's intentional about reframing old narratives that may have painted us in a less than positive light, in ways that challenge all to rethink what we may have thought to be true. According to Oprah Winfrey, "Ava has the rare ability to capture humanity in all of its beauty, ugliness, and truth. . . . She has a gift for illuminating the stories of the underrepresented and unseen."

When They See Us, for example, "takes boys who were . . . reduced to an indistinguishable pack of animals . . . and insists that they be viewed as individuals, children worthy of love, and then years later, men worthy of justice," writes film critic Emily Nussbaum in a *New Yorker* review. "If they're free, we're free." In recalling meeting with the men whose stories she captured in the Netflix series, DuVernay reflects, "I think of the day that the men wept in my arms and I wept in theirs as they told me that I told their story better than they could have imagined."

Hers is one of these stories. From the tough streets of Compton, California, she has arrived at a pinnacle where she is doing the groundbreaking artistic work she loves, with purpose and impact. "There's a lot of really beautiful work that's left by the wayside because it just hasn't pierced through the cultural consciousness," says DuVernay. She's committed to doing more of the piercing through the authentic telling of more stories of those who have been overlooked and misunderstood.

"I'm really fortunate to be in a position now to make work that I love, with my own independent vision. . . . [This] is a rarified honor . . . especially for someone who looks like me, someone who looks like us."[2]

NELSON MANDELA WAS NOT BROKEN

EMOTIONAL RESILIENCE ▪ *Fayruz Kirtzman, New York City*

Not too long ago, I stood in front of cell number 5, a seven-by-nine-foot room in desolate maximum security prison Robben Island, five miles offshore from Cape Town, South Africa. There, Nelson Mandela had slept naked on a damp and cold concrete floor, a lightbulb burning bright twenty-four hours a day, seven days a week, for thirteen of his twenty-seven years behind bars, for fighting against the racist apartheid regime. In addition, he had done forced labor, breaking rock at the quarry for many hours a day. He could only receive one visitor a year, for thirty minutes, and one letter every six months.

To this day, I still cannot shake the juxtaposition between the cruelty and dehumanizing treatment Mandela received over such a long period of time and his refusal to succumb to dehumanizing his own captors.

How did he manage to accomplish this?

Mandela demonstrated emotional resilience in every aspect of his life. His composure amid the most dire of circumstances was singular. He did not crack. He did not riot. Instead, he lobbied for pajamas, he petitioned for medical care when needed, he influenced the slowing of the walking pace to the quarry to a more sustainable one. He often used disarming humor to win his captors over, like the time when he referred to the eight guards who had escorted him to an interrogation as his "honor guard." And whatever concessions he won he did not accept for himself, unless his fellow prisoners also received them.

Mandela also exemplified situational awareness; while never giving up his fight for human rights, he sought to truly understand his opponent. He urged his fellow inmates to study Afrikaans, despite their objection that it was the language of the oppressor. His reasoning was clear: "We are in for a protracted war. You can't dream of ambushing the enemy if you can't understand the general commanding the forces. You have to read their literature and poetry, you have to understand their culture so that you get into the mind of the general."[3]

The impact on those around him was profound. In 1978, an eighteen-year-old pro-apartheid prison guard, Christo Brand, was assigned to guard Mandela. He says, "When I came to the prison, Nelson Mandela was already sixty. He was down-to-earth and courteous. He treated me with respect and my respect for him grew. After a while, even though he was a prisoner, a friendship grew. It was a friendship behind bars." This friendship lasted even after Mandela was released, and it extended to Brand's family.[4]

Mandela's situational awareness extended far into his postprison life. He knew that despite the widespread support he was receiving, there was an element of "White fear" in his country, and he worked to alleviate rather than ignore it. He entered into a government of national unity with Frederik Willem de Klerk, the former president of South Africa's National Party. Mandela invited for lunch Percy Yutar, the man who had once headed the prosecution against him and who had called for his death sentence. After this meeting, Yutar called Mandela "a saintly man." Both Mandela and de Klerk won the Nobel Peace Prize in 1993 for their efforts to reform their country.

In 2002, Mandela wrote, "Today when I look at Robben Island I see it as a celebration of the struggle and a symbol of the finest qualities of the human spirit . . . rather than as a monument to the brutal tyranny and oppression of apartheid."[5]

This is emotional resilience—the key to Mandela's inclusive leadership. And that is why his country to this day calls him Madiba, "Father of the Nation."

MINDY KALING HAS NO APOLOGIES

SELF-ASSURANCE ▪ *Karen Huang, Philadelphia*

Shortly after Molly Patel (played by Mindy Kaling on *Late Night*, the Amazon original comedy written by her) lands her dream job as the sole woman on a team of White male comedy writers, she overhears Tom (played by Reid Scott) complaining about her getting hired instead of his brother. "Right now is a hostile environment in which to be an educated White male . . . It's staggering how unfair it is . . . They completely overlooked my brother. She's like a diversity hire or something." Tom, we later learn, inherited his job from his father.

Much to his chagrin, he turns around midconversation to see Molly glaring at him. She snaps, "I'd rather be a diversity hire than a nepotism hire, because at least I had to beat out every minority and woman to get here. He just had to be born."

In fact, Kaling herself was hired through NBC's diversity writing program, but she did not possess the wherewithal, at age twenty-four, to confidently speak up for what she deserved. She explains, "For a long time I was really embarrassed about that. No one [on *The Office*] said anything to me about it, but they all knew and I was acutely aware of that. It took me a while to realize that I was just getting the access other people had because of who they knew."[6] In the years since, Kaling has won awards, critical acclaim, and fans and become one of the few women of color to achieve Hollywood success for herself and for inclusion.

Rather than let others box her in with her race, ethnicity, gender, or appearance, Kaling has expanded the mainstream ideals of beauty, introduced noncéd, diverse characters to a broad audience, challenged the diminishing assumptions that thwart women of color, and demonstrated that including diverse perspectives is "actually valuable and a better way to make money and to reach more people."[7] Crucial to these accomplishments is her self-assurance, a belief that she can succeed by being herself because her original ideas, talent, personality, and appearance have value just as they are. Like Molly, she had the confidence to defy typecasting and to unapologetically take a seat at the table for herself and for other people of color by writing characterful, diverse roles and stories that simply didn't exist in Hollywood.

For *The Mindy Project*, a romantic sitcom that Kaling created and starred in, she invented Dr. Mindy Lahiri, a hilarious, unabashedly boy-crazy, fashion-obsessed, self-proclaimed "hottie" ob-gyn doctor who confidently grabs attention, unlike the stereotypically thin, smart, "model minority" Asian female characters favored by Hollywood. As such, Dr. Lahiri was hailed as the most subversive female lead of 2014.[8]

Kaling's self-assurance has also led her to champion inclusive diversity behind the camera. Her cadre of writers is always diverse. Kaling explains, "For many years, I thought that hard work was the only way you could succeed, but it's simply not true . . . Particularly if you're a woman of color, you need people to give you opportunities, because otherwise it won't happen."[9]

Finally, Kaling has used her self-assurance to challenge people—primarily male interviewers—to examine their exclusionary ideas and assumptions about women and success.

While doing press for *Late Night*, a journalist asked Kaling if she has "impostor syndrome." She replied, "I actually don't, because I've really put in the time," and she questioned his implicit assumptions by noting that a thirty-nine-year-old man would never be asked if he felt like an impostor for writing a movie.[10]

In response to the *Where do you get your confidence?* question that male journalists frequently ask her, she notes the insulting reasoning behind it: "You [Mindy] don't look like a person who should have any confidence. You're not White, you're not a man, and you're not thin or conventionally attractive. How were you able to overlook these obvious shortcomings to feel confident?"[11]

Mic drop, Kaling.

SEEING WELL BEYOND THE SURFACE

INQUISITIVENESS ▪ *Sahar Sarreshtehdari, Berlin*

How did the Korn Ferry executive search senior partner figure out that a doctoral candidate finishing her thesis on memory cultures of diaspora communities, using second-generation Iranian immigrants in Germany as the case study, had what it took to be an executive search consultant?

A few years ago, the person who is my manager today saw me in action in Berlin at an annual convention for Iranian diaspora business-people in technology. More than two thousand Iranians, Germans, and North Americans had come together to network, exchange ideas, and work together.

My team and I were in charge of looking after the speakers and making sure the sessions ran smoothly. A Korn Ferry partner was attending the conference, given his long-standing interest in Iran. We spoke briefly, and that's when I shared information about the thesis I was working on. He asked me some insightful questions about why I had picked the topic and how I had gone about the research.

We stayed in touch over the next year while I continued to live in Munich, and one day, via LinkedIn, he reached out to ask me what my plans were. It was good timing. I had not quite settled on an academic career track yet, but I did not know much about what else was out there. He asked whether I would be interested in exploring a career in executive search. At the time, I didn't even know what that was!

Nevertheless, being the adventurous type, and given that he kept telling me he saw qualities in me that would be valuable in executive search, I accepted his invitation to visit Korn Ferry's Frankfurt office. It would be the first time for me seeing a corporation from the inside. As I flew to the interview, I wondered how someone like me, who was not corporate in demeanor and thinking, could be effective in a fast-paced, commercially driven environment.

After a full day of interviews, the partner actively sought to understand how I was experiencing the process. What was I thinking and feeling about the people I was meeting? Could I see myself doing the work? He pointed out how someone with my curiosity and research abilities would do very well in finding greater diversity for our clients' candidate pools.

I found myself learning new things about myself in this new context.

The partner's curiosity about what motivated me, my own different cultural background, and the unique ways in which I saw the world was a demonstration of his inclusive leadership. Through his inquisitiveness, I felt valued and appreciated precisely because of my own diversity.

Here was a leader who wanted to learn from me but was also very effective at helping me learn new things about myself. It completely changed my professional life.

———————■———————

FLEXIBILITY IS NOT JUST GOOD FOR YOGA

FLEXIBILITY ■ *Kristin Hibler, Portland*

Performing improv, explains comedian Ryan Stiles of the American improvisation show *Whose Line Is It Anyway?*, is like jumping out of an airplane and knitting your parachute on the way down. Improvisers make up a story in real time, with other people, in front of a live audience. It requires an extreme openness to ambiguity and the unknown.

Inclusive organizational leaders also must be great at improvising. It makes me think of two leaders—one who did it well and one who didn't—and the impact it had on their ability to achieve business objectives.

"Maria" (name and identifying details changed), a general manager at a global hotel chain, is a corporate improviser. After successfully establishing three US-based hotels, she was sent to Japan to open the hotel chain's first hotel in the Asia-Pacific region. When she arrived, she quickly learned that the rules were different.

For example, she noticed that decisions didn't get made during meetings. It was as if all the strategic ones had been made well in advance. She learned that if she wanted to get buy-in and move forward with big decisions, she would have to spend more time having "meetings before the meetings," building engagement and consensus in advance to ensure there would be no loss of face during an actual meeting. She changed her approach, and it worked. Her team appreciated the time she had taken to learn their way of doing things, instead of forcing her way. This built inclusion and, with that, trust.

In essence, Maria improvised to manage the diversity around her. She jumped in and tried things, even though the path ahead was not clear. The key to her improvised flexibility was getting to know and understand the differences around her; it provided the necessary guidance through uncharted waters.

While Maria's flexibility enabled her success, the lack of flexibility shown by her colleague "Jason" hindered his. Jason was the general manager for the chain's Boston location and had been tapped to open its first hotel in Africa. Ethiopia was a risky location, given its slow (but growing) tourist and business footprint. But if anyone could do it, management thought, Jason could. In Boston, he was known as a logistics rock star who excelled at cutting through red tape.

However, within several months, it became clear that what worked in Boston wasn't going to work in Addis Ababa. The red tape was all too familiar, but cutting through it was a different story. Jason hit road-blocks at every turn. His quick, decisive, and tough style had led to stellar results in Boston. In Addis, though, he was way behind sched-ule and not getting much done.

Jason was perplexed and frustrated that what had been surefire ways for getting things done was not working. He had put together an operational plan with an aggressive timeline, established key per-formance indicators for each of his teams, and empowered them to implement. Meanwhile, he assumed responsibility for engaging their senior stakeholders.

His inflexibility was his downfall. As someone used to getting straight to the point with his contemporaries, he had seen little value in the Ethiopian cultural ways of doing things. He judged it as wasting time through recurring and protracted ceremonial coffee sessions.

Not surprisingly, the local politicians and business leaders, whose buy-in was critical for the hotel chain, ended up calling him "the Steamroller."

In contrast, halfway around the world, Maria, despite also being in a culturally different environment, was called "the Improviser."

———— ▪ ————

FILMMAKER ALFONSO CUARÓN HAS US SEE WHAT OTHERS SEE

EMPATHY ■ *Gustavo Gisbert, Chicago and Caracas*

Mexican director Alfonso Cuarón's 2019 Oscar-winning story *Roma*, told through the eyes of Cleo, an indigenous domestic worker in a middle-class home in Mexico City, was a cinematic and societal breakthrough.

At the core of Cuarón's tour de force was his powerful debiasing approach: empathy. He chose to not use his own middle-class perspective to tell the story. Instead, he took the more difficult route of telling it through the perspective of his real-life nanny, Liboria "Libo" Rodriguez. He spent hours with her to capture how she remembered the past. The many surprises in how different their memories were led to a much more powerful film.

Cuarón used empathy to shed light on what makes us both the same and different to one another. He reflects on how a unique and differentiated story can paradoxically uncover universal human experiences: "[*Roma*] is a film about a very specific family, in a very specific society, in a very specific time in history, but at the end . . . it's about something that we all share as humans."[12]

"I see [life] as a crack in the wall," says Cuarón. "The crack is whatever pain happened in the past. We tend to put several coats of paint over it, trying to cover that crack. But it's still there."[13]

Cuarón's empathy is grounded in knowing his own story. From street vendor scenes in Mexico City's plazas to political violence interrupting mundane activities, he shows awareness of his unique cultural experiences and humility in not trying to cover the cracks. The pain, the perplexing experiences, the things he valued most, he opens these up to audiences to explore freely on their own.

Now Cuarón's empathetic art is significantly influencing change. Cleo's story is a look at an era intimately known by Mexicans but never narrated from the perspective of someone historically ignored. The movie character represents the more than 2.4 million domestic workers across present-day Mexico, more than 95% of whom are female and from indigenous areas and who have been discriminated against through abuse and injustice. And the story within the story is that lead actress Yalitza Aparicio, who gave a breakout performance as Cleo, had never been in a movie before. Cuarón discovered her acting skills in rural Mexico.

Cuarón's nonmainstream approach led to blockbuster ratings among a diverse array of audiences and has influenced millions—in fact, the whole culture—to consider embracing those who have traditionally been excluded. To do so, he found ways to make the strange familiar, the differences valued, the discomfort comfortable.

"The emotional reaction of people that watched the film," says Cuarón, "gives me hope for diversity."[14]

■

LAUNCHING ONE THOUSAND INCLUSIVE LEADERS

STRUCTURAL INCLUSION ▪ *Marji Marcus, Boston*

To make the transformation toward greater diversity and inclusion, leaders at the very top must become inclusive leaders. But they cannot create an inclusive culture alone. What they need is one thousand inclusive leaders in every corner of the organization.

Imagine if one thousand inclusive leaders could learn to recognize different learning and thinking styles, build rapport and trust with those both alike and different from them, invite new people to the table, and actively seek out contributions from those who bring different experiences to the discussion, and thus elicit the personal best from each individual.

Imagine if one thousand inclusive leaders were practicing inclusion in talent review discussions, when deciding whom to bring onto a team, or when assigning a plum developmental opportunity.

Imagine if one thousand inclusive leaders were rewarded for desired inclusive behaviors just as they were rewarded for achieving other goals, such as winning clients or meeting sales targets.

But how can an organization exponentially multiply its number of inclusive leaders?

It requires the ability to provide knowledge and develop skills in a scalable way. While the top twelve or the top one hundred will have access to deep assessments measuring inclusive leadership, as well as executive coaching and other reinforcing interventions, the large group of middle managers must be ramped up differently. One of the most intractable unresolved obstacles to advancing diversity and inclusion is the mindset of the middle manager—you know, the one who hires and fires, and develops and promotes. Or not.

For sure, training is foundational. But so is access to just-in-time tools they can use to interrupt their unconscious biases. They need structurally inclusive processes and systems so that job requirements, behaviorally based interviews, success profiles, and other evaluative tools are bias free. They need methodologies such as inclusive design approaches that they can capably apply to remedy department-specific inequities. And they need to be as capable as many have become in Six Sigma and safety procedures.

Finally, managers need to be understood by their organizations. They face myriad pressures that compete for their time and attention. They, too, need to feel included, valued, respected, and supported in ways that help them to perform *and* to become inclusive leaders. As organizations demonstrate greater empathy toward their middle managers, those managers will be more curious about their own team members and will better see the unique value that each person brings.

When this type of behavior proliferates across an organization, the true benefits of a diverse and inclusive organization will start to be realized and sustained—one manager, one team, one department, one function at a time.

It's time to unleash one thousand inclusive leaders in your organization.

■

Appendix B

RESEARCH METHODS BEHIND KORN FERRY'S INCLUSIVE LEADER MODEL

THE FINDINGS IN THIS BOOK DRAW ON multiple original research methods used to collect and analyze data that includes psychometric-based assessments, surveys, interviews, and focus groups. The results provide a rich, scientifically grounded lens with which to define and measure inclusive leadership. Throughout this book, we have used general language to describe key concepts, while explaining technical terms where necessary.

More detailed descriptions of the various scientific and field-based research methods we used to develop the inclusive leader model are presented here.

ASSESSMENT DATA ANALYSIS

In collaboration with the Korn Ferry Institute, we developed an Inclusive Leader model based on Korn Ferry's "whole person" assessment data, especially the data on competencies and traits, and on the deep subject matter expertise of Korn Ferry's diversity and inclusion consultants. Then, we conducted analyses to test the model and to use it to better understand inclusive leadership.

TESTING THE INCLUSIVE LEADER COMPETENCIES AND TRAITS COMPOSITES

The process was as follows: Based on deep field experience doing diversity and inclusion strategy and programmatic and coaching work, and on the growing literature on cultural agility, we delved into the Korn Ferry library of competencies and traits to develop a hypothesis of what an inclusive leader would look like. Next, we conducted analyses to test our hypothetical model by validating the competency and trait composites. Specifically, we tested whether observed data fit the proposed mapping of competencies and traits. That is, we analyzed data to evaluate whether our proposed map of competencies accurately portrayed how scores on our competency measures relate to each other. Similarly, we analyzed data to evaluate whether our proposed trait clusters reflected relationships among trait scores.

Both the competencies and traits were measured with Korn Ferry assessments that use forced choice response options, combined with item response theory–based scoring. The forced choice response option format reduces the opportunity to either consciously or unintentionally distort responses, while the scoring method used helps avoid a problem that has affected most forced choice tests in the past. This problem, known as ipsativity, involves an individual's scores being inappropriately restricted. In essence, scores on one part of an ipsative assessment fix or determine the scores on another. Scores that are ipsative should not be used for some statistical analyses or for comparing one person to another.

We consistently find that leaders who score higher on Korn Ferry assessments are more highly engaged in their jobs. For example, leaders who closely fit with traits and drivers in client-customized profiles are up to thirteen times more likely to be highly engaged in their jobs.[1] Our longitudinal research also has found that executives' scores on Korn Ferry competencies, traits, and drivers also are related to job performance about one year later.[2] Therefore, the Korn Ferry Inclusive Leader model includes competencies and traits that are relevant to leadership roles and predictive of leaders' success in their roles.

Analyses also previously demonstrated that Korn Ferry's assessments have good reliability. This means that the assessments meet or exceed guidelines for how consistently people are expected to score on them.[3] For example, all things being equal, if a person takes the assessment multiple times, the scores will be similar across those times.

The specific analysis we used to test the fit of the observed data to our models is called confirmatory factor analysis, which is a type or subset of analysis within structural equation modeling. We used commercially available software to execute these analyses (IBM's SPSS module, called AMOS). Comparable analyses could be executed on other software, including R, which is in the public domain.

Best practice guidelines for interpreting the results of structural equation models, including confirmatory factor analyses, call for computing multiple fit indexes. Different indexes have different strengths and limitations, providing different insights on fit. Those we examined, including the root mean square error of approximation (RMSEA), the Tucker-Lewis index (TLI), and comparative fit index (CFI), were within standards indicating good fit. (For competencies, $RMSEA = 0.05$, $CFI = 0.94$, Tucker–Lewis index [TLI] $= 0.91$; for traits, $RMSEA = 0.06$, $CFI = 0.95$, $TLI = 0.90$.)

Consequently, this research provides support for the validity of the Inclusive Leader model. When rolled together as the model indicates, scores on the competency and trait clusters provide meaningful insights.

Thus, Korn Ferry's Inclusive Leader assessment is a scientifically supported and field-researched instrument informed by analysis of Korn Ferry's database. The Inclusive Leader assessment captures thirteen competencies and eleven traits, each organized in five key clusters. The five trait clusters are referred to as the enabling traits, and the five competency clusters make up the five disciplines.

INCLUSIVE LEADERS BY REGION, INDUSTRY, AND FUNCTION

One of the questions we were curious about was where the inclusive leaders are. Are there more (or fewer) inclusive leaders in different regions, industries, or functional areas?

To address this question, we again utilized a data set compiled by Korn Ferry from individuals around the globe, who typically had been invited by an organization to complete our assessments. We computed scores on the five enabling trait composites and the five disciplines of inclusive leadership for approximately twenty-four thousand leaders, who ranged from C-suite leaders to first-level team leads.

Then we examined the scores to see what proportion of leaders scored in the top twenty-fifth percentile on all ten composites. Interestingly, we found that no one did. Leaders who score high across many of the inclusive leader disciplines and enabling trait composites are rare. Only about 5% of leaders are in the top twenty-fifth percentile on six or more composites. This means the model sets a very high standard.

Of course, there were variations. Nearly 10% of leaders working for nonprofits are in the top twenty-fifth percentile on six or more composites, followed by about 9% in government and 7% in health-care delivery. By country, New Zealand (13%), Australia (11%), the United Arab Emirates (10%), and the United States (10%) have the highest percentage of inclusive leaders. Note that these results reflect the leaders in our data set who are working in these countries, not the culture of the country itself.

As for the functional roles, the highest percentage of inclusive leaders was in creative and among executives/general management. The functional roles with the next higher percentage of inclusive leaders are technology, human resources, and financial services. Those with the lowest percentages of inclusive leaders were administrative services, legal, and sales.

HEAD AND HEART INCLUSIVE LEADERS

Using the same data set, we examined, via cluster analysis, the patterns of scores to see if there tended to be any typical profiles of strengths across the ten inclusive leader composites. A number of distinct patterns emerged.

One pattern involves high average scores on two enabling trait composites (**flexibility** and **inquisitiveness**) and two competency composites (**applies an adaptive mindset** and **achieves transformation**). This cluster can be described as more mindset- and action-oriented, and people with score profiles like this one may be thought of as leading inclusively with their heads.

In contrast, a second cluster stood out for high average scores on people-related constructs. With high scores on two trait clusters (**authenticity** and **emotional resilience**) and three competency clusters (**optimizes talent, integrates diverse perspectives,** and **builds interpersonal trust**), these leaders can be described as leading with their hearts.

Taken together, our research shows that we can assess inclusive leadership in a sound, psychometrically based way using Korn Ferry's world-renowned leadership assessment tool, and then coach accordingly. The head and heart clusters provide additional ways to interpret the assessment results and to interpret their implications for individual leadership and coaching, as well as organizational strategy for greater inclusion.

INCLUSIVE LEADER SURVEY WITH DIVERSITY AND INCLUSION, HUMAN RESOURCES, AND TALENT EXPERTS

Once we had our scientifically tested model, we applied traditional work analysis methods and sought out the opinions of diversity and inclusion, HR, and talent management experts, asking whether, in their experience and knowledge, what we had identified as core competency and trait clusters are important to being an effective inclusive leader.

This approach is a well-established step in the process of describing jobs and figuring out the tasks and/or knowledge, skills, and other abilities that are needed to successfully perform a particular job or role. In conventional work analysis, the ratings are provided by those familiar with the role—typically job incumbents or their supervisors. We adapted the method to evaluate by asking D&I, HR, and talent management leaders and professionals what competencies and traits are important to being an effective inclusive leader.

An invitation to complete the survey was sent out via email to a group of leaders and professionals on Korn Ferry's diversity and inclusion newsletter mailing list. The survey was set up in Qualtrics. We received insights from twenty-five participants, and although the sample size is not quite large enough to meet minimum thresholds for certain types of statistical analyses (conventionally, $n = 30$), it is robust from a qualitative perspective.

To help understand who responded, the survey included questions about people's background, jobs, and careers. Not everyone completing the survey answered these questions about themselves. Of those who did:

- 57% identified as female, 39% identified as male, and 4% chose not to say;
- 13% were 31 to 40 years old, 39% were 41 to 50, 39% were 51 to 60, 9% were 61 and over; and
- 96% were from North America.

Most of the respondents were seasoned experts. Thirty percent were senior executives who report to the CEO, 43% were senior leaders, 9% were midlevel managers, 9% were first-level supervisors, and 9% were individual contributors. And a majority of those who reported their experience had worked more than ten years in human resources, diversity and inclusion, or talent management.

The results, which have been summarized throughout this book, reinforce the importance of the inclusive leadership traits and competencies. Almost all respondents rated all of the inclusive leader competencies as extremely important or very important to being an effective inclusive leader. A somewhat smaller but still substantial majority saw all the inclusive leader traits as extremely important or very important to being an effective inclusive leader. This pattern is consistent with traits being enablers of inclusivity.

GATHERING PERSPECTIVES ON INCLUSIVE LEADER IMPACT ON TALENT

Among the survey respondents, there was complete or near consensus on the positive impact inclusive leaders have on their talent, including helping talent to feel free to bring their authentic selves to work, giving them a sense of empowerment, reassuring them that there is fairness, and ensuring that they will be challenged with stretch opportunities (see table B-1).

GATHERING PERSPECTIVES ON INCLUSIVE LEADER IMPACT ON ORGANIZATIONAL GOALS

Consensus also showed up in the survey participants' beliefs about the impact inclusive leaders have on their organizations, including leading

Table B-1: How Inclusive Leaders Help Individuals

INCLUSIVE LEADERS HELP INDIVIDUALS FEEL:	STRONGLY AGREE (%)	AGREE (%)	STRONGLY AGREE + TOTAL AGREE (%)
Safe and free to be their authentic self	72	28	100
Committed, believing that everybody is working toward a common cause	40	60	100
Clarity around what is expected from them	40	60	100
Empowered to take risks	64	32	96
Sense of fairness that rewards and recognition are linked directly to performance	64	28	92
Consistent sense of stretch from challenging yet attainable goals being set for them	32	60	92

Source: Korn Ferry Inclusive Leader survey, 2019–2020.

their organization to greater innovation, fostering marketplace growth, creating more inclusive management practices, and influencing their organizations to embrace diversity as a vital part of an economic business case (see table B-2).

GATHERING PERSPECTIVES ON IMPACT OF EXPERIENCES ON INCLUSIVE LEADERSHIP

Among the survey respondents, diverse experiences were not considered as important to being an inclusive leader as were the inclusive leader competencies and traits. Yet it was still rated extremely or very important by 24% to 48% of respondents (table B-3). The range was due to the type of experience. The highest vote getter was having had the experience of working in an organization with a meaningful amount of diversity; 48% said this was extremely or very important. The lowest

Table B-2: How Inclusive Leaders Help Organizations

INCLUSIVE LEADERS HELP ORGANIZATIONS:	STRONGLY AGREE (%)	AGREE (%)	STRONGLY AGREE + TOTAL AGREE (%)
Leverage diversity to build a strong innovation portfolio and capitalize on new business opportunities	64	36	100
Create momentum for an initiative by incorporating inclusive change management practices	68	24	92
See demographic diversity as a growth opportunity	84	16	100

Source: Korn Ferry Inclusive Leader survey, 2019–2020.

scored experience (24%) was having lived in a different country or in a heterogeneous region within one's own country.

Table B-3: Why Leaders Should Seek New Experiences

VALUE OF DIFFERENT TYPES OF EXPERIENCES FOR INCLUSIVE LEADERSHIP EFFECTIVENESS	EXTREMELY IMPORTANT (%)	VERY IMPORTANT (%)	EXTREMELY IMPORTANT + VERY IMPORTANT (%)
Working in an organization with a meaningful amount of diversity	12	36	48
Leading a key change initiative across different levels	4	36	40
Working in different organizations, sectors, or functions	8	24	32
Having lived in a different country or a heterogeneous region within one's own country	20	4	24
Looks to new and diverse experiences for personal development and organizational benefit	68	32	100

Source: Korn Ferry Inclusive Leader survey, 2019–2020

While there were mixed opinions about the importance of *past* diverse experiences, there was unanimous consent (when combining the *extremely important* and *very important* answers) that inclusive leaders must seek to gain new and diverse experiences in the *present* and the *future*. Additional experiences that were seen as valuable were those where leaders not only received something but also were actively involved in giving something back. Specifically, sixty-eight percent said sponsoring and mentoring people from different backgrounds was extremely or very important.

LEADER INTERVIEWS

Using the Inclusive Leader model to obtain examples of inclusive leadership in action, we conducted interviews with inclusive leaders who were nominated by others from various organizations across the globe. We interviewed inclusive leaders from Austria, Brazil, China, France, Germany, Hungary, India, Norway, Saudi Arabia, Spain, the United States. (For the full list of leaders, titles, companies, and countries see the acknowledgments.)

In conducting the interviews, we used a behavioral-based interview protocol that sought examples of how these leaders had demonstrated inclusive leadership behaviors in each of the competencies within each of the five disciplines. We also obtained formative biographical and career information from each of them to better contextualize who they were as inclusive leaders.

We did not formally probe these leaders on the enabling traits, though we were able to infer a good amount of how certain traits manifested for these leaders. Nevertheless, the main objective of these interviews was to obtain qualitative data around the five disciplines.

YOUNG PROFESSIONALS FOCUS GROUPS

At the back end of our research, we went out to test how our assumptions and findings would play out with young professionals of the Millennial and Gen Z generations, who are not yet fully in positions of power and broad influence in critical mass numbers but who soon will be.

We did this by desk research, examining trends as documented in various journalistic and academic publications on how these two younger generations (who will make up over 70% of the workforce by 2025 and will keep increasing their percentage every year after that) choose to be inclusive. We then heard it in their own words during five mixed-gender focus groups, in Africa, Asia, Europe, Latin America, and the United States. These focus groups were all conducted virtually, as detailed in chapter 12.

Appendix C

RESOURCES

H ERE ARE SOME RESOURCES TO FURTHER DEVELOP inclusive leadership skills. For help from Korn Ferry contact us at:

clientsupport@kornferry.com

CONSULTING

Korn Ferry offers consulting services related to every dimension of diversity, equity, and inclusion, to companies and organizations in every sector, at any level of their organizational diversity and inclusion maturity.

ASSESSMENT AND COACHING

Korn Ferry's Inclusive™ Leader assessment, debrief, and coaching can be done at the executive, senior leader, manager, and individual contributor level, at varying levels of depth and application.

LEARNING

- The Inclusive™ Leader executive learning suite
- Conscious Inclusion™ workshop
- Making Inclusive Hiring Decisions™ workshop
- Inclusive Recruiting™ workshop
- The Inclusive™ Leader Digital Journeys is an experience that takes a learner through a short series of learning assets, such as assessments, coaching sessions, videos, courses, readings, and activities, that each focus on one task, behavior, or competency.
- FastStart Pairs™ is paired coaching with various tools to help a leader hiring someone from an underrepresented group ensure their successful onboarding.

JUST-IN-TIME TOOLKITS

Just-in-time toolkits intended to disrupt bias include:

- *Disrupting Bias in Hiring*
- *Disrupting Bias in Developing Talent*
- *Disrupting Bias in Managing Performance*

WHITE PAPERS/ARTICLES

To access our white papers and articles, go to https://www.kornferry.com/insights. Scroll down on the left-hand bar to the Filters menu. Under "By Topic," select "Diversity and Inclusion."

BOOKS

Altered Traits: Science Reveals How Meditation Changes Your Mind, Brain, and Body, by Daniel Goleman and Richard J. Davidson

Applied Empathy: The New Language of Leadership, by Michael Ventura

The Art of Empathy: A Complete Guide to Life's Most Essential Skill, by Karla McLaren

Auténtico: The Definitive Guide to Latino Career Success, by Robert Rodriguez, PhD, and Andrés T. Tapia

Blindspot: Hidden Biases of Good People, by Mahzarin R. Banaji and Anthony G. Greenwald

Blink: The Power of Thinking Without Thinking, by Malcolm Gladwell

The Diversity Bonus: How Great Teams Pay Off in the Knowledge Economy, by Scott Page

The Emotional Life of Your Brain: How Its Unique Patterns Affect the Way You Think, Feel, and Live—and How You Can Change Them, by Richard J. Davidson and Sharon Begley

Erasing Institutional Bias: How to Create Systemic Change for Organizational Inclusion, by Tiffany Jana and Ashley Diaz Mejias

Everyday Bias: Identifying and Navigating Unconscious Judgments in Our Daily Lives, by Howard J. Ross

The Inclusion Paradox: The Post-Obama Era and the Transformation of Global Diversity, by Andrés T. Tapia

One Second Ahead: Enhance Your Performance at Work with Mindfulness, by Gillian Coutts, Jacqueline Carter, and Rasmus Hougaard

The Pause Principle: Step Back to Lead Forward, by Kevin Cashman

The Person You Mean to Be: How Good People Fight Bias, by Dolly Chugh

The Power of Choice: Embracing Efficacy to Drive Your Career, by Michael Hyter

Thinking, Fast and Slow, by Daniel Kahneman

Triggers: Sparking Positive Change and Making It Last, by Marshall Goldsmith and Mark Reiter

We Can't Talk About That at Work!: How to Talk About Race, Religion, Politics, and Other Polarizing Topics, by Mary-Frances Winters

Whistling Vivaldi: How Stereotypes Affect Us and What We Can Do, by Claude M. Steele

White Fragility: Why It's So Hard for White People to Talk About Racism, by Robin DiAngelo

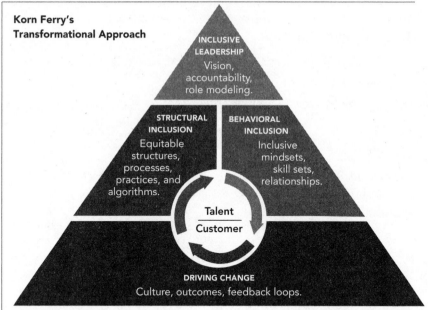

Korn Ferry's Transformational Approach

INCLUSIVE LEADERSHIP
Vision, accountability, role modeling.

STRUCTURAL INCLUSION
Equitable structures, processes, practices, and algorithms.

BEHAVIORAL INCLUSION
Inclusive mindsets, skill sets, relationships.

Talent
Customer

DRIVING CHANGE
Culture, outcomes, feedback loops.

A systemic approach to building an inclusive organization. Korn Ferry, 2020.

How We Help

Build Inclusive Leadership	Architect Structural Inclusion	Shape Behavioral Inclusion	Drive and Sustain Change
■ **Help CEOs** shape their Diversity, Equity & Inclusion (DE&I) commitments. Coach them on how to lead change.	■ **Rapid as well as comprehensive diagnosis of talent management practices** to uncover areas of bias.	■ **Help people become more inclusive in their daily work** through learning experiences such as: Conscious Inclusion, Managing Inclusion, Inclusive Hiring and the Race Matters series.	■ Provide **pragmatic and action-oriented guidance** on how to make change happen–including what to prioritize and **how to get started** fast.
■ Develop evidence-based **DE&I strategies** aligned to business and talent priorities.	■ **Build transparent, equitable talent processes** through inclusive design techniques.	■ **Reinforce inclusive behaviors** though Korn Ferry Activators (tools, guides, micro-eLearning, videos).	■ Develop a **communication strategy** and plan that incorporates listening channels and feedback loops.
■ **Assess senior leaders** against the **Korn Ferry Inclusive Leader model**. Make recommendations on development areas.	■ **Accelerate the talent pipeline** by attracting and recruiting diverse talent at all levels, and uncovering internal hidden talent via increased access, opportunity, development, and rewards.	■ **Unleash the power of underrepresented groups** through a wide range of high-impact development programs including:	■ Help facilitate dialogue and **difficult conversations**.
■ **Provide training and development** to help leaders become fully equipped and accountable for the implementation of the DE&I strategy.	■ **Pay equity analysis** and design of inclusive reward strategies.	■ Power of Choice for racially underrepresented and other groups	■ Establish governance mechanisms to **track and measure outcomes**.
	■ Build agile, smart, and **inclusive teams** that harness their diversity to outperform.	■ Advancing women worldwide	■ Embed DE&I in the organization's DNA through use of **tools, technology, processes**, and **structures**.
		■ FastStart pairs onboarding	
		■ 3 new modules specific to Race Matters series	

How we help clients build diverse and inclusive organizations. Korn Ferry, 2020.

NOTES

Foreword

1. Ajay Banga, "MasterCard CEO Ajay Banga's Six Lessons on Leadership—as Told to the IIM-A Class of 2015," *Quartz India*, April 7, 2015, https://qz.com/india/377104/ajay-bangas-six-lessons-on-leadership-as-told-to-the-iim-a-class-of-2015.

2. Carl DiOrio, "Jackson Pushes Biz on Diversity," *Hollywood Reporter*, February 22, 2007, https://www.hollywoodreporter.com/news/jackson-pushes-biz-diversity-130667.

3. Andrew Sullivan, "Anderson Cooper: 'The Fact Is, I'm Gay,'" *The Dish*, July 2, 2012, http://dish.andrewsullivan.com/2012/07/02/anderson-cooper-the-fact-is-im-gay.

Preface

1. McKinsey & Company, *Diversity Wins: How Inclusion Matters*, May 2020, https://www.mckinsey.com/~/media/McKinsey/Featured%20Insights/Diversity%20and%20Inclusion/Diversity%20wins%20How%20inclusion%20matters/Diversity-wins-How-inclusion-matters-vF.ashx.

2. The global business certification standard for equality, https://edge-cert.org/.

3. See Deb DeHaas, Linda Akutagawa, and Skip Spriggs, "Missing Pieces Report: The 2018 Board Diversity Census of Women and Minorities on Fortune 500 Boards," Harvard Law School Forum on Corporate Governance, https://corpgov.law.harvard.edu/2019/02/05/missing-pieces-report-the-2018-board-diversity-census-of-women-and-minorities-on-fortune-500-boards; and Matt Orsagh, "The Current State of Women on Boards in 2016: A Global Roundup," CFA Institute, https://www.cfainstitute.org/en/advocacy/market-integrity-insights/2016/10/the-current-status-of-women-on-boards-in-2016-a-global-roundup. The MSCI ESG Research global director universe is a compilation of 4,218 companies from around the world.

4. See Khristopher J. Brooks, "Why So Many Black Business Professionals Are Missing from the C-Suite," *CBS News*, December 10, 2019, https://www.cbsnews.com/news/black-professionals-hold-only-3-percent-of-executive-jobs-1-percent-of-ceo-jobs-at-fortune-500-firms-new-report-says; Stefanie K. Johnson and Thomas Sy, "Why Aren't There More Asian Americans in Leadership Positions?," December 19, 2016, https://hbr.org/2016/12/why-arent-there-more-asian-americans-in-leadership-positions; Hispanic Association on Corporate Responsibility, "HACR Released 2016 Corporate Inclusion Index, Produces Findings for Hispanic Inclusion in Corporate America," March 16, 2018, https://www.hacr.org/2016/12/19/hacr-releases-2016-corporate-inclusion-index; and Drew DeSilver, "Women Scarce at Top of US Business—and in the Jobs That Lead There," Pew Research Center Fact Tank, April 30, 2018, https://www.pewresearch.org/fact-tank/2018/04/30/women-scarce-at-top-of-u-s-business-and-in-the-jobs-that-lead-there.

Introduction. Defining the Inclusive Leader

1. Data in figure 1 is from *Diversity and Inclusion in Corporate Social Engagement*, CEO Force for Good, 2018, p. 4, https://cecp.co/wp-content/uploads/2018/12/ cecp_di_whitepaper_FINAL.pdf (70% higher growth); Sylvia Ann Hewlett, Melinda Marshall, and Laura Sherbin, with Tara Gonsalves, *Innovation, Diversity, and Market Growth*, executive summary, Center for Talent Innovation, 2013, p. 6, https://www.talentinnovation.org/_private/assets/IDMG-ExecSummFINAL-CTI.pdf (75% faster time to market); Erik Larson, *Infographic: Diversity + Inclusion=Better Decision Making At Work*, Cloverpop, September 19, 2017, https://www.cloverpop. com/blog/infographic-diversity-inclusionbetter-decision-making-at-work (87% better decisions); Vivian Hunt, Sara Prince, Sundiatu Dixon-Fyle, and Kevin Doan, Diversity wins: How inclusion matters, May 2020, https://www.mckinsey.com/~/media/McKinsey/Featured%20Insights/Diversity%20and%20Inclusion/Diversity%20wins%20How%20inclusion%20matters/Diversity-wins-How-inclusion-matters-vF.ashx (36% better profitability); Rocío Lorenzo, Nicole Voigt, Miki Tsusaka, Matt Krentz, and Katie Abouzahr, *How Diverse Leadership Teams Boost Innovation*, January 23, 2018, https://www.bcg.com/publications/2018/how-diverse-leadership-teams-boost-innovation.aspx (19% better innovation); and "Korn Ferry Partners with *Fortune* for the 21st Year on World's Most Admired Companies List," Korn Ferry, January 30, 2019, https://www.kornferry. com/about-us//press/korn-ferry-partners-with-fortune-for-the-21st-year-on-worlds-most-admired-companies-list (87% impact on performance). Also see *Inclusive Mobility: How Mobilizing a Diverse Workforce Can Drive Business Results*, Deloitte, 2018, p. 4, https://www2.deloitte.com/content/dam/Deloitte/us/Documents/Tax/us-tax-inclusive-mobility-mobilize-diverse-workforce-drive-business-performance.pdf.

2. Nancy J. Adler, *International Dimensions of Organizational Behavior*, 4th ed. (Cincinnati, OH: Thomson South-Western, 2002).

The Core of Inclusive Leadership: The Enabling Traits

1. Erving Goffman, *Stigma: Notes on the Management of Spoiled Identity* (New York: Simon & Schuster, 1963), 102–104.

2. Christie Smith and Kenji Yoshino, *Uncovering Talent: A New Model of Inclusion*, Deloitte Development, 2019, https://www2.deloitte.com/content/dam/Deloitte/us/Documents/about-deloitte/us-about-deloitte-uncovering-talent-a-new-model-of-inclusion.pdf.

3. Milton J. Bennett, "A Developmental Approach to Training for Intercultural Sensitivity," *International Journal of Intercultural Relations* 10, no. 2 (1986): 179–196. This full model, specifically, is measured by the Intercultural Development Inventory.

4. Andrés T. Tapia, *The Inclusion Paradox: The Obama Era and the Transformation of Global Diversity*, 3rd ed. (Los Angeles: Korn Ferry Institute, 2016).

5. Jeanine Prime and Elizabeth R. Salib, "The Secret to Inclusion in Australian Workplaces: Psychological Safety," Catalyst, 2015, https://www.catalyst.org/wp-content/uploads/2019/02/the_secret_to_inclusion_in_australian_workplaces.pdf.

6. Brent W. Roberts and Daniel Mroczek, "Personality Trait Change in Adulthood," *Current Directions in Psychological Science* 17, no. 1 (2008): 31–35.

7. J. J. A. Denissen, M. Luhmann, J. M. Chung, and W. Bleidorn, "Transactions Between Life Events and Personality Traits Across the Adult Lifespan," *Journal of Personality and Social Psychology* 116, no. 4 (2019): 612–633.

8. Melinda Gates, *The Moment of Lift* (New York: Flatiron Books, 2019), 19.

9. Ann Scott Tyson, "Melinda Gates: What She's Learned," *Christian Science Monitor*, September 18, 2019, https://www.csmonitor.com/World/Making-a-difference/2019/0918/Melinda-Gates-What-she-s-learned.

Chapter 1. Discipline 1: Builds Interpersonal Trust

1. Robert M. Sapolsky, *Behave: The Biology of Humans at Our Best and Worst* (New York: Penguin, 2017).

Chapter 2. Discipline 2: Integrates Diverse Perspectives

1. Katherine W. Phillips, "How Diversity Makes Us Smarter," *Scientific American*, October 1, 2014, https://www.scientificamerican.com/article/how-diversity-makes-us-smarter.

Chapter 3. Discipline 3: Optimizes Talent

1. These terms are from the founder of the field of intercultural communication, anthropologist Edward T. Hall. A high-context communication style relies on implicit communication and nonverbal cues. In high-context communication, a message cannot be understood without a great deal of background information. Asian, African, Arab, Central European, and Latin American cultures are generally considered to be high-context cultures. A low-context communication style relies on explicit communication. In low-context cultures, more of the information in a message is spelled out and defined. Cultures with Western European roots, such as the United States and Australia, are generally considered to be low-context cultures. See Hall, *The Silent Language* (New York: Anchor Books, 1959).

2. Survey results from 170 companies, with 6.6 million employees across 172 countries and a variety of industries.

3. Barnabas Piper, "The 40 Best Quotes from *Creativity, Inc.*," September 10, 2015, https://barnabaspiper.com/2015/09/the-40-best-quotes-from-creativity-inc.html.

4. "Leadership Lessons from Ed Catmull's *Creativity, Inc.*," Slack blog, August 20, 2018, https://slackhq.com/leadership-lessons-from-ed-catmulls-creativity-inc.

5. Alex Samur, "Collaborative Leadership: Moving from Top-Down to Team-centric," Slack blog, March 19, 2019, https://slackhq.com/collaborative-leadership-top-down-team-centric.

6. Beth Stackpole, "Why Pixar Founder Ed Catmull Wants You to 'Fail the Elevator Test,'" MIT Management Sloan School, May 8, 2019, https://mitsloan.mit.edu/ideas-made-to-matter/why-pixar-founder-ed-catmull-wants-you-to-fail-elevator-test.

7. Anita Woolley, Thomas W. Malone, and Christopher F. Chabris, "Why Some Teams Are Smarter Than Others," *New York Times*, January 16, 2015, https://www.nytimes.com/2015/01/18/opinion/sunday/why-some-teams-are-smarter-than-others.html.

Chapter 4. Discipline 4: Applies an Adaptive Mindset

1. Justin Bariso, "This Is the Book That Inspired Microsoft's Turnaround, According to CEO Satya Nadella," *Inc.*, November 26, 2018, https://www.inc.com/justin-bariso/this-is-book-that-inspired-microsofts-turnaround-according-to-ceo-satya-nadella.html.

2. "Mission and Vision," Microsoft, https://www.microsoft.com/en-us/about. Accessed September 2, 2019.

3. Amit Chowdhry, "Microsoft CEO Satya Nadella Apologizes for Comments on Women's Pay," *Forbes*, October 10, 2014, https://www.forbes.com/sites/amitchowdhry/2014/10/10/microsoft-ceo-satya-nadella-apologizes-for-comments-on-womens-pay/#61730d436d2b.

4. Chowdhry, "Microsoft CEO Satya Nadella Apologizes."

5. Amelia Lester, "The Roots of Jacinda Ardern's Extraordinary Leadership After Christchurch," *New Yorker*, March 23, 2019, https://www.newyorker.com/culture/culture-desk/what-jacinda-arderns-leadership-means-to-new-zealand-and-to-the-world.

6. Suzanne Moore, "Jacinda Ardern Is Showing the World What Real Leadership Is: Sympathy, Love and Integrity," *Guardian*, March 18, 2019, https://www.theguardian.com/commentisfree/2019/mar/18/jacinda-ardern-is-showing-the-world-what-real-leadership-is-sympathy-love-and-integrity.

7. Charlotte Graham-McLay, "Jacinda Ardern Pitched New Zealand's Charms. Now She Speaks of Its Pain," *New York Times*, March 16, 2019, https://www.nytimes.com/2019/03/16/world/asia/jacinda-ardern-new-zealand-christchurch.html.

8. Michael Hirtzer, "Cotton Makes a Comeback in U.S. Plains as Farmers Sour on Wheat," *Reuters*, May 29, 2018, https://www.reuters.com/article/us-usa-cotton-plantings-idUSKCN1IU0E4.

9. "Microsoft CEO Satya Nadella: How Empathy Sparks Innovation," *Knowledge@Wharton*, February 22, 2018, https://knowledge.wharton.upenn.edu/article/microsofts-ceo-on-how-empathy-sparks-innovation.

Chapter 5. Discipline 5: Achieves Transformation

1. Matthew J. Gibney and Randall Hansen, eds., *Immigration and Asylum: From 1900 to the Present*, vol. 2 (Santa Barbara, CA: ABC-CLIO), 405.

2. Iain Walker, "Saudi Arabia and Its Immigrants," Centre on Migration, Policy, and Society (COMPAS), August 13, 2013, https://www.compas.ox.ac.uk/2013/saudi-arabia-and-its-immigrants.

3. Justin Wolfers, "Fewer Women Run Big Companies Than Men Named John," *New York Times*, March 2, 2015, https://www.nytimes.com/2015/03/03/upshot/fewer-women-run-big-companies-than-men-named-john.html.

4. "'One Hundred Percent Wrong Club' Speech," January 20, 1956, Library of Congress, Manuscript Division, Branch Rickey Papers, https://www.loc.gov/collections/jackie-robinson-baseball/articles-and-essays/baseball-the-color-line-and-jackie-robinson/one-hundred-percent-wrong-club-speech.

5. David Oshinsky, "The Man Who Hired Jackie Robinson," *New York Times*, March 25, 2011, https://www.nytimes.com/2011/03/27/books/review/the-man-who-hired-jackie-robinson.html.

6. Vivian Nunez, "Monica Ramirez Talks the Bandana Project, Her Latinidad, and Her Career in Farmworkers Advocacy," *Forbes*, April 25, 2019, https://www.forbes.com/sites/viviannunez/2019/04/25/monica-ramirez-talks-the-bandana-project-her-latinidad-and-her-career-in-farmworkers-advocacy/#442155153ecb.

7. Mónica Ramírez, interview, available at *Today*, "America Ferrera Speaks Out About 'Time's Up' Anti-Harassment Plan," video, 4:57, January 4, 2018, https://www.youtube.com/watch?v=9qQNn9Ip-nE.

8. Tamara Best, "Mónica Ramírez's #MeToo Lesson for Hollywood, Straight from the Farm," *Daily Beast*, March 12, 2018, https://www.thedailybeast.com/monica-ramirezs-metoo-lesson-for-hollywood-straight-from-the-farm.

9. Intel Newsroom, "Intel Diversity in Technology Initiative," press kit, December 10, 2019, https://newsroom.intel.com/press-kits/intel-diversity-in-technology-initiative/#gs.xoflyu.

10. Ben Hubbard and Vivian Yee, "Saudi Arabia Extends New Rights to Women in Blow to Oppressive System," *New York Times*, August 2, 2019, https://www.nytimes.com/2019/08/02/world/middleeast/saudi-arabia-guardianship.html.

11. Bonnie Reilly Schmidt, "Women on the Force," *Canada's History*, March 15, 2016, https://www.canadashistory.ca/explore/women/women-on-the-force.

12. Manitoba Status of Women Division, *Women and Policing in Canada: A Status Brief and Discussion Paper* (Winnipeg: Manitoba Status of Women Secretariat, 2014).

13. Manitoba Status of Women Division, *Women and Policing in Canada*, 4.

14. Bonnie Ann Reilly Schmidt, "Women in Red Serge: Female Police Bodies and the Disruption to the Image of the Royal Canadian Mounted Police" (PhD diss., Simon Fraser University, 2013).

Chapter 7. John Deere: Inclusive Leadership Feeds the World

1. Roberto Baldwin, "John Deere Wants to Remind the World That It's a Tech Company," *Engadget*, January 17, 2019, https://www.engadget.com/2019/01/17/john-deere-autonomous-technology.

2. John Deere, "Feed the World: A Challenge and an Opportunity," *John Deere Journal*, December 2, 2015, https://johndeerejournal.com/2015/12/smallholder-farmers-big-challenges.

Chapter 8. Marriott: Where Everyone Belongs

1. Sarah Clemence, Ed Frauenheim, and Christopher Tkaczyk, "A New Marriott—for All and By All," Great Place to Work Institute, https://www.greatplacetowork.com/resources/reports/a-new-marriott-for-all-and-by-all.

2. Abha Bhattarai, "Lavish Indian Weddings Help DC-Area Hotels Turn Handsome Profit," *Washington Post*, https://www.washingtonpost.com/business/2015/02/13/89e874e8-b210-11e4-886b-c22184f27c35_story.html.

3. Meredith Barack, "Muncie-Based Program Urging Employers to Hire More People with Disabilities," *Hiring Hoosiers*, January 3, 2019, https://www.theindychannel.com/news/hiring-hoosiers/muncie-based-program-urging-employers-to-hire-more-people-with-disabilities.

4. Danielle Douglas, "Marriott's Next Boss May Sound Like Its Namesake, but Arne Sorenson Is No Clone," *Washington Post*, December, 18, 2011, https://www.washingtonpost.com/business/economy/marriotts-next-boss-may-sound-like-its-namesake-but-arne-sorenson-is-no-clone/2011/12/15/gIQAqQ1220_story.html.

Chapter 10. Structural Inclusion: Confronting the Reference Man Norms That Leave Most of Us Out

1. Zahra Mulroy, "Chilling Reason Why Women Are More Likely to Die in a Car Crash Then [*sic*] a Man, *Mirror*, February 26, 2019, https://www.mirror.co.uk/news/world-news/chilling-reason-women-more-likely-14056777.

2. Sukhvinder S. Obhi, email message to authors, March 15, 2020.

3. *Inclusive Microsoft Design*, Microsoft, 2016, https://download.microsoft.com/download/b/0/d/b0d4bf87-09ce-4417-8f28-d60703d672ed/inclusive_toolkit_manual_final.pdf, 8.

4. Kat Holmes, *Mismatch: How Inclusion Shapes Design* (Cambridge, MA: MIT Press, 2018), 4.

5. Kate Clark, "Female Founders Have Brought In just 2.2% of US VC This Year (Yes, Again)," *TechCrunch*, November 4, 2018, https://techcrunch.com/2018/11/04/female-founders-have-brought-in-just-2-2-of-us-vc-this-year-yes-again.

6. "Our Mission," Kapor Capital, https://www.kaporcapital.com/who-we-are.

7. "SMASH Academy," SMASH, https://www.smash.org/programs/smash-academy.

8. Lauren A. Rivera, "The Paper" in *Pedigree: How Elite Students Get Elite Jobs*, 83–112. Princeton; Oxford: Princeton University Press, 2015. Accessed June 8, 2020. https://www.jstor.org/stable/j.ctv7h0sdf.

9. Neal Goodman, "Unconscious Bias," *Training*, July 16, 2014, https://trainingmag.com/trgmag-article/unconscious-bias.

Chapter 11. Identity Inclusion: The Perennial Unfinished Business of Race and Gender

1. Content on colorism and race in this chapter is heavily influenced by thinking and excerpts from Katherine W. Phillips, Paul Calello, and Andrés T. Tapia, "Does Race Still Matter?: Moving Toward a New Global Conversation on Race and Colorism," *Diversity Best Practices News*, special issue, July 2013, https://www.diversitybestpractices.com/sites/diversitybestpractices.com/files/import/embedded/anchors/files/does_race_still_matter.7.2013.pdf; Robert Rodriguez and Andrés Tomás Tapia, *Auténtico: The Definitive Guide to Latino Career Success* (Chicago: Latinx Institute Press, 2017); and various blog posts and articles put out by the Korn Ferry Black, Latino, and Asian think tanks.

2. Don Gonyea, "Majority of White Americans Say They Believe Whites Face Discrimination," NPR, October 24, 2017, https://www.npr.org/2017/10/24/559604836/majority-of-white-americans-think-theyre-discriminated-against.

3. ANI, "Tackling the 'Snow White Syndrome' in India," *Rediff.com*, April 12, 2010, http://getahead.rediff.com/report/2010/apr/12/tackling-the-snow-white-syndrome-in-india.htm.

4. Phillip Martin, "Why White Skin Is All the Rage in India," PRI, November 25, 2009, https://www.pri.org/stories/2009-11-25/why-white-skin-all-rage-asia.

5. "Brazil 2010 Census Shows Changing Race Balance," BBC, November 17, 2011, https://www.bbc.com/news/world-latin-america-15766840.

6. Marianne Bertrand and Sendhil Mullainathan, "Are Emily and Greg More Employable Than Lakisha and Jamal? A Field Experiment on Labor Market Discrimination," *American Economic Review* 9 (September 4, 2004), 991–1013.

7. Devah Pager, Bruce Western, and Bart Binikowski, "Discrimination in a Low-Wage Labor Market: A Field Experiment," *American Sociological Review* 75, no. 5 (2009): 777–799.

8. Brando Simeo Starkey, "Why We Must Talk About the Asian-American Story, Too," *The Undefeated*, November 3, 2016, https://theundefeated.com/features/why-we-must-talk-about-the-asian-american-story-too.

9. "Korn Ferry Study Reveals United States Black P&L Leaders Are Some of the Highest Performing Executives in the US C-Suite," *Business Wire*, October 10, 2019, https://www.businesswire.com/news/home/20191010005567/en/Korn-Ferry-Study-Reveals-United-States-Black.

10. Karen Huang, "Asian American Women as Leaders Abolish So Many Stereotypes," LinkedIn, July 12, 2019, linkedin.com/pulse/asian-american-women-leaders-abolish-so-many-karen-huang-ph-d-/.

11. Huang, "Asian American Women as Leaders."

12. Claire Zillman and Emma Hinchliffe, "Where Are Wall Street's Women CEOs? The Broadsheet," *Fortune*, September 19, 2019, https://fortune.com/2019/09/19/where-are-wall-streets-women-ceos-the-broadsheet.

13. Corilyn Shropshire, "Women in the Workplace: The Glass Ceiling May Be Breaking—But Now the 'Broken Rung' Blocks Advancement," *Chicago Tribune*, October 18, 2019, https://www.chicagotribune.com/business/ct-biz-lean-in-mckinsey-women-work-survey-20191018-nq2hykzxqnbitata7ge5sbdlvy-story.html.

14. World Economic Forum, "Closing the Gender Gap Accelerators," https://www.weforum.org/projects/closing-the-gender-gap-accelerators.

15. Korn Ferry, "New Report by Korn Ferry and the Conference Board," March 6, 2019, https://www.kornferry.com/about-us/press/new-report-by-korn-ferry-and-the-conference-board.

16. Sheryl Sandberg and Rachel Thomas, "Sheryl Sandberg: The Gender Gap Isn't Just Unfair, It's Bad for Business," *Wall Street Journal*, October 15, 2019, https://www.wsj.com/articles/sheryl-sandberg-the-gender-gap-isnt-just-unfair-its-bad-for-business-11571112300.

17. American Express, "Number of Women-Owned Businesses Increased Nearly 3,000% Since 1972, According to New Research," August 21, 2018, https://about.americanexpress.com/press-release/research-insights/number-women-owned-businesses-increased-nearly-3000-1972-according.

18. Nadya A. Fouad and Romila Singh, "Stemming the Tide: Why Women Engineers Stay in, or Leave, the Engineering Profession," in *Career Choices of Female Engineers: A Summary of a Workshop*, ed. Sara Frueh, appendix D (Washington, DC: National Academies Press, 2011), 30–37. https://www.nap.edu/read/18810/chapter/11.

19. Marcus Noland and Tyler Moran, "Study: Firms with More Women in the C-Suite Are More Profitable," *Harvard Business Review*, February 8, 2016, https://hbr.org/2016/02/study-firms-with-more-women-in-the-c-suite-are-more-profitable; "Globally, Companies Lose $160 Trillion in Wealth Due to Earnings Gaps Between Women and Men," World Bank, May 30, 2018, https://www.worldbank.org/en/news/press-release/2018/05/30/globally-countries-lose-160-trillion-in-wealth-due-to-earnings-gaps-between-women-and-men; Jodie Gunzberg, Beth Ann Bovino, and Jason Gold, "Adding More Women to the US Workforce Could Send Global Stock Markets Soaring," S&P Global, 2018, https://www.spglobal.com/_Assets/documents/corporate/Adding-More-Women-To-The-US-Workforce.pdf.

20. Kal Raustiala and Chris Sprigman, "Who Owns the Korean Taco?," *Freakonomics*, July 2, 2010, https://freakonomics.com/2010/07/02/who-owns-the-korean-taco/.

21. Andrea Johnson, comment on Andrés T. Tapia's "Is Identity in Our Blood? What 23andMe Says—and Does Not Say—About Us," LinkedIn, https://www.linkedin.com/feed/update/urn:li:article:7665017998265119983?commentUrn=urn%3Ali%3Acomment%3A%28article%3A7665017998265119983%2C6575127729765789696%2.

22. Robinson Richard, "Creating an Inclusive Workplace: Integrating Employees with Disabilities into a Distribution Center Environment [Professional Safety]," *Insurance News Net*, June 14, 2012, https://insurancenewsnet.com/oarticle/Creating-an-Inclusive-Workplace-Integrating-Employees-With-Disabilities-Into-a-a-346155.

Chapter 12. Sociopolitical Inclusion: When the Outside Comes Inside

1. Andrew Ross Sorkin, "BlackRock CEO Larry Fink: Climate Crisis Will Reshape Finance," *New York Times*, January 14, 2020 (updated February 24, 2020), https://www.nytimes.com/2020/01/14/business/dealbook/larry-fink-blackrock-climate-change.html; Aimee Picchi, "Goldman Sachs' New IPO Rule: No More All-White, Male Boards," CBS News, January 24, 2020, https://www.cbsnews.com/news/goldman-sachs-diversity-ipo-women-minorities-david-solomon-davos.

2. United Airlines, "Protecting Immigrant Families and Defending the Rights of Asylum Seekers," October 29, 2019, https://donate.mileageplus.com/Charity/Details/334818.

3. Trevor Noah, *Born a Crime: Stories from a South African Childhood* (New York: Spiegel & Grau, 2016), 209.

4. Issa Rae, *The Misadventures of Awkward Black Girl* (New York: Atria, 2015), 163.

5. Heather Holland, comment on Andrés T. Tapia, "Inclusive Leadership: Standing Up for Those Who Take a Knee," LinkedIn, https://www.linkedin.com/feed/update/urn:li:article:7717680481133295045?commentUrn=urn%3Ali%3Acomment%3A%28article%3A7717680481133295045%2C6321089528652185600%2.

Conclusion. Creating Inclusive Organizations—Who Has the Last Word?

1. All of the focus groups were conducted virtually. The Africa focus group, with participants from Botswana, Côte d'Ivoire, Ghana, South Africa, Tanzania, and Zimbabwe, was conducted on February 12, 2020; the Latin America focus group, with participants from Chile and Colombia, was conducted on November 26, 2019; the Europe focus group, with participants from Germany, Spain, and Sweden, was conducted on December 16, 2019; the US focus group, with participants from California, Louisiana, New York, Texas, and Washington, DC, was conducted on December 18, 2019; and the India focus group was conducted on December 19, 2019.

2. Capital Global Employment Solutions, "Millennials and Gen Z—The New World of Work," December 13, 2018, https://www.capital-ges.com/millennials-and-generation-z-the-new-world-of-work.

3. Eliza Barclay and Brian Resnick, "How Big Was the Global Climate Strike? 4 Million People, Activists Estimate," *Vox*, September 22, 2019, https://www.vox.com/energy-and-environment/2019/9/20/20876143/climate-strike-2019-september-20-crowd-estimate.

4. Adam Hayes, "Genuine Progress Indicator (GPI)," *Investopedia*, July 8, 2019, https://www.investopedia.com/terms/g/gpi.asp.

Appendix A. Bonus Tracks: Spotlights on the Enabling Traits

1. Kellee Terrell, "#LocLife: Ava DuVernay Encourages Black Folks to Show Off Their Luxurious Locs with Pride," *Hello Beautiful*, September 6, 2019, https://hellobeautiful.com/playlist/loclife-ava-duvernay-encourages-black-folks-to-show-off-their-luxurious-locs-with-pride/item/29.

2. All quotes from Elaine Welteroth, "Ava DuVernay Is Going to Fix Our Country, One Film at a Time," *Glamour*, October 23, 2019, https://www.glamour.com/story/women-of-the-year-2019-ava-duvernay.

3. Mike Woolridge, "Mandela Death: How He Survived 27 Years in Prison," BBC News, December 11, 2013, https://www.bbc.com/news/world-africa-23618727.

4. Andrew Meldrum, "The Guard Who Really Was Mandela's Friend," *Guardian*, May 19, 2007, https://www.theguardian.com/world/2007/may/20/nelsonmandela.

5. Matthew Taub, "Nelson Mandela's Prison Cell, Through His Eyes," *Atlas Obscura*, https://www.atlasobscura.com/articles/nelson-mandela-prison-cell-drawing.

6. Hadley Freeman, "Mindy Kaling: 'I Was So Embarrassed About Being a Diversity Hire,'" *Guardian*, May 31, 2019, https://www.theguardian.com/film/2019/may/31/mindy-kaling-i-was-so-embarrassed-about-being-a-diversity-hire.

7. Brent Lang, "Mindy Kaling Created Her Own Opportunities (and Doesn't Plan on Stopping)," *Variety*, January 23, 2019, https://variety.com/2019/film/features/mindy-kaling-late-night-sundance-1203112400.

8. Antonia Blyth, "Mindy Kaling on How 'Late Night' Was Inspired by Her Own 'Diversity Hire' Experience & the Importance of Holding the Door Open for Others—Deadline Disruptors," *Deadline*, May 18, 2019, https://deadline.com/2019/05/mindy-kaling-late-night-the-office-disruptors-interview-news-1202610283.

9. Laura Berger, "Quote of the Day: Mindy Kaling & Nisha Ganatra on the Importance of Opening Doors for Others," *Women and Hollywood*, January 23, 2019, https://womenandhollywood.com/quote-of-the-day-mindy-kaling-nisha-ganatra-on-the-importance-of-opening-doors-for-others.

10. Freeman, "Mindy Kaling."

11. Mindy Kaling, *Why Not Me?* (New York: Crown Archetype, 2015), 216.

12. Kirk Semple, " Mexico City as the Director of 'Roma' Remembers It and Hears It," *New York Times*, January 2, 2019, https://www.nytimes.com/2019/01/02/movies/alfonso-cuaron-roma-mexico-city.html.

13. Kristopher Tapley, "Alfonso Cuarón on the Painful and Poetic Backstory Behind 'Roma,'" *Variety*, October 23, 2018, https://variety.com/2018/film/news/roma-alfonso-cuaron-netflix-libo-rodriguez-1202988695.

14. Gustavo Gisbert, "The Overlooked Inclusive Oscars," Korn Ferry, April 19, 2019, https://www.kornferry.com/insights/articles/oscar-academy-award-inclusion.

Appendix B. Research Methods behind Korn Ferry's Inclusive Leader Model

1. James L. Lewis and Jeff Jones, "Executive Insights: Fit Matters," Korn Ferry Institute, https://www.kornferry.com/content/dam/kornferry/docs/article-migration/Korn-Ferry-Institute-Fit-matters.pdf.

2. E. Susanne Blazek, Jeff A. Jones, James L. Lewis, and J. Evelyn Orr, "Proof Point: Leading Indicators," Korn Ferry Institute, https://www.aesc.org/sites/default/files/uploads/documents-2015/Korn-Ferry-Institute-ProofPoint-CEO-outcomes.pdf.

3. James L. Lewis, "Korn Ferry Four Dimensional Enterprise Assessment: Research Guide and Technical Manual," August 20, 2019, https://www.kornferry.com/content/dam/kornferry/docs/article-migration//KF4D_Executive_Manual_FINAL.pdf.

GLOSSARY

THIS GLOSSARY IS NOT INTENDED TO PROVIDE an exhaustive list of terms used in the work of diversity and inclusion. Neither is it intended to provide an authoritative definition to cover all circumstances and contexts. Here, we limit ourselves to the definitions of core, and at times differentiated, concepts used in this book.

available labor force The demographic representation of those in different job categories and professions who have the necessary qualifications in skills, education, and experience to do the job.

collective intelligence The positive cumulative and synergistic impact on an organization of the thinking, input, and ideas of the array of diverse individuals within it, working inclusively together.

diversity The mix.

equality A promise that no one will be favored or disfavored based on who they are.

equitable organization An organization in which there is no inequity in access, opportunity, support, and reward, and where outcomes in terms of promotions, achievements, recognitions, and representation are representationally reflective of the available labor force.

equity Examination if the promises of equality were fulfilled; if not, the steps taken to rectify the inequality.

inclusion Making the mix work.

inclusive design for talent systems A methodology for ensuring that talent systems are structured in ways that do not inadvertently or intentionally favor or disfavor any individual or groups of people based on who they are. It also is an approach in which those from all backgrounds have input, influence, and decision-making power.

Latinx Contemporary American English term increasingly used to refer to Latinos and Latinas who are members of Gen Y and Gen Z within the US. It's gaining in popularity—thought has not reached universal acceptance—for not being gender specific and therefore mitigates the use of the masculine form ("Latinos") when referring to a group made up of both Latinos and Latinas.

In this book, we used Latinos and Latinas when referring to male and female defined groups, Latinos when referring to the overall demographic group, and Latinx when specifically referring to Gen Y and Gen Z Latinos and Latinas. We chose not to use Latinx to refer to the overall demographic group due to Latinx not being embraced yet by a majority of Latinos as the all-encompassing term, though there's a growing acceptance to use this term when describing the intersectionality of being a Gen Y or Gen Z Latina or Latino.

overlooked user Talent whose needs, aspirations, and preferences have not been taken into account when talent systems have been designed.

Reference Man The default user around which talent systems have been designed. This default user is defined by those who have traditionally been in the majority and in power.

talent management disparities Areas in the talent management process and in work experience where specific demographic groups have fewer opportunities, access, development, and/or rewards compared to the majority, based on quantitative and qualitative data.

traditionally underrepresented talent Talent from demographic groups that are not reflected in proportional numbers in the workforce relative to their availability in talent pools.

BIBLIOGRAPHY

Banaji, Mahzarin, and Anthony G. Greenwald. *Blindspot: Hidden Biases of Good People*. New York: Delacorte Press, 2013.

Bennett, Milton J., ed. *Basic Concepts of Intercultural Communication*. Yarmouth, ME: Intercultural Press, 1998.

Bock, Lazlo. *Work Rules: Insights from Inside Google That Will Transform How You Live and Lead*. New York: Grand Central, 2015.

Bohnet, Iris. *What Works: Gender Equality by Design*. Cambridge, MA: The Belknap Press of Harvard University Press, 2016.

Broom, Michael F., and Donald C. Klein. *Power: The Infinite Game*. Ellicott City, MD: Sea Otter Press, 1999.

Carreyrou, John. *Bad Blood: Secrets and Lies in a Silicon Valley Startup*. New York: Random House, 2018.

Carr-Ruffino, Norma. *Managing Diversity: People Skills for a Multicultural Workplace*. 6th ed. Boston: Pearson, 2003.

Cashman, Kevin. *Leadership from the Inside Out: Becoming a Leader for Life*. San Francisco: Berrett-Koehler, 2008.

Catalyst. *The Bottom Line: Connecting Corporate Performance and Gender Diversity*. New York: Catalyst, 2004.

Coates, Ta-Nehisi. *Between the World and Me*. New York: Spiegel & Grau, 2015.

Cobbs, Price M., and Judith L. Turnock. *Cracking the Corporate Code: The Revealing Success Stories of 32 African American Executives*. New York: AMACOM, 2003.

Daugherty, Paul R., and James H. Wilson. *Human + Machine: Reimagining Work in the Age of AI*. Cambridge, MA: Harvard Business Press, 2018.

Davidds, Yasmin. *Take Back Your Power: How to Reclaim, Keep It, and Use It to Get What You Deserve*. Los Angeles: Atria, 2006.

Díaz, Junot. *The Brief Wondrous Life of Oscar Wao*. New York: Riverhead, 2008.

Eggers, Dave. *The Circle*. New York: Vintage, 2013.

Ellison, Ralph. *Invisible Man*. New York: Random House, 1952.

Eubanks, Virginia. *Automating Inequality: How High-Tech Tools Profile, Police, and Punish the Poor*. New York: St. Martin's, 2017.

Fraser, George C. *Click: Ten Truths for Building Extraordinary Relationships*. New York: McGraw-Hill, 2009.

García Márquez, Gabriel. *One Hundred Years of Solitude*. New York: Alfred A. Knopf, 1995.

Gladwell, Malcolm. *Blink: The Power of Thinking Without Thinking*. New York: Little, Brown, 2005.

Gladwell, Malcolm. *Outliers: The Story of Success*. New York: Little, Brown, 2008.

Gladwell, Malcolm. *The Tipping Point: How Little Things Can Make a Big Difference*. London: Abacus, 2000.

Griffin, John Howard. *Black Like Me*. London: Penguin, 1976.

Holmes, Kat. *Mismatch: How Inclusion Shapes Design*. Cambridge, MA: MIT Press, 2018.

Hyter, Michael, and Judith L. Turnock. *The Power of Inclusion: Unlock the Potential and Productivity of Your Workforce*. Toronto: Wiley, 2006.

Hyun, Jane. *Breaking the Bamboo Ceiling: Career Strategies for Asians*. New York: HarperCollins, 2005.

Kahneman, Daniel. *Thinking Fast and Slow*. New York: Farrar, Straus and Giroux, 2011.

Kochman, Thomas. *Black and White Styles in Conflict*. Chicago: University of Chicago Press, 1981.

Korn Ferry Institute. "The Power of Culture Transformation." March 5, 2015. http://www.kornferry.com/institute/power-culture-transformation.

Korn Ferry. *FYI For Your Improvement: Competencies Development Guide*. Minneapolis: Korn Ferry, 2014.

Leguizamo, John and illustrated by Christa Cassano and Shamus Beyale. *Ghetto Klown*. New York: ABRAMS, 2015.

Lewis, Michael. *Moneyball: The Art of Winning an Unfair Game*. New York: W. W. Norton, 2004.

Libert, Barry, John Spector, et al. *We Are Smarter than Me: How to Unleash the Power of Crowds in Your Business*. Upper Saddle River, NJ: Wharton School Publishing, 2007.

Malone, Thomas W. *Superminds: The Surprising Power of People and Computers Thinking Together*. Boston: Little, Brown, 2018.

Markus, Hazel Rose, and Alana Conner. *Clash!: 8 Cultural Conflicts That Make Us Who We Are*. New York: Hudson Street Press, 2013.

McIntosh, Peggy. "White Privilege: Unpacking the Invisible Knapsack." From *White Privilege and Male Privilege: A Personal Account of Coming to See Correspondences Through Work in Women's Studies.* Working Paper 189. Wellesley, MA: Wellesley College Center for Research on Women, 1988.

Page, Scott E. *The Diversity Bonus: How Great Teams Pay Off in the Knowledge Economy*. Princeton, NJ: Princeton University Press, 2019.

Paulson, Henry, Jr. *On the Brink: Inside the Race to Stop the Collapse of the Global Financial System*. New York: Grand Central, 2011.

Perez, Caroline Criado. *Invisible Women: Exposing Data Bias in a World Designed for Men*. New York: Abrams Press, 2019.

Pfeffer, Jeffery. *Dying for a Paycheck: How Modern Management Harms Employee Health and Company Performance—and What We Can Do About It*. New York: HarperCollins, 2018.

Shelton, Chuck. *Leadership 101 for White Men: How to Work Successfully with Black Colleagues and Customers*. Garden City, NJ: Morgan James, 2008.

Tapia, Andrés. *The Inclusion Paradox: The Obama Era and the Transformation of Global Diversity*. 3rd ed. Korn Ferry Institute, 2016.

Thomas, David A., and John Gabarro. *Breaking Through: The Making of Minority Executives in Corporate America*. Boston, MA: Harvard Business School Publishing, 1999.

Thomas, R. Roosevelt, Jr. *Beyond Race and Gender: Unleashing the Power of Your Total Workforce by Managing Diversity*. New York: AMACOM, 1992.

Thurnberg, Greta. *No One Is Too Small to Make a Difference*. London: Penguin, 2019.

Trompenaars, Fons, and Charles Hampden-Turner. *Riding the Waves of Culture: Understanding Diversity in Global Business*. McGraw-Hill Companies, 2012.

Vargas Llosa, Mario. *Conversations in the Cathedral*. New York: Harper and Row, 1975.

Wallace-Wells, David. *The Uninhabitable Earth: Life After Warming*. New York: Tim Duggan Books, 2019.

Wu, Frank H. *Yellow: Race in American Beyond Black and White*. New York: Basic Books, 2002.

Wyche, Keith R., and Sonia Alleyne. *Good Is Not Enough: And Other Unwritten Rules for Minority Professionals*. New York: Portfolio, 2009.

ACKNOWLEDGMENTS

HERE, YOU WILL SEE THAT IT TOOK a global village to pull this book together. There also were various work streams, each with its unique needs and dynamics, so for the most part we list our contributors within the work stream to which they contributed. Since some contributed in more than one work stream, they will show up more than once. First, however, there are some individuals who merit very special appreciation.

Nia-Imani Heslop: You are the epitome of commitment, smarts, attention to detail, partnership, collaboration, stick-to-itiveness, friendliness. You were at our side from the first word to the last, providing all the editorial support through and through. This book basically does not happen without you! You are off to a very promising start to your career.

Sarah Hezlett and Maynard Goff: The scientists, the industrial/organizational PhDs from the Korn Ferry Institute who did the research behind what ended up being the five disciplines and the enabling traits model. Not only did you have the handle on coefficients but also you so cared about the work of how this would be used, how our clients would benefit, and how we could be the best possible consultants with the most accurate research-based tools we could have. Also a shout-out to Sarah for all the careful editorial review in the introductory and part 1 chapters.

Jessy James: You have been a valuable partner in our Inclusive Leader journey as a member of the core Inclusive Leader team, and also thank you so much for all your energy in the introductions to those in India.

Karen Huang: What a thinking partner you have been! You so thoughtfully read the manuscript, surfaced areas on lack of clarity or bad transitions. You offered new sources of research. And then you offered and delivered a top-to-bottom edit that added shine and further clarity to the work.

Sahar Sarreshtehdari: What a joy to meet and experience your connections, smarts, and passion as you so proactively jumped in to help the cause of this book. Thank you for the various inclusive leaders you surfaced in EMEA and helped us interview.

Barry Callender: Thank you for all your careful deliberation as you thoughtfully read key parts of the manuscript to ensure they made sense and were as helpful as possible to the practitioners.

Cara Boratto: Without your calendaring prowess and attention to detail, Andrés would end up marooned in the middle of the Pacific Ocean. You kept me together!

Neal Maillet: As our overall editor, you believed in this book's message and purpose and were key in advocating for it. Your guidance throughout ensured our ideas were presented in the clearest and most succinct way possible.

INTERVIEW ACKNOWLEDGMENTS
Inclusive Leader Interviewees

You inspired us as you shared your insights, methods, and stories!

Anil Sachdev, Founder and Chairman of the School of Inspired Leadership, India

Anna Jonen, Business Unit Manager Digital Transformation, Live Reply DE, Cologne area, Germany

Cristina David, VP Business CIO—Head of Solution Area Develop, Sell, Deliver, Ericsson, Stockholm, Sweden

Deena Al-Faris, CEO and Founder of Qamrah and Cofounder of Caviar Court sturgeon fish farm and caviar factory, Saudi Arabia

Freada Kapor Klein, PhD, Partner at Kapor Capital and Founder/Board Chair of SMASH, San Francisco

Frode Berg, Managing Director Nordics, Experian, Oslo, Norway

Gabor Gonda, Managing Director–Central Europe, Hewlett Packard Enterprise, Hungary

Hengliang Pan, General Manager–Global After-market Business, LiuGong Machinery, China

Jenny Ni, Dow China HR Director, Dow Chemical, China

Johannes Koch, Managing Director Germany, SVP Global Sales DACH region, Austria

Luis Nieto, Retired CEP Executive, Chicago

Martin Moser, Senior Director Hybrid IT Hardware in CERTA (Central Europe, Russia, Turkey, and Africa), Hewlett Packard Enterprise, Austria

Melissa Donaldson, SVP and Chief Diversity Officer, Wintrust, Chicago, US

Mervi Lampinen, Director IT, OneIT Country Lead Germany, MSD Sharp & Dohme GmbH, Haar, Germany

Rita Estevez Luaña, CEO Market President for Spain and Portugal, Experian, Madrid, Spain

Tram Trinh, CEO and Founder, VITANLINK, Paris, France

Vladimir Alves, Diversity and Inclusion Manager LATAM Talent Acquisition South America Manager, John Deere LATAM, São Paulo, Brazil

Wellington Silverio, Human Resources Director, John Deere LATAM, São Paulo, Brazil

Welz Kauffman, President and CEO, Ravinia Festival, Chicago, US

INTERVIEW SETUP
Nominations and Introductions

Cecilia Pinzón, Senior Principal, Bogotá, Colombia (Latin American contacts)

Charles Shao, Senior Client Partner, Beijing, China (Asia-Pacific contacts)

Jessy James, Senior Consultant, San Francisco (India contacts)

Margot Zielinska, Associate Client Partner, London (Middle East and European contacts)

Monick Evans, Senior Client Partner, London (Experian contact)

Sahar Sarreshtehdari, Senior Associate, Berlin, Germany (Germany, Eastern Europe contacts)

Note Taking and Administration
Nia-Imani Heslop
Cara Boratto

RESEARCH ACKNOWLEDGMENTS
You fully grounded the Inclusive Leader model in science. You guided us in the inferences that could and couldn't be made. You listened to the stories of our experiences. You challenged us. You supported us. You helped us grow. You made the work stellar and rock solid.

Korn Ferry Institute
(Analyses to test the Inclusive Leader competency and trait clusters, cluster analyses, and regional/industry analyses)

Heather Barnfield, Director of Intellectual Property Development, Chicago

Maynard Goff, Retired Senior Scientist, Prescott, Arizona

Sarah Hezlett, Senior Director, IP and Assessment Science, Minneapolis

Yu-Ann Wang, Data Scientist, Singapore

Surveys
(Global Inclusive Leaders benchmark analysis and the diversity and inclusion and talent leader opinion survey)

Alexa Stepien (Korach), Senior Global Marketing Specialist, Philadelphia

Jessy James, Senior Consultant, San Francisco

Karen Opp, Vice President, Deputy General Council, Minneapolis

Sarah Bond, Director D&I in Business Council (Europe) at the Conference Board, Bristol

Sarah Hezlett, Senior Director, IP and Assessment Science, Minneapolis

Nia-Imani Heslop, Analyst, Washington, DC

Focus Groups
(Facilitation, set-up, management)

Carice Anderson, Senior Principal, Johannesburg, South Africa

Cecilia Pinzón, Senior Principal, Bogotá, Colombia

Jessy James, Senior Consultant, San Francisco

María José Rovira, Associate Principal, Santiago, Chile

Nia-Imani Heslop, Analyst, Washington, DC

Sahar Sarreshtehdari, Senior Associate, Berlin, Germany

SIDEBAR AUTHOR ACKNOWLEDGMENTS

You found exemplars in history, corporations, nonprofits, civil rights movements, the arts, sports, comedy. You plumbed their stories for precise insights into how each of them lived one of the competencies or traits that make up inclusive leadership. Others of you offered reflections on key concepts in organizational inclusion. You know your stuff, and you care deeply about diversity, equity, and inclusion. You deliver results. And you, too, inspire.

With the exception of the two CEOs and the one identified book author, all are current or former Korn Ferry consultants.

"African American Women: Refueling Our Spirits"
Audra Bohannon, Senior Client Partner, Boston

"As White Women, We Need to Admit We Have Not Been Fully Inclusive of Women of Color"
Shannon Hassler, Principal Consultant at Yardstick Management

"Ava DuVernay: Seeing the Real Us"
Johné Battle, Vice President of Diversity and Inclusion, Dollar General

"Can Humor Help Deal with the Outside Coming In?"
Pamela O'Leary, Principal, San Francisco

"The Canadian Mounted Police: How Women on the Force Led to Safer Communities"
David Herrera, Principal, Mexico City and Toronto

"The Challenge with Traits: Can People Really Change Who They Are?"
Sarah Hezlett, Senior Director, Korn Ferry Institute, Minneapolis

"The Counterintuitive Power of Slowing Down"
Peggy Hazard, Senior Client Partner, New York City

"Filmmaker Alfonso Cuarón Has Us See What Others See"
Gustavo Gisbert, Principal, Chicago and Caracas

"Flexibility Is Not Just Good for Yoga"
Kristin Hibler, Principal, Portland

"From Star to Director: How Inclusive Leaders Leverage Differences"
Wayland Lum, Founder/Managing Director, Copperbox; formerly of Korn Ferry Executive Development/Transformational Leadership, Austin

"The Globetrotter Who Thought He Had a Global Perspective"
Margot Zielinska, Associate Client Partner, London

"How Mónica Ramírez Persuaded Millions to Join the Time's Up Movement"
Michael Hyter, Chief Diversity Officer, Washington, DC

"Imaginative Collaboration at Pixar"
Brandon Farrugia, Associate Principal, Cincinnati

"Inclusive Leaders Successfully Enroll Middle Managers"
Barry Callender, Senior Principal, Atlanta

"Inspiring Models of Leadership in Overlooked Places"
Cecilia Pinzón, Senior Principal, Bogotá

"Jackie Robinson's Advocate"
Barry Callender, Senior Principal, Atlanta

"Labor Day Reflection: Ismeta's Story"
Arne Sorenson, CEO, Marriott, Bethesda

"Launching One Thousand Inclusive Leaders"
Marji Marcus, Senior Principal, Boston

"Leading a Nation Inclusively After the Horror of a Mass Shooting"
Juliet Warne, Senior Principal, Sydney

"Listening Has Been a Key Part of My Being More Inclusive"
Welz Kauffman, President and CEO, Ravinia Festival, Chicago

"Mindy Kaling Has No Apologies"
Karen Huang, Director of Search Assessment, Philadelphia

"Nelson Mandela Was Not Broken"
Fayruz Kirtzman, Senior Principal, New York City

"Rohini Anand at Sodexo: Making Social Justice Relevant to the Business"
Ömer Ongun, Senior Consultant, Ottawa

"Seeing Talent: Life-Altering Experience"
Darryl A. Smith, Senior Client Partner, Chicago

"Seeing Well Beyond the Surface"
Sahar Sarreshtehdari, Senior Associate, Berlin

"Storytelling Goes to the Heart of Trust"
Kevin Cashman, Global Leader, CEO and Executive Development, Minneapolis

"To Think Different Goes Against Most of What We've Been Taught"
Tej Singh Hazra, Associate Client Partner, Toronto

"What Korean Barbecue Tacos Tell Us About Asian–Latinx Crossover"
Andrés T. Tapia, Global Diversity and Inclusion Strategist, Chicago, and **Karen Huang**, Director of Search Assessment, Philadelphia

"The World Is Still Built for Men"
Caroline Criado Perez, Author

CONTENT, EDITORIAL, AND PRODUCTION ACKNOWLEDGMENTS

Peer Review from Korn Ferry

Barry Callender

Karen Huang, PhD

Sarah Hezlett

Peer Review from outside Korn Ferry

Mary Kay Chess

Ella Mason

Ellyn Kerr

Editing

Danielle Goodman, Developmental Editor

Jeevan Sivasubramaniam, Managing Director, Editorial, Berrett-Koehler Publishers

Neal Maillet, Commissioning Editor, Berrett-Koehler Publishers

Production

Nia-Imani Heslop, Project Management

Jeff Anderson, Fact checking

Daniel Tesser, Studio Carnelian, Cover Designer

Richard Whitaker, Seventeenth Street Studios, Book Producer

Michael Crowley, Marketing

Katie Sheehan, Publicist

Sohayla Farman, Production Coordinator

Valerie Caldwell, Art Director

René Ruiz, Audio Book Narrator

INDEX

ABOUT THE AUTHORS

Andrés T. Tapia

Andrés is a senior client partner and Global Diversity and Inclusion Strategist at Korn Ferry, a leadership and talent consultancy. He has more than twenty-five years of experience as a C-suite management consultant, diversity executive, organizational development and training professional, and journalist.

Prior to Korn Ferry, he was the president of Diversity Best Practices, a diversity and inclusion think tank and consultancy, and the chief diversity officer and emerging workforce solutions leader for Hewitt Associates. He has worked with dozens of Global 500 organizations, such as John Deere, Marriott, United, MassMutual, Allstate, Target, Cigna, HPE, Capital Group, Apple, LinkedIn, and Novartis, as well as non-US multinationals in Brazil, South Korea, and India.

Andrés is the author of *The Inclusion Paradox: The Post-Obama Era and the Transformation of Global Diversity* (Korn Ferry Institute, 2016), coauthor with Robert Rodriguez of *Auténtico: The Definitive Guide to Latino Career Success* (Latinx Institute, 2017), and a regular contributor of articles, white papers, and blog posts. He specializes in working with executive teams on developing data-grounded global enterprise-wide diversity and inclusion strategies while also providing one-on-one executive coaching on inclusive leadership. He is a sought-after speaker, the recipient of numerous leadership awards, Ravinia Festival trustee chair, Diversity, Equity, & Inclusion Working Group, and board member of Leadership Greater Chicago.

Andrés received a bachelor's degree in modern history from Northwestern University with an emphasis in journalism and political science.

He grew up in a bilingual/bicultural home in Lima, Perú. Andrés is married to Lori, a musician. They have one grown daughter, Marisela, who is a professional flamenco dancer.

Alina Polonskaia

Alina is a senior client partner and a global leader of the diversity and inclusion practice at Korn Ferry. Alina specializes in diversity and inclusion, organizational design, and large-scale organizational transformation. She is a trusted adviser to a number of leading organizations. She works with executive teams and HR leaders to help them develop data-driven diversity and inclusion strategies and to design work in a way that enables structural and behavioral inclusion. Alina has worked with dozens of large organizations across industries and geographies.

Prior to Korn Ferry, Alina was a global leader of Mercer's diversity and inclusion executive peer client networks, where she engaged senior human resources and diversity and inclusion executives from Fortune 500 companies such as Merck, Marriott, Hilton, Unilever, Sodexo, Novartis, Johnson & Johnson, BNY Mellon, World Bank, Goldman Sachs, PwC, Microsoft, Cisco, and many others in collective problem solving on critical issues around diversity and inclusion and talent risk management.

Prior to Mercer, Alina was with the organizational transformation practice at Oliver Wyman, a leading management consulting firm, and prior to that she worked at IBM Business Consulting Services.

Alina coined the term *structural and behavioral inclusion* and has authored several publications on the importance of evidence-based approach to diversity and inclusion, structural inclusion, and inclusive design application to talent systems.

Alina holds a master of business administration degree from the Ivey School of Business at the University of Western Ontario and a bachelor's degree in psychology from Irkutsk State University, Eastern Siberia, Russia.

Alina is fluent in Russian and English and speaks basic Portuguese. She resides in Toronto, Canada, with her husband and two children.

 KORN FERRY®

ABOUT KORN FERRY

K ORN FERRY IS A GLOBAL ORGANIZATIONAL CONSULTING firm. We
help clients synchronize strategy and talent to drive superior
performance. We work with organizations to design their structures,
roles, and responsibilities. We help them hire the right people to bring
their strategy to life. And we advise them on how to reward, develop,
and motivate their people.

Korn Ferry's diversity, equity, and inclusion practice is the largest in
the world. We cover the full spectrum of DE&I strategic and programmatic solutions. This includes organization-wide strategy, deep quantitative and qualitative diagnostics, inclusive design of talent systems,
training and learning, in all modalities, with a vast library of content,
and various other programmatic interventions, such as establishing
DE&I councils, employee resource groups, mentoring, and sponsorship programs.

The Korn Ferry Institute, our research and analytics arm, was established to share intelligence and expert points of view on talent and
leadership. Through studies, books, and quarterly magazine briefings,
we aim to increase understanding of how strategic talent decisions
contribute to competitive advantage, growth, and success.

Korn Ferry in Numbers

- Work with 98% of the Fortune 100
- More than 69 million assessments taken
- More than 4 billion data points collected
- Rewards data on more than 20 million professionals
- Place a candidate every 3 minutes, each business hour

- Located in more than 100 offices in more than 50 countries
- Nearly 9,000 employees
- Assess and coach around 100,000 leaders a month

Korn Ferry Resources

kornferry.com

kornferry.com/diversity

kornferryinstitute.com

Berrett–Koehler
Publishers

Berrett-Koehler is an independent publisher dedicated to an ambitious mission: *Connecting people and ideas to create a world that works for all.*

Our publications span many formats, including print, digital, audio, and video. We also offer online resources, training, and gatherings. And we will continue expanding our products and services to advance our mission.

We believe that the solutions to the world's problems will come from all of us, working at all levels: in our society, in our organizations, and in our own lives. Our publications and resources offer pathways to creating a more just, equitable, and sustainable society. They help people make their organizations more humane, democratic, diverse, and effective (and we don't think there's any contradiction there). And they guide people in creating positive change in their own lives and aligning their personal practices with their aspirations for a better world.

And we strive to practice what we preach through what we call "The BK Way." At the core of this approach is *stewardship,* a deep sense of responsibility to administer the company for the benefit of all of our stakeholder groups, including authors, customers, employees, investors, service providers, sales partners, and the communities and environment around us. Everything we do is built around stewardship and our other core values of *quality, partnership, inclusion,* and *sustainability.*

This is why Berrett-Koehler is the first book publishing company to be both a B Corporation (a rigorous certification) and a benefit corporation (a for-profit legal status), which together require us to adhere to the highest standards for corporate, social, and environmental performance. And it is why we have instituted many pioneering practices (which you can learn about at www.bkconnection.com), including the Berrett-Koehler Constitution, the Bill of Rights and Responsibilities for BK Authors, and our unique Author Days.

We are grateful to our readers, authors, and other friends who are supporting our mission. We ask you to share with us examples of how BK publications and resources are making a difference in your lives, organizations, and communities at www.bkconnection.com/impact.

Dear reader,

Thank you for picking up this book and welcome to the worldwide BK community! You're joining a special group of people who have come together to create positive change in their lives, organizations, and communities.

What's BK all about?

Our mission is to connect people and ideas to create a world that works for all.

Why? Our communities, organizations, and lives get bogged down by old paradigms of self-interest, exclusion, hierarchy, and privilege. But we believe that can change. That's why we seek the leading experts on these challenges—and share their actionable ideas with you.

A welcome gift

To help you get started, we'd like to offer you a **free copy** of one of our bestselling ebooks:

www.bkconnection.com/welcome

When you claim your **free ebook**, you'll also be subscribed to our blog.

Our freshest insights

Access the best new tools and ideas for leaders at all levels on our blog at ideas.bkconnection.com.

Sincerely,

Your friends at Berrett-Koehler